CHINA'S GLOBAL STRATEGY

China's Global Strategy

Towards a Multipolar World

Jenny Clegg

PLUTO PRESS
www.plutobooks.com

First published 2009 by Pluto Press
345 Archway Road, London N6 5AA and
175 Fifth Avenue, New York, NY 10010

Distributed in the United States of America exclusively by
Palgrave Macmillan, a division of St. Martin's Press LLC,
175 Fifth Avenue, New York, NY 10010

www.plutobooks.com

British Library Cataloguing in Publication Data
A catalogue record for this book is available from the British Library.

ISBN 978 0 7453 2519 4 Hardback
ISBN 978 0 7453 2518 7 Paperback

Library of Congress Cataloging in Publication Data applied for.

This book is printed on paper suitable for recycling and made from fully managed and
sustained forest sources. Logging, pulping and manufacturing processes are expected to
conform to the environmental standards of the country of origin. The paper may contain up
to 70 per cent post-consumer waste.

10 9 8 7 6 5 4 3 2 1

Designed and produced for Pluto Press by
Curran Publishing Services, Norwich

Printed and bound in the European Union by
CPI Antony Rowe, Chippenham and Eastbourne

CONTENTS

ACKNOWLEDGEMENTS

This book originated in discussions with Keith Bennett. Whilst I take full responsibility for what follows, I am indebted to him for his contributions in many different ways to the project. Most particularly, I would like to mention the political acuity of his advice on some of the more controversial matters.

I am very grateful to my brother, Peter Clegg, for his diligent assistance, which was a great help in the final stages of the writing process.

I also benefited from the advice of Jun Li on Chapters 6 and 9, and from Ian Cook on Chapter 7, and I would also like to thank them for this.

ABBREVIATIONS AND ACRONYMS

ABM	anti-ballistic missile
ACFTA	ASEAN-China Free Trade Area
ACFTU	All-China Federation of Trade Unions
AFTA	ASEAN Free Trade Area
APEC	Asia-Pacific Economic Cooperation
ASEAN	Association of South-East Asian Nations
ASEAN+1	ASEAN plus China
ASEAN+3	ASEAN plus, China, South Korea and Japan
ASEM	Asia-Europe Meeting
CIS	Commonwealth of Independent States
CNOOC	China National Offshore Oil Corporation
COE	collectively owned enterprise
CNP	comprehensive national power
CPC	Communist Party of China
CTBT	Comprehensive Test Ban Treaty
DPRK	Democratic People's Republic of Korea
DWSR	Dollar Wall Street Regime
EU	European Union
FDI	foreign direct investment
FIE	foreign invested enterprise
FMCT	Fissile Materials Cut-Off Treaty
FTA	free trade agreement
FTAA	Free Trade Area of the Americas
G-7	Group of 7
G-8	Group of 8
G-77	Group of 77
GATT	General Agreement on Trade and Tariffs
GDP	gross domestic product
IAEA	International Atomic Energy Authority
ICBM	intercontinental ballistic missile
IMF	International Monetary Fund

IPR	intellectual property rights
KMT	Kuomintang
MD	missile defence
MFA	Multi-Fibre Agreement
MNC	multinational corporation
MTCR	Missile Technology Control Regime
NAFTA	North American Free Trade Agreement
NAM	Non-Aligned Movement
NATO	North Atlantic Treaty Organisation
NGO	nongovernment organisation
NIEO	New International Economic Order
NIPEO	new international political and economic order
NPC	National People's Congress
NPL	non-performing loan
NPT	Non-Proliferation Treaty
NSC	New Security Concept
NSS	National Security Strategy
NWFZ	nuclear weapons-free zone
OECD	Organisation for Economic Cooperation and Development
PAROS	Prevention of an Arms Race in Outer Space
PLA	People's Liberation Army
PNAC	Project for a New American Century
PRC	People's Republic of China
PSI	Proliferation Security Initiative
QDR	*Quadrennial Defense Review*
R&D	research and development
RMB	renminbi
SAARC	South Asia Association for Regional Cooperation
SAIC	Shanghai Automotive Industry Corporation
SCO	Shanghai Cooperation Organisation
SIPRI	Stockholm International Peace Research Institute
SOB	state-owned bank
SOE	state-owned enterprise
TNC	transnational corporation
TRIPS	Trade-Related Intellectual Property Rights
TVE	township or village enterprise
UN	United Nations
UNCTAD	UN Conference on Trade and Development
UNSC	United Nations Security Council
WMD	weapons of mass destruction
WTO	World Trade Organization

INTRODUCTION

1 A WORLD TURNING UPSIDE DOWN

China is emerging as a powerful player on the world stage and the contours of another world are taking shape. The neocon vision of a unipolar world dominated by the United States as the sole superpower is starting to give way as China's rise signals the emergence of a new kind of multipolar international order with a more democratic determination of world affairs.

China, it seems, is coming out of nowhere. Just five years ago, George W. Bush launched into the war on Iraq in a bid for US supremacy which was, as Arrighi has observed, the most ambitious project of world rule ever conceived.[1] At the time China was widely portrayed as verging on collapse, its corrupt one-Party state a hollow sham, at odds with a capitalist economy being driven to bankruptcy by the endless pumping of funds into the dying dinosaurs of its state-owned enterprises (SOEs).

Instead, China has kept growing from strength to strength, following its own plans to quadruple its GDP between 2000 and 2020, lifting millions of people out of poverty. Today, with the United States unable to win the wars it so disastrously started and its economy riddled with bad debt, dragging the rest of the world towards recession, many are increasingly looking to China's development as a source of global economic stability.

China's international influence is growing rapidly and everyone knows that it is becoming a major international power. But what kind of a power will China be? What kind of a role will it play in shaping the world? A look back over the developments of recent years can start to provide an answer.

ANOTHER WORLD IS HAPPENING

Broadly, the anti-war movement has viewed Bush's war on Iraq as about the control of the global oil spigot. This was true, but it was also always about much more than this. For the neocons, the war was to be a first move in a long-term strategy. Some commentators realised this: for example, Dan Plesch, when in 2002 he raised the prospect, 'Iraq, Iran, and China next'.[2]

The real significance of the decision to go to war on Iraq lay in the way the United States openly flouted the United Nations. Bush's unilateralist pre-emptive strike doctrine went further than any previous US interventionism in that it overtly challenged the basic principles of the UN Charter and interna-tional law. What Bush understood was firstly that, in order to preserve US dominance, it was necessary not only to defend, but to extend, the US model of 'freedom, democracy and free enterprise', and secondly that this in turn necessitated overturning the whole global consensus on non-intervention enshrined by the United Nations. The US strategy to prevent the rise of any potential challenger was to be set as the new international norm in order to pursue a 'one size fits all' model of neoliberal globalisation.[3] The concern of the neocons to prevent the emergence of any 'peer competitor' to the United States was a tacit admission that they saw the main threat as coming from the growing multipolar world trend.

Discussion about a 'unipolar versus multipolar' world came to the fore-front of world debate in 2003 as the US decision to go to war on Iraq produced a rift across the Atlantic. As the European Union, Russia and China drew closer, Condoleezza Rice struck out, warning that multipolarity was a 'theory of rivalry'. 'We have tried this before', she declared. 'It led to the Great War ....'[4] Clearly in her eyes, multipolarisation presaged violent inter-imperialist struggles for the redivision of the world. Her words were to be echoed shortly afterwards by Tony Blair when, speaking of multi-polarity, he proclaimed that there was 'no more dangerous theory in international relations today'.[5]

China's leaders have long grasped the significance of multipolarisation as *the* counter-hegemonic trend breaking superpower monopoly on world affairs. Discussion by Chinese analysts since the mid-1980s has focused on the emergence of multipolarity with rifts between the major developed powers potentially opening political space for new initiatives from within the developing world to reflect the world's diversity and allow a multifaceted approach to development.

When Bush first took office he made China policy a top priority but 9/11 changed that. With the United States preoccupied with its wars in Afghanistan and Iraq and the major powers increasingly divided, the massive anti-war opposition from governments and people around the world, helped to unleash a new mood of Third World solidarity, presenting China with a huge opportunity to step up its strategic diplomacy worldwide.

While Bush used the 'war on terror' as a pretext to increase US military and diplomatic engagement in Asia, causing China concern for its own security, China itself began to promote South–South cooperation in a big way.

Pursuing mutually beneficial win–win economic exchange agreements and security dialogues, China found considerable success in deepening its relations in the developing world. In 2004, high-profile tours by China's most senior leaders to Latin America took in Brazil, Argentina, Chile, Cuba,

Peru, Venezuela, Trinidad and Jamaica. 2005 saw Chinese President Hu Jintao mark the 60th anniversary year of the Bandung Conference by visiting India as well as a number of African states. The China–Africa Summit was held in Beijing in November 2006, with representatives from 48 African countries including many heads of state. China also initiated negotiations on trade agreements with ASEAN, the Gulf States and Pakistan as well as with Australia and New Zealand. It is in this context of the upsurge in Third Worldism that the recent rapid strengthening in China's global position must be situated.

China conceives its own future to be as one power amongst an increasing number of others within a wider multipolar context, as it develops alongside other developing countries and their regional organisations. Its leaders have recognised that their country cannot be developed in isolation from the rest of the world, and have sought integration into the existing international order, not as a one-way process of adaptation, but rather as a means to influence it from within. Where others see uncertainty and propensity for chaos, for China the multipolar trend potentially opens the way for a more democratic organisation of world affairs, one of equal partnerships holding power rivalries in check, so creating room to develop South–South cooperation and North–South dialogue to shape a fair globalisation.

With its own development driving world development, and its internationalist stance of support for a multipolar world, China's rise seems inevitably to bring it into conflict with the US hegemonic project. As Lanxin Xiang has wryly noted, it is just as China considers joining in the current international system that the United States decided to force changes in the international rules.[6] In 2006, China was for the first time openly named by the second Bush administration as the future potential competitor with which the United States was most concerned.

CHINA THREAT OR US THREAT?

The absence of discussion about China's development in the West has created a vacuum of knowledge in which fears of a China 'threat' can freely take hold. In recent years China's rise, with its seemingly endless supplies of cheap labour, has been blamed for the loss of jobs especially across the developed world, and China is now readily seen to be emerging as a coercive superpower with scant regard for people's wants and needs. Stereotyped notions, however, draw more on nineteenth-century images of the 'Yellow Peril' than on actual conditions in China. Huntington's notion of a 'clash of civilisations', it should be recalled, was as much about the conflicts between 'the West' and Confucianism as about the 'the West' and Islam.[7]

'China threat' theories emanate from a neo-McCarthyite, neocon vision which compares China's rise with that of Germany and Japan in the first half of the twentieth century.[8] The United States then should 'do what it can to slow the rise of China'.[9]

The portrayal of China as a serial human rights abuser provided a constant backdrop as 'humanitarian intervention' evolved into the central theme of US foreign policy in the post-Cold War period. Now as the West seeks to use the 'democracy' agenda as the latest tool to maintain its weakening control over the rest of the world, China is construed as the main obstacle to progress.

In the Sinophobic view, China is in the grip of an ideologically bankrupt communist dictatorship, which, clinging to power through xenophobic aggressive nationalism, pursues internal and foreign policies that are actively hostile to human rights and upholding international law. China's new diplomacy is characterised as a selfish pursuit of national interests, backed by a growing military power, as its voracious appetite for resources drives it abroad in search for oil and minerals for its own exclusive use. China is seen to be rising at the expense of the wider global good. Apparently displaying no qualms in dealing with what are cited as being some of the world's worst human rights offenders in order to further its own commercial and political ends, China stands accused of frustrating the advance of UN work on issues of human rights and legitimate government, considered vital to international stability.

In this portrayal the real situation is turned on its head: it is not the rise of China but the United States and its pursuit of unipolarity that constitutes the main source of world destabilisation. War, after all, is the greatest abuse of human rights. At the same time, the United States constantly places the UN non-interventionist system under stress; dumps its junk currency on world markets and insists on pursuing a foreign policy of democratic utopianism to impose its own model on others regardless of their actual conditions, exacerbating global inequalities. The United States, and indeed most of the rest of the world, buys its oil from corrupt states in Africa and human rights abusers in the Middle East. China's long-standing willingness to deal with states that the West regards as pariahs is based in part on a reluctance to make judgements about other countries' domestic policies as well as a concern about the power politics behind the exercise of pressures and intervention.

The United States has developed 'a military apparatus of unparalleled and unprecedented destructiveness';[10] China, itself nearly destroyed by military interventions in the nineteenth and first half of the twentieth century, seeks to avoid direct confrontation with the superpower.

China's power should not be exaggerated. Over the last 30 years, it has indeed been the world's fastest-growing economy, currently lying equal third with Germany in the world rankings. However, China remains a developing country, and will continue to be so for decades to come. Its average per capita gross national income in 2007 was a mere \$2,360, according to the World Bank, ranking 132 in world,[11] and tackling poverty remains its major preoccupation. Its economy is less than a quarter the size of the United States, and although it is developing as a huge manufacturing base, it lacks technological power, leaning heavily in this respect on intellectual input from outside.

As China looks to multipolarisation to open up the world progressive trend, it differs in its approach from the USSR. Rather than directly challenging the US superpower, it employs a more subtle diplomacy, aimed at reducing tensions with the West in order to create a stable and predictable world environment favourable to its own, as well as the wider world's development.

A NEW VIEW FROM THE LEFT

The Western Left offers little to counter the neocons' Sinophobia, and in some ways even subscribes to it. For some sections, China is seen as a new 'resource colonialist',[12] and as an emerging imperialist power whose rise is bringing on an increasingly chaotic period of inter-imperialist rivalries.[13] On the other hand, others from the Left argue that China has been recolonised and recompradorised,[14] operating under the sway of the United States and the multinational companies (MNCs), driving a 'race to the bottom' of intensifying competition and exploitation to undermine the conditions of workers all around the world.[15] Vanaik, for example, regards China as too wishy-washy – anything but a serious pillar of resistance to US global ambitions,[16] while Roden argues that China is falling into line with US policy goals, serving to enhance US structural power in the global economy, reversing the superpower's decline.[17]

However, from within the more mainstream debate, analysts such as the neo-Keynesian Stiglitz[18] and the world sociologist Arrighi[19] reject the widespread assumption that China's development has followed the neoliberal paradigm. Ramo, too, has posited the notion of a 'Beijing consensus', following a more equitable, high-quality growth path using both economics and government to improve society, as the antithesis of the much-discredited 'Washington consensus'.[20]

This book follows the view that China's strategists have far from 'allowed imperialist circles to think for them'. However, it differs from the above mentioned theorists by addressing questions of strategy, drawing in particular on the work of Samir Amin.[21] The strategic perspective is taken as essential in evaluating the significance and potential of China's rise in the changing world order.

Focusing on China's part in the changing international order, especially over the last decade, this book seeks to highlight how its leaders have responded to US interventionism and unilateralism and to explore the ways in which China's vision of peaceful development is starting to transform world politics.

The problem generally with China's critics is that they fail to engage seriously with its realities – its historical background, its level of development and the problems of developing such a huge country, as well as the international space within which it seeks to manoeuvre. Many of China's failings identified by its critics do indeed need to be addressed. However, what is rarely acknowledged is that Chinese policymakers not only know this, but are actively taking measures to address the problems. Instead, the policies of the Chinese government are dismissed as 'empty rhetoric'.

This book, on the other hand, attempts to capture China's wide-angle view as it looks to the long term precisely by examining China's past and current policies. It draws not only on Western scholarship and reportage but also on the speeches of China's leaders and the analytical approaches of its scholars and strategists. In this way the discussion aims to throw light on China's own political perspectives and future directions as it faces new domestic and international challenges in the twenty-first century.

The argument sees the United States and China positioned at opposite poles in an international order shaped by a unipolar–multipolar dynamic, with the United States as the largest developed and China as the largest developing country. It is this difference in positioning in the international order that is seen to define the nature of their strategic conflict as one centred on the question of world development.

As this book seeks to demonstrate, China's development challenges the whole structure of global hegemony and global inequality. Where the United States attempts through intervention to monopolise world affairs to preserve the dominance of Western finance and monopoly capital, China's commitment, as it struggles to lift itself out of poverty, is to a more democratic rules-based international order with greater equity in development as the fundamental condition for its own, as well as global, security.

This then is an examination of China's pursuit of a progressive agenda for a new international political and economic order (NIPEO). The purpose is not merely to show that China's growing influence can serve as a restraint on US hegemonic action, but to look at how China tackles the realities of world power relations, how it seeks to play an instrumental role in a fair globalisation through its own widespread win–win economic diplomacy, and how it pursues equal partnerships based on mutual benefit in order to contribute to a world of multipolar stability with a strong United Nations at its centre. In these ways, by creating a new cooperative system of international relations to facilitate world development, China's strategy offers a concrete alternative to the US neocons' vision of the New American Century based on US military might.

The book is organised into three parts. Part 1 sets out to explore China's rise in the broad context of the unipolar–multipolar dynamic with the Sino–US relationship at its core. Chapter 2 highlights the role of the US 'war on terror' in encircling China, arguing that the new US militarism and interventionism is a strategic response to the multipolarisation trend opening up in the 1990s with China's rise. To reveal the Sino–US relationship as the crux of the world's structural patterning, the discussion looks back on the history of Sino–US relations since 1949, as well as examining the more recent influence of the neocon Project for a New American Century (PNAC) on US foreign policy.

Chapter 3 then applies a multipolar approach to analyse the world development pattern since the Second World War, and proceeds to situate China's development in the emerging multipolarity with the rise of the Third World as well as the popular movements against the Vietnam War and the nuclear arms race. It goes on to examine the evolution of China's strategic outlook in this wider historical context as it sought to emerge from Cold War embargo and isolation.

Chapter 4 explores China's strategic analysis of the world situation in the post-Cold War period, examining its efforts to engage with the other major world powers as a response to the conditions of US dominance, seeking to adjust the imbalance between the unipolar and multipolar trends. The chapter focuses on China's cooperative security approach as set out by its New Security Concept (NSC) which is seen to provide an alternative basis for international relations in contrast with the Bush doctrine.

Chapter 5 provides a more theoretical dimension to the discussion of multipolarisation. Unlike the Western conception of rival blocs of power, in China's view, multipolarisation involves much more than a readjustment in relative strengths of different powers with their rise and decline, but rather spells the end of imperialism. Without denying the potential role of second-order powers, including European powers, China sees developing countries as the main force for world peace and development, playing a determining role in countering the US pursuit of hegemonism to underpin the West's monopoly of world markets and world affairs. At the same time globalisation, viewed from the Chinese perspective as a 'double-edged sword', not only a threat but also an opportunity, is seen as central to the multipolarisation trend. In examining the debates here, this chapter argues that China's strategy represents a Leninism for the twenty-first century, adapted to the new dynamics of imperialism in conditions of growing interdependence and regionalism in the post-Cold War period.

The Asian region is the major focus for China's diplomatic efforts. Chapter 6 looks at three case studies – the Shanghai Cooperation Organisation

(SCO), the six-party talks on the denuclearisation of the Korean peninsula and China's economic relations with South-East Asia – to examine in greater detail how, region by region, China's initiatives set out to counter US encirclement by creating a new style of cooperative international relations based on mutual benefit, in which security is linked to development.

The argument that China plays a positive role in the world today operating as an independent pole in a multipolarising world cannot be sustained without an examination of the overall economic, political and social dimensions of its own development. This forms the theme of Part 2 as it explores the processes and mechanisms of China's socialist path.

Faced with the enormous challenges of simultaneously managing a transition economy like Russia as well as a developing economy like Bangladesh,[22] China's development has steamed ahead, largely avoiding the problems of debt crisis, deficits and financial crashes which have destabilised other reforming and developing countries. Not to be written off as dinosaurs, China's SOEs are now becoming profitable dynamos of an economic development to which the rest of the world increasingly looks to sustain global growth.[23]

China has followed an essentially self-reliant path, free from the dictates of foreign capital, rooted in its basic system of public ownership and shaped by a reform path which has sought to preserve and strengthen the state to give the developing market a long-term socialist orientation. China is undergoing an industrial revolution of unprecedented scale, and Part 2 of this book finds the government and the Communist Party of China (CPC), despite many failings not least of corruption, responding in some innovative and creative ways as they face the challenges, continuing to enhance their political capacity to maintain a peaceful and stable order as the basis for economic and social development.

Chapter 7 traces the evolution of China's path of development through its various stages, the differing approaches of Mao and Deng as well as its current phase of more radical economic reforms. Taking up the controversial issue of China's WTO membership, it reveals China's 'embrace' of globalisation as an audacious move to join the world technological revolution and become part of the global knowledge economy, as well as to open up a wide reaching economic diplomacy.

Putting the spotlight on China's engagement with foreign capital and the development of private capital, the chapter considers the measures taken by the government to minimise the risks and dangers of exposure to international competition whilst using globalisation to upgrade from a cheap labour economy, foster its own globally competitive 'national champions' and generally strengthen China's position in the world order.

Chapter 8 sets out to examine the downside of China's 'growth first' strategy. The remarkable achievements in development and reductions in poverty have been taking place alongside and in conditions of widening gaps in wealth, in particular with growing rural–urban inequality; poor, sometimes appalling, work environments; inadequacies in rural health care; environmental degradation; problems of corruption and compradorisation, all raising concerns about social unrest.

To argue that China is a progressive force is not to deny these problems: it is not the aim here to advocate a Chinese model of development for others to follow. The social costs of China's growth do indeed pose challenges to the socialist credentials of the Party and state. However, the difficulties need to be set in the context of China's national conditions as it has had to adapt its development in difficult circumstances.

Chapter 8 goes on to look at how these problems are being addressed as the current leadership shifts direction towards a more equitable and ecologically sustainable 'people first' approach. It also seeks to address the question of political reform. Unlike the disastrous attempt by the USSR to carry out glasnost and perestroika, economic liberalisation and political openness at the same time, China's leaders have kept political reform on the back burner while focusing on economic restructuring. With no existing model to follow, China has had to create a path that suits its own conditions, proceeding cautiously. But now political modernisation is rising up the agenda and, as this chapter argues, an awakening at the grass roots holds the promise of a more vibrant people's democracy.

Part 3 returns to the international stage, where a 'smokeless war' is taking place between the United States and China across a range of fronts over the rules of the global order. Part 3 sets out to identify more clearly the parameters of China's vision of an NIPEO and to look more specifically at how China, as it starts to take a more proactive role in the multilateral order, is beginning to shape the rules of the global order, contributing to a progressive global agenda for stability, development and dialogue.

Chapter 9 addresses issues of political and military concern, looking at the current trial of strength in the United Nations as the United States continues its onslaught on UN principles of non-intervention and international law from within. The chapter takes up a number of controversial issues, including the situation over Darfur, Iran and the question of nuclear non-proliferation as well as China's military spending, at the same time setting out China's stand on UN reform and nuclear disarmament.

Chapter 10 takes up the question of global economic instabilities and a fair globalisation. Claims that China is an unfair trader and currency manipulator, stealing manufacturing jobs from the West, have been used by the Bush administration to exert economic pressure on China. This chapter considers China's responses to the US global economic hegemonic drive, looking at how the dominance of Western monopoly and finance capital is starting to come under challenge as it develops. The question of South–South exchange is also considered here, particularly in terms of China's role in Africa. In examining China's stance on issues of trade and investment, the discussion shows how these are opening up novel approaches to risk- and resource-sharing for a fair globalisation based on financial stability, market coordination and technological sharing in place of imperialist practices of exporting crises and monopolising resources.

Chapter 11 looks to the future, providing some final considerations on the question of the emergence of a global progressive alliance against the US militarist and dollar-based hegemonism.

ENDLESS WAR?

'We are at the beginning of the biggest geopolitical shift since the dawn of the industrial era,' wrote Martin Jacques at the start of 2008.[24] At the crux of this shift, as this book argues, lies the Sino–US relationship. China may not be perceived right now as a 'clear and present danger' by Washington, but if the neocons have their way, a conflict with China seems inevitable.

Across the political spectrum in the West, the widespread view of the future, with the decline of the United States, is one of ceaseless chaos and wars as the big powers battle it out to carve up the world's scarce resources. On the other hand, the sustainability of the planet demands international cooperation. This book aims to show that what is at stake with China's rise is not a future of endless resource wars but a real choice over the future model of the international order: the US strategic goal of a unipolar world to uphold and extend existing patterns of exploitation, or a multipolar and democratic one for a more equitable, just and peaceful world.

The key role that China is playing in limiting US hegemonism and war deserves far more debate among progressives in the West. This book is written in the conviction that if the Western peace and progressive movements are to strengthen their influence in a complex and changing world, they need to recognise this significance of China's rise, as well as its positive contribution to a progressive international agenda.

China's human rights record is far from perfect, yet its problems are often misrepresented and taken out of context by the Western media. According to the UNDP's 2005 Human Development Index, China ranks 29th among 108 developing countries, standing significantly higher than many other countries at similar levels of per capita GDP.[25] Whilst the Western discourse on human rights and democracy has been constructed within the liberal paradigm, China's stand is a reminder that a nation's right to develop, and the right to choose its own path of development suited to its own needs and conditions, is also essential to the realisation of social and economic rights. At the same time, for China, the point of the Open Door policy was to 'learn from the outside world'. There is scope here for constructive dialogue, exchange and practical cooperation with the broadest range of progressive forces from both the global North and South, the East as well as the West.

A Note on Terminology

Hegemony

As Arrighi notes, what differentiates a hegemonic power from a dominant one is its capacity or will to lead the system of states 'in ways that enhance the collective power of the system's dominant groups'.[26] In Gramscian terms, hegemony is exercised through consent as well as coercion, and in order to lead, dominant groups must 'present their rule as credibly serving not just their own interests but those of subordinate groups as well'.[27] This in turn involves not only economic and technological dominance, which allows scope to provide material incentives, but also the political and ideological dimensions of influence.

US supremacy in the international order is then not just a matter of the threat or use of force. The US hegemonic project seeks to shape the overall pattern of international relations, laying down general rules for the behaviour of states, in order to secure solutions to global problems which both privilege its own particular interests in maintaining primacy, and foster consensual relations with the other major capitalist states as well as the compradorised elites in the developing world.

US hegemonism may be seen to extend globally through an invisible government of corporations, banks and international organisations such as the IMF and World Bank, or through the cultural 'soft power' of the 'American Dream'. However, the power of the United States should not be overestimated as an all-embracing empire. The US hegemonic project is in fact aspirational, contested and potentially contradictory, its relationships with its allies both consensual and conflictual. As Amin notes, to secure its global position, the United States has to strike compromises with other states, even dominated ones, especially if they reject its position.[28] The approach adopted in this book follows Amin in therefore placing the emphasis on the political and strategic aspects of hegemonic leadership. The debates around the US hegemonic role are explored further in the section on Western debates on globalisation and imperialism in Chapter 5.

Unipolarity

A unipolar world is one in which the pattern of inter-state relations centres on a single dominant hegemon such that it is able to concentrate power in its own hands. In pursuit of a unipolar world, the United States seeks to shape power and forge rules so as to make it impossible for any other power or coalition of forces to challenge its pre-eminence. It is, as Bromley puts it, a 'prescription of perpetual dominance for perpetual leadership'.[29]

The fact that US hegemonism can only achieve its objectives by working with other powers does not signify in itself that the world is becoming more multipolar. Unipolarity should not be confused with unilateralism. As argued in Chapter 9, the second Bush administration paid more attention to multilateralism in so far as it sought support from its allies. Nevertheless, its main aim was still to achieve a unipolar world, to secure the dominance of Western MNCs through the deployment of a US military empire, with the participation of these allies in a subordinate role.

Multipolarity

In contrast, a multipolar world involves a pattern of multiple centres of power, all with a certain capacity to influence world affairs, shaping a negotiated order. Multipolarisation involves not only readjustments in the relations between the major powers with the growing role of Europe and Japan but also the rise of developing countries, their regional associations such as ASEAN, the African Union, the South American communities as well as the Shanghai Cooperation Organisation, and their international organisations such as the G77 and the non-aligned movement (NAM). The rising forces of the Third World in fact play the key role in multipolarisation, with the support of the world's other progressive forces and states, to provide the basis for a genuine multilateralism coordinated through the United Nations.

Since the hegemonist strategy of the United States and its allies is today, as Amin puts is, the main enemy of social progress, democracy and peace, admitting no toleration of any other project,[30] a multipolar world is a necessary framework for alternative projects for greater global equity. At the same time, in narrowing the scope for US aggression, multipolarity enhances the possibilities of peaceful solutions to conflictual situations.

The Third World

It is the contention of this book that the nature of the political contradictions being worked out in today's world through the unipolar–multipolar dynamic lies in the ongoing historical struggle of Third World countries, in a world dominated by imperialism led by US hegemonism, to consolidate their political independence so as to develop their own economies and social and cultural lives. This is both the condition of, and requirement for, a more peaceful and more evenly developed world.

Third World collectivism, put forward as an aspiration at the Bandung

Conference of 1955, was forged in the 1960s and 1970s around a development agenda to restructure North–South relations. This agenda, again as Amin highlights, was the product of 'powerful social movements against the logic of capitalist expansion' and set against a background of major social reforms within the newly independent states, including nationalisations, welfare programmes and land reforms.[31]

Recently, however, the notion of a Third World as a collectivity has become increasingly contested as developing countries have been growing more diverse, not only in terms of economic strength and size, and levels of development, but also displaying a great range of development strategies, as well as very different political systems. Nevertheless, as Parkins argues, while the idea of the Third World needs to be viewed critically, it remains valid because it captures a fundamental and enduring division within the global system.[32]

Furthermore, as Marchand points out, through institutions such as the G77 and NAM, developing countries have continued to maintain a common identity around the development agenda, while the scope for South–South exchange has been expanding bit by bit, albeit based on varying achievements in development and nation-building across the developing world.[33] There is then potential to reclaim and recreate the collectivist Third World identity, and it is precisely the argument here that China, with its socialist orientation, is playing a key role in this, increasingly using its leverage in the global economy to promote win–win exchanges.

Win–win

Developmentalists have long argued not only that South–South exchange would be of mutual benefit to developing countries but also that the advanced industrialised countries stand to gain from assisting the more impoverished regions of the world, since development there would expand the demand for the goods and services of the developed countries.[34]

Similarly, the 'China opportunity' argument advocates that, rather than representing a threat, China's development offers a win–win scenario creating new openings not only for itself but also for the rest of the world, whether developed and developing, as it becomes a key driver of the world economy.

Today, growing global interdependencies, while raising the prospects of conflicts ending in lose–lose scenarios, make the need to find win–win solutions to global problems all the more urgent. However, such solutions to global problems of equitable, sustainable and peaceful development are still a work in progress. There is then no single comprehensive progressive political programme presented here to end imperialism.

What is important are the principles and methods to be adopted in working out win–win solutions in practice: principles of equal treatment and methods which focus on finding common ground in interests and complementarities in economic structures to counter the zero-sum win–lose approach of imperialism and a hegemonic drive for primacy.

To illustrate these principles and methods and to clarify China's role in the evolving progressive agenda, various examples of win–win solutions are considered throughout the book. Chapter 7 discusses China's approach of 'exchanging markets for technology' in making deals which allow Western MNCs to gain a share in China's growing markets, while also aiming to ensure technology transfer. Western companies then win in absolute terms from the growth in markets, but face the prospects of a diminishing relative share in the markets of the future as Chinese companies develop their own capacities and break up the West's monopoly control.

The issue of China's competitive threat producing a 'lose' for other workers and industries around the world is an important theme in Chapter 10, and the negotiations on the Sino–EU textile trade in that chapter provide a particular illustration of how a win–win scenario might be worked out here. Win–win is also central to China's concept of 'cooperative security' and the methods of achieving this are discussed in detail in the section in Chapter 6 which deals with the six-party talks on the denuclearisation of the Korean peninsula.

Table 2 sets out key themes and objectives for a new international and political order (NIPEO), which for the most part are discussed and explored in Chapters 9 and 10, to be achieved through win–win strategies.

International democracy

Multipolarity is fundamentally about the democratisation of international affairs, of the global system – the strengthening of international institutions, and of the United Nations in particular, to transform the hold of the developed world over decision-making power in international institutions, instead allowing multiple voices to shape world agendas and put forward alternative solutions to global problems. Upholding the principles of non-intervention and sovereign equality is central to this.

This emphasis on international democratisation in the current period is the exact reverse of the Bush–Blair paradigm which takes the spread of Western political institutions as the fundamental condition in making the world more democratic, so making internal patterns of national governments the concern of the 'international community'.

Critics of the approach of this book will no doubt argue, as indeed it is argued in criticism of China's foreign policies, that it fails to engage with the problems of the unrepresentativeness of corrupt and dictatorial regimes. Yet Western-style democracies, in the developed as well as the developing worlds, often struggle to represent the interests of their people in the face of the demands of big business as well as US foreign policy. There is an important distinction to be made here between the formal institutions of democracy and the processes of democratisation which ensure 'real and growing equality of access [for all people] to the material means available in the modern world'.[35] International democratisation is in this sense a necessary condition for real democratisation, to break the grip of corporate capital over the world economy and to create more room for nations to determine their own path in the world appropriate to their needs.

The goals of democratisation and the realisation of human rights around the world are not in question here. The issue is rather: how can progress be made? What sorts of international initiatives are possible and workable? It is here that the liberal perspective displays its greatest weakness, calling for punitive and interfering methods, even interventionism, which tend to exacerbate problems and obviate the chances of peaceful political solutions.[36]

The intractable situations in many failed or failing states around the world are not amenable to quick-fix solutions, but generally require patient, steady negotiation and conflict resolution. As is argued in particular in Chapter 6, China's more practical approach in fact has much to offer in terms of building trust through the construction of cooperative frameworks for stability and development at a regional level in place of the power struggles inherent in the system of imperialism and hegemonism.

PART 1

THE UNIPOLAR–
MULTIPOLAR DYNAMICS

2 US–CHINA RELATIONS IN THE GLOBAL DYNAMICS

This chapter addresses the strategic dimension of the new US militarism. Since 2001, Bush has set US military doctrine on a completely different footing in a quest for absolute military advantage. The doctrine of preventive strike represented a change from a stance of defence and maintenance of the status quo to an offensive aggressive position, matched by a shift from a nuclear weapons policy of mutual deterrence to one preparing for their actual use in war.

The policy of the Bush administration from the outset was the containment of China but this then modified to a dual approach of engagement and containment, intensifying both at the same time. On the one hand, Sino–US dialogue has deepened, yet the United States has used the 'war on terror' to encircle China with military bases. Its military build-up in the Pacific is greater than it has ever been since the Second World War, setting the stage for a potential collision between the United States and China over Taiwan.

This chapter sets out to explain the developments in US hegemonic strategy, as it has unfolded under the influence of the neocons with the wars in Afghanistan and Iraq, in the context of the growing successes of China's diplomacy, especially since the end of the 1990s, as these started to open up the multipolarisation trend in Asia.

An examination of the historical development of Sino–US relations since the Second World War reveals the long-term nature of US strategy as well as the underlying importance of the US–China relationship in the shaping of the global order. Recent developments have shown the importance of controlling the Eurasian region for a US unipolar world, but the historical context also shows the strategic importance of Taiwan not only for China but also for US control over the Pacific and hence its claim to global hegemony.

US GLOBAL MILITARY STRATEGY FOR A UNIPOLAR WORLD

The end of the Cold War unleashed a new age of imperialism with the United States emerging as the world's sole superpower. The fall of the USSR was seen to have opened a 'window of opportunity' for the United States to shape the world in its own interests, freed from the limits imposed by the rival superpower. But the end of the Cold War had contradictory effects. While the US economy was in recession in the early 1990s, Europe and Japan were continuing to develop as powerful economic entities. Europe in particular was becoming more assertive in demanding more say in world affairs. The Asia-Pacific was clearly emerging as a strong economic region, with China as the fastest-growing world economy.

The post-Cold War goal of the United States, as revealed by Wolfowitz's infamous Defense Planning Guidance (1994–99) document for the Pentagon, has been to reshape the global order to prevent the rise of regional competitors so as to guarantee US supremacy in world affairs.

To make sure that no foreign power can dictate the terms of regional or global security, the US intention is to maintain a military 'without peer' in order to 'dissuade potential adversaries from pursuing a military build up in the hopes of surpassing, or equalling the power of the United States'. Should any military competitor succeed in developing 'disruptive or other capabilities that could enable regional hegemony' the United States' declared intention is to 'deny a hostile power its strategic and operational objectives'.[1]

The US pursuit of absolute military primacy amounts to the following:

- *Strengthening the Cold War military alliances*, primarily with NATO and Japan from the mid-1990s, using them to form what Chinese strategists call a 'python strategy', to control and incorporate Europe and Japan, and suppress and contain Russia and China.[2]
- *Extending its military control across the entire globe, seeking 'full-spectrum dominance'* whereby US forces would by 2020 be able to defeat any adversary in all domains: land, sea, air, space and information. From above, this consists of the intention to 'control and dominate' space and 'deny' other countries access, as spelt out in the US Space Command's 1997 Vision for 2020, in effect, turning space into a new theatre of war.[3] From below, this involves a 'revolution in military affairs' to create a hi-tech flexible forward-deployed rapid reaction military operating from small 'lily pad' bases networked across the globe from Africa to the Middle East and Asia. This global force alignment aims to 'take the fight to the enemy'.[4]
- *The development of missile defence* (MD) which is intended not just as a deterrence, as the name suggests, but to operate as a shield to reinforce US nuclear first-strike capacity, making MD part of an actual preparation for using nuclear weapons in war. By effectively allowing the Pentagon to launch a nuclear strike with impunity, its aim is to establish US military supremacy beyond challenge.

- *Pursuing nuclear primacy*, increasing long-range nuclear strike capabilities by improving its ICBMs and submarines with more accurate high-yield nuclear warheads, at the same time lowering the nuclear threshold. The 2001 US Nuclear Posture Review set out a number of contingencies for the use of tactical nuclear weapons 'in the event of surprising military developments'. This, together with plans to develop low-yield bombs, represents the aim of upgrading nuclear weapons from a 'weapon of last resort' to a potentially usable part of the US military arsenal.

The Bush doctrine of pre-emptive – or preventive – military intervention, adopted as the core principle of the US National Security Strategy (NSS) in 2002, was then the final stage of US policy transformation to secure its ambition to dominate the whole world. Effectively declaring the whole world as a zone of US national interest, it aimed to bring into play all these military preparations, giving the US military complete freedom to intervene.

Even under the second Bush administration from 2006, more favourable to multilateralism, the United States has continued to pursue its goals of global military primacy, affirming the unilateral doctrine of pre-emptive strike in the 2006 US National Security Strategy. Renewed US multilateralism has been directed primarily at integrating all major and emerging powers as 'stakeholders' in an international system that fundamentally guarantees US primacy.

US STRATEGY AS CHINA ENCIRCLEMENT

By the 1990s, it was clear that the United States was becoming increasingly concerned with the rise of China as a potential competitor. In 1992, as the Wolfowitz document was leaked to the press, Bush senior had pressed ahead with the sale of 150 F-126 fighters to Taiwan. Violating the 1982 joint Sino–American Communiqué in which the United States had agreed to scale back arms sales to Taiwan, this signalled a new more hostile approach to China in the post-Cold War period.

However, it was the Taiwan Strait crisis of 1995/6 which was to prove a turning point. This, the most serious to occur since the normalisation of Sino–US relations in 1979, escalated as Clinton gave permission in 1995 for the Taiwanese president to visit the United States on an unofficial basis. China, which had been pursuing a softer line towards reconciliation with Taiwan since January 1995, now shifted to a harder stance in the early months of 1996 when the People's Liberation Army (PLA) proceeded to conduct exercises to coincide with the island's first presidential elections. If China's actions in firing missiles, albeit without warheads, to land within

25 miles of Taiwanese ports, was an indication of its intention to become a more assertive power, the US dispatch of two aircraft carrier battle groups into the Strait, each comprising nearly 20 warships, far in excess of China's own naval capacity, left no doubt as to the extent of US hostility to China as a future adversary.

With both sides demonstrating their preparedness to use force to resolve the Taiwan issue, the crisis caused each to seriously consider the real possibility of armed conflict between them in the Strait. Almost instantly, the United States started to upgrade its alliances both with Australia and Japan. The alliance with Japan in particular had served as the linchpin of US strategy in East Asia since 1952, and when new defence guidelines were finalised in 1997, they were no mere updating of long-standing security ties but committed Japan to remilitarisation, with its forces to play a role beyond self-defence in an active support capacity in the event of US involvement in any 'areas surrounding Japan'. What was left unclear was whether this would include Taiwan, and whether Japan, which has strong links to leading members of Taiwan's elite, would be involved in collaboration with the United States to promote Taiwan's independence.

But Clinton stepped back from immediate confrontation, signing a significant agreement with China in October 1997 to work towards a 'constructive strategic partnership'. For him, Europe remained the focal point of foreign policy. Nevertheless, US strategists stayed alert to developments in the Asia-Pacific region as China continued to grow. As the commander of the US forces in the region made clear in 1999, 'We do not advertise it a lot but we're looking at making a little bigger show of our presence [in the South China Sea] than we have in the past.'[5]

Whether or not the bombing of the Chinese Embassy in Belgrade in 1999 was by accident or designed to punish China's opposition to the US-led war on Yugoslavia is a matter of dispute. However, the new NATO 'out of area' policy indicated a clear intention to expand the remit of the Atlantic military and nuclear alliance eastwards across Asia, matching Japan's own new 'out of area' guidelines, with China in the middle.

On the other hand, Clinton remained weak on MD and had given way to rapprochement with North Korea (the Democratic People's Republic of Korea). In the run-up to the 2000 election, the neocons went into action to condemn his policy as being 'soft on China'.[6]

Bush came to office with the clear strategic objective to achieve permanent military dominance and to make the Wolfowitz doctrine of preventive strike the official US global military policy. Once elected as president, he quickly declared China to be not a 'strategic partner' but a 'potential peer competitor'. The US spy plane incident off Hainan Island in April 2001 brought further military manoeuvres as three destroyers were sent to the waters off Hainan to assert the US 'right' to intrude into the airspace and waters of other nations. The incident occurred on the eve of a decision about whether to advance US anti-missile and air defence systems to Taiwan, and was swiftly followed by Bush's statement that he would be prepared to 'do whatever it takes' to help Taiwan defend itself. The subsequent $4 billion deal was to be the largest arms package since 1992. It was backed by a commitment to sell to Taiwan the Aegis system vital to MD, although this was not actually included in the package.[7]

The crisis served as a backdrop for Bush's speech just a few weeks later when he declared the Anti-Ballistic Missile (ABM) Treaty a 'relic of the Cold War' giving clear indication of his commitment to MD. In an implicit repudiation of Clinton's North-East Asia rapprochement, North Korea was the overt target, but the system was widely seen as directed against China.

The ratcheting up of tensions with China all attested to a US design to shift the focal point of its military strategy step by step towards the Asia-Pacific, and indeed much of US nuclear targeting was being shifted from Russia to China in 2001.[8]

However, following 9/11, as the United States sought to tighten its grip in the Middle East and Central Asia, Bush shifted his stance in October 2001 from regarding China as a 'strategic competitor' to accepting it as a partner in the 'war on terror'. Was global terrorism to replace China as the primary potential threat to the United States? As Chinese analysts argued, the United States was actually pretending 'to advance along one path while secretly going along another', that is, launching an anti-terrorist struggle in name only while accelerating its military deployment in Asia and the Pacific, laying out a hegemonic strategy.[9]

The US *Quadrennial Defense Review* (QDR) issued in October 2001 called for a massive escalation of military power across Asia from Baghdad to Tokyo in order to address 'new geopolitical trends shaping the world'.[10] Asia was seen as 'gradually emerging as a region susceptible to large scale military competition' with the possibility that 'a military competitor with a formidable resources base will emerge'. Particularly challenging was the area of the East Asia littoral from the Bay of Bengal to the Sea of Japan, covering the major oil routes from the Middle East to North-East Asia and across the Pacific to the US West Coast.

The December 2001 *Nuclear Posture Review* identified China amongst a nuclear 'hit list' including Iraq, Iran, North Korea, Syria, Libya and possibly Russia, specifically highlighting China's 'ongoing modernisation of its nuclear and non-nuclear forces' as a cause for concern. Alongside the possibilities of an Iraqi strike on Israel and a North Korean attack on South Korea, a confrontation over Taiwan was seen as one of three scenarios of immediate contingency in which nuclear weapons might be used.

The withdrawal of the United States from the ABM Treaty and the commitment of funds to develop MD were quickly followed by the publication of the *National Security Strategy* in 2002. Enshrining the right to preventive strike, the document noted the danger of the renewal of 'old patterns of great power competition', and directed a severe warning to China specifically to desist in its 'outdated path' of pursuing 'advanced military capabilities that can threaten its neighbours in the Asia-Pacific region'.[11]

The 'war on terror' indeed became a pretext for the United States not only to insert itself into Central Asia and the Middle East more decisively, but to strengthen its strategic hold across Asia. The establishment of a string of US bases across Central Asia, in particular in Kyrgyzstan, brought its military to just 200 miles from the borders of Xinjiang province, where China's sensitive nuclear weapon installations are sited. At the same time, the United States sought to strengthen military ties with Pakistan, India, Sri Lanka and Mongolia, and in South-East Asia with Singapore, Thailand and Malaysia as well as Indonesia.

With Japan and Australia already established as the 'northern and southern anchors' of the US East Asian security strategy, these new developments in Central, South and South-East Asia are an indication that an incipient anti-China containment strategy is virtually complete. The new advances in the US hegemonic project, focused as they were on the Middle East and Central Asia, were evidence not so much of a change of strategic orientation away from Europe and East Asia as of a shift in tactics from the 'python strategy' based on NATO and the US–Japanese alliance to close in on Russia and China from both east and west, to a Eurasian focus to contain Russia from below and China from the west.

CHINA'S MULTIPOLAR DIPLOMACY STARTS TO UNFOLD

For China, the end of the Cold War between the United States and USSR represented both a threat and an opportunity. On the one hand, it was left more vulnerable, facing the sole remaining superpower alone as Bush Senior endeavoured to orchestrate a campaign to isolate China through severe sanctions following the military crackdown in Tiananmen Square in June 1989. On the other hand, although the East Asian region still suffered the legacies of Cold War division, the general thaw opened opportunities for China to improve relations with South Korea, Singapore and Indonesia as well as with the Association of South-East Asian Nations (ASEAN) as a whole, and also with the states in Central Asia. In the face of the US embargoes, China's foreign policy took an Asian turn to follow up these new openings as the focus of governments in the region shifted from military to economic and development concerns.

Following the Taiwan Strait crisis in 1995/6, China extended its pursuit of good neighbour relations into a strategy of diplomacy which reached globally. As shall be discussed in more detail in Chapter 4, this response to the US assertion of its overwhelming power saw China stepping up its commitment to multilateralism and adopting a new approach to forge partnerships with the major world powers, whilst seeking to rebuild its relations with the United States.

Efforts began to pay off as China emerged from this difficult period: in 1996, a Sino–Russian strategic partnership of cooperation was formed, while negotiations on partnership agreements were opened with the United States in 1997; and with both the European Union and Japan in 1998. These not only helped to stabilise China's environment for development, offering a framework to manage differences through dialogue, but also helped to pave the way for significant shifts in the balance of power in the Asian regions.

The success of China's strategy in Asia caught the United States unawares. The 1997 Sino–Russian partnership agreement declared itself against the Cold War militarist mentality of division, favouring instead the promotion of a multipolar world and the establishment of a just and equitable new international political and economic order. This provided the basis for the formation of the Shanghai Five – a confidence-building grouping with Kazakhstan, Kyrgyzstan and Tajikistan. Aimed at creating a zone of stability in the Central Asian region, this group was in effect geared to fill the power vacuum which had emerged with the break-up of the USSR and the weakening position of Russia against NATO expansion.

As a part of this process, China was beginning to emerge as a significant player in the new energy markets opening in the Central Asian region. The United States received a shock when its top oil companies, including Amoco, Texaco and Unocal, were sidelined by the China National Petroleum Company in July 1997 in a deal to develop production rights of the Uzen oilfield, the second largest in Kazakhstan. The deal included a plan for a 1,900 mile pipeline stretching through Xinjiang province across China to fuel its rapidly industrialising coastal belt.[12]

Meanwhile, in South-East Asia, China's esteem rose significantly when it refused to devalue its currency during the Asian financial crisis of 1997/8. China's position was in sharp contrast to that of the United States, which insisted on imposing IMF conditions, only to make the crisis worse. Also unexpected was the summit meeting between leaders of North and South Korea in 2000 which indicated a shift in the balance of relations in North-East Asia. The prospect of rapprochement on the Korean peninsula – which owed not a little to China's diplomacy – threatened to call into question not only the existence of 37,000 US troops in South Korea but also the 60,000 in Japan and indeed the entire US security structure in the Asia-Pacific region.

July 2001 saw another critical move with the upgrading of the Shanghai Five to the more formal Shanghai Cooperation Organisation (SCO) against terrorism, separatism and extremism in the region. In its opening statement, the SCO declared opposition to US missile defence plans and support for the ABM Treaty, calling for adherence to UN principles. The formation of the SCO was made possible when Uzbekistan, concerned with mounting instability and terrorism in the region, agreed to join the Shanghai Five. Of course, it may be hard to see this as a positive global trend, given Uzbekistan's extremely poor human rights record. However, the point being made here is that this change in the power relations in Central Asia away from NATO was a serious blow to the US hegemonic strategy, given that Uzbekistan was one of the alliance's partners for peace. As Brzezinski had noted, the control of Uzbekistan is the key to controlling the Central Asian Republics, and the control of the Central Asian Republics is the key to controlling Eurasia.[13]

Brzezinski had warned in 1997 against the emergence of a 'hostile coalition' from Germany and Russia across to China that could eventually seek to challenge US primacy. He argued that the United States' worst fear should be marginalisation in Eurasia, a region containing two of the world's three most advanced and economically productive regions.[14] Now, the formation of the SCO together with the moves towards Korean rapprochement raised the real prospect of stronger ties right across this continent. The United States was losing the initiative in these two vital areas. The successes in China's diplomacy made plans for a new 'energy Silk Road' of oil and gas pipelines linking Europe and Japan with Central Asia and the Middle East, with China at the centre, a more viable proposition. Such a link would not only make China but also Europe, Japan and Korea less dependent on the US military's ability to guarantee oil supplies from the Middle East by securing the world's sea lanes.

Critics of the recent US-led wars have argued that US control of oil has been the main motivating factor. As Rees has pointed out, the region of South Central Eurasia from the Balkans to Afghanistan accounts for some three-quarters of world energy resources. Yet his account, taking energy as the focus and so viewing the Middle East and Gulf areas as the pivot of international action, passes over China at the periphery, included only as a new player in a 'Great Energy Game' of inter-imperialist rivalries.[15]

The control of oil has indeed been a key factor in US strategy. Bush made this clear in May 2001 when, noting the growing demand for energy from China along with India, he unleashed a panic that the United States was running out of oil and determined to make 'darned sure' to find more supplies.[16]

China became an oil importer for the first time in 1993. Calculations vary but Yi Xiaoxiong estimates that imports account for one-third of China's oil consumption, with 58 per cent of the supply coming from the Middle East.[17] By using the 'war on terror' to strengthen its strategic control over the world's major oil-producing regions and to extend its role in patrolling the world's sea lanes, the United States has gained new pressure points to apply to China. The control of the Malacca Strait is of particular strategic significance since over half of the world's oil passes through it each year, including much of US supplies from the Middle East and up to 80 per cent of China's imported oil.

The issue of oil, however, does not provide the whole story. The US endeavour to establish a military presence east of the Gulf is part of a much bigger strategy. By linking the wars in Afghanistan in Central Asia and Iraq in the Middle East with the 'war on terror' in South-East Asia and the pressures to destabilise North Korea, the plan is to draw the entire Asian region together in a Washington-led world security structure surrounding China in order to ensure its global integration under US primacy.

To answer the question why the United States has turned to increasing militarism in recent years, it is necessary to appreciate the significance of the shifting power balances in Asia. These, brought about not least by China's multipolar diplomacy between 1996 and 2001, showed the weakness of United States in a global strategy which left Eurasia exposed, placing the whole of its hegemonic unipolar project in potential jeopardy.

To understand further the strategic implications involved, it is necessary to look beyond China's increasing appetite for energy and examine the nature and centrality of the US–China relationship in the international order in historical context.

CHINA AND THE UNITED STATES: HISTORICAL BACKGROUND

The US 'Loss' of China

Just as the United States was about to assume the mantle of leadership of the Western capitalist world, following victory in the Second World War, it was to meet the ultimate limit of its hegemonic reach in the East. Precisely as the United States stepped into the vacuum left by Japan's defeat and a crumbling European colonial empire to claim Asia for the new 'free world', the Communist Party of China (CPC) swept to power in China in 1949 at the head of a radicalised anti-imperialist people's war movement. This victory thwarted the United States in the realisation of its long-held global ambitions.

In its own view, the appeal of US leadership lay in its ability to remake the world in its liberal image, thereby creating an international order far better than what had gone before, bringing in place of colonialism, war and totalitarianism, universal wealth and peace. But the Chinese people evidently had their own ideas about freedom.

Although US economic power was weighted towards its Atlantic seaboard, its leaders had long calculated that if their country was to succeed

Britain as the world's leading power, it must first dominate Asia. Participation in the First World War had assured the United States of a major role in the world but only to act in concert with the other great powers. For Brzezinski, Eurasia was the most crucial area of global geopolitics, where the United States had to sustain its preponderance, but in fact it was US dominance over the Pacific in the mid-twentieth century that would give it the edge over its Atlantic partners and serve as the springboard in its bid for global hegemony. Indeed, for the United States the *raison d'être* of the Second World War, the greatest overseas conflict in its history, was to stake its claim to the Pacific Ocean as 'our lake' against the Japanese rival.

For almost a century, the United States had regarded the Pacific Ocean, reaching right across to China, as its natural zone of influence. US traders had first appeared in the Pacific following Britain's success in forcibly opening China to trade through the Opium Wars. Indeed many of the leading families in the United States, including the grandfather of Franklin D. Roosevelt, had a hand in opium trafficking and made their fortunes through trade with Asia.[18]

The Second World War had itself been immensely profitable for US capital and its post-war search to maintain and increase profits fuelled a new phase in its ever westward imperialist expansion, as it looked to South-East Asia and especially China, with rich resources and the prospects of new markets opening, to support the continued growth of the US economy. The imperative was to protect this vital capitalist periphery from Communism, which the United States aimed to do with an invasion of dollars, industrial machinery and technical talent. This would help to secure governments pliable to the will of the US economy and ready to permit its military to build up a chain of bases in the region to provide the foundation for the US superpower status.

In China, following Japan's defeat in 1945, the United States manoeuvred behind a façade of mediating between two sides in a civil war in order to put in place a pro-Western government under Chiang Kaishek's Kuomintang (KMT). Although the CPC had in fact worked closely with the US military to fight the Japanese, it was clearly Chiang, an inveterate anticommunist, who would make China safe for the US dollar. So, with 100,000 of its own personnel in China, the United States helped to move Chiang's troops into north and north-east China, to prevent the CPC forces from taking over key positions.

Once set up in government, Chiang signed up to a free trade treaty with the United States in 1946 and US companies began to expand their already considerable interests in China. But the Chinese people had not fought so hard and at such cost to resist Japanese imperialism only to have put in place a highly corrupt government under the sway of US imperialism.

The CPC victory was the first defeat for the United States' new liberal international political and economic order. Two years previously India's negotiated path to independence through reform had been rushed through by the British to serve as an example for other Asian nationalists. In South-East Asia, the British, French and Dutch, with much material backing from the United States, were seeking to re-establish their hold at least for as long as it took to install pro-Western regimes equally supportive of the demands of free trade. The Chinese revolutionary path, however, now offered a radical alternative which raised hopes throughout the whole of Asia for a complete uprooting of the imperialist order and the establishment of economic as well as political independence. US plans to secure the resource-rich South-East Asian periphery for capitalism were now also placed in jeopardy.

The success of the Chinese anti-imperialist movement was a tremendous blow to the newly ascendant US power. The US westward expansion had been missionary-led, and the conquering of new frontiers across the Pacific to China had been infused with all the character of a moral crusade. Deeply interwoven into the chauvinistic belief in 'US exceptionalism' is a whole mythology about saving the souls of the 'heathen Chinese' from Fu Manchu-like despots. The 'loss of China' was a trauma then that struck at the heart of the nation's psyche, at its own conception of its 'unprecedented character' and 'manifest destiny' to light the way for the rest of the world to freedom.

Isolation and Encirclement

On the face of it, the Truman administration prevaricated in deciding how to handle the situation once Chiang Kaishek had retreated to the island of Taiwan (then known as Formosa). Roosevelt had committed himself to the return of Taiwan to China at the end of the war in a joint declaration with Britain and China at the Cairo Summit conference in 1943, and the matter was never questioned whilst the KMT was in government.[19] At the same time, although Mao had announced the policy of 'leaning to one side' to rely on friendship with the USSR in June 1949, CPC leaders had simultaneously sought some assurance of cooperation from the United States as they prepared to establish a New Democratic government in alliance with China's own business sector.[20] Only at the end of 1949 did Mao go to Moscow to negotiate an alliance with the USSR.

However, while Truman gave assurances in January 1950 that the US government would not provide military aid or advice to the KMT forces on Formosa, the press reported continued shipments of tanks at knock-down prices.[21] Despite its apparent neutrality, the United States had in fact been acting as Chiang's unofficial adviser, and now US businessmen were being pressed to leave China while US shipping was banned from entering Chinese ports. War-battered China was in desperate need and these restrictions on trade were clearly hostile.

It was ultimately Senator Joe McCarthy's apocalyptic vision of the Soviet superpower poised for global dominance that was to provide the rationale for reversing the Cairo Declaration. In his inflammatory speech on 9 February 1950, McCarthy attacked Truman's administration for having 'sold China into atheistic slavery'. Unable to accept that China had 'gone communist', many US citizens were ready to believe that the CPC-led victory was the handiwork of a Soviet conspiracy designed to subvert US foreign policy in Asia, rather than the expression of nationalist resistance and opposition to a highly corrupt regime.

When just days later, Stalin, after keeping Mao waiting around in Moscow for weeks, decided to sign a Sino–Soviet pact, a wave of anti-communist hysteria engulfed US politics and the Cold War became for the United States a fully fledged ideological crusade.

In June 1950, when North Korean troops entered into South Korea crossing the 38th parallel,[22] Truman promptly sent the 7th Fleet up through the Taiwan Strait, in a clear message of support for the KMT government against 'invasion'. The desire of the People's Republic of China (PRC) for unification with Taiwan was seen not so much as the logical conclusion of the civil war, but a part of a 'godless communist world conspiracy'. For a United States now on a crusade to reverse the tide of 'communist aggression', determined to prevent the unification of Korea under a left-wing government and intent on reversing the Chinese revolution, Taiwan was suddenly a vital geopolitical base, a stronghold from which the PRC could be challenged.

As MacArthur readied his forces[23] to roll back the North Korean troops, the United States prepared Chiang to reconquer China with massive infusions of aid. Throughout the first two years of the Korean War, the United States continued to back the KMT in Taiwan to the hilt through aid at a rate of $1 million a day.[24]

Driving back the North Korean army and moving his forces right up to the Chinese border, MacArthur declared openly that the Yalu River was neither a boundary between Korea and China, nor an end to the US Army's advancement.[25] Chinese volunteer soldiers then began to pour wave upon wave over the border to prevent the threat.[26] Although it was Truman's hostile use of the 7th Fleet that in effect took the first step in involving China in the conflict, it was the PRC that was portrayed in the West as the aggressor.

Now an international pariah in Western eyes, China faced a worldwide ban on trade. The US media unleashed a stream of frenzied ideological assaults against the 'Red Peril'; mainland Chinese assets in the United States were frozen; and Chiang's Republic of China in Taiwan was installed at the United Nations in PRC's place.

The United States set about helping the KMT to organise raids into the mainland from the small Taiwanese islands just off the Chinese coast as well as from Burma in 1951. It threatened nuclear attack against Chinese and North Korean cities.[27] Meanwhile, in Japan, it reversed its occupation plans to break up the military–industrial complex and rebuilt big business instead to produce arms for the war needs of the US-led troops in Asia.

The United States was beginning to put in place a security architecture in North-East Asia under its command, one which still continues to shape the region. Japan was reconfigured under the 1952 Security Treaty with the United States as the keystone of US power for the whole Asia-Pacific region; Taiwan was to be used as an 'unsinkable aircraft carrier', and to this day some 37,000 US troops remain in South Korea, Chinese troops having been withdrawn shortly after the 1953 armistice was agreed.

The Korean War was used to put the newly established Chinese government to the test. China was in economic ruin but although its volunteer troops, alongside those of the North Koreans, felt the full force of the US military brutality, they did not give way. The fighting ended in stalemate in 1953 and the United States was stopped from taking over all of Korea. This made the Korean War the first in history in which US troops fought and did not win.

The hostilities on the Korean peninsula having ceased, the PRC announced its intention to pursue reunification by launching a barrage on Taiwan's offshore islands. The United States, now under the Eisenhower administration, once again sent its 7th Fleet armada of nuclear-capable aircraft carriers and destroyers into the Taiwan Strait. Chivvying Chiang to retake the mainland, Eisenhower pledged in a military treaty of December 1954 to defend Taiwan and its offshore islands 'by all means necessary' including the use of nuclear weapons. China was then placed under continued threat of nuclear attack for several months.

China was yet again to face US nuclear blackmail in 1958 when Eisenhower reacted once more to a barrage of Taiwan's islands by a PRC growing impatient to resolve the issue, by sending the Pacific Fleet back up the Taiwan Strait. This time, with Dulles threatening 'massive retaliation', the United States mobilised for a nuclear first-strike attack by deploying surface-to-surface nuclear missiles from both South Korea and Taiwan.

Eisenhower had continued to build up Chiang's government ready to destabilise the PRC when the opportunity arose. His strategy of containment encircled China with a string of US military bases in South Korea, Japan, Okinawa, Taiwan, South Vietnam, Burma and Thailand. This was reinforced by a series of bilateral alliances with South Korea, Thailand, Australia and New Zealand extending the US-led security architecture, with the US–Japan Security Agreement forming the linchpin and the Taiwan Defence Agreement at the centre.

In the early 1960s, Kennedy began to intensify US presence on China's southern border, warning of the influence of an expansionist China in Vietnam. By 1965, the situation had escalated into war. As with the Korean War, the Vietnam War was essentially a war against China, which the United States regarded at this time as far more dangerous than the USSR under Khrushchev. However by the end of 1969, it was clear that the United States, facing mounting opposition at home, was losing this war to a powerful popular resistance. The US strategy of encirclement, embargo and isolation to destabilise the PRC was failing. Although this had caused severe difficulties for China's development, far from collapsing, the PRC had proved able to consolidate its national strength. Support for China's UN recognition was building up as more and more newly independent African and Asian states joined the organisation, and continued opposition by the United States to this was becoming an embarrassment. The myth of a monolithic Communist conspiracy had been completely exploded by the Sino–Soviet split in the 1960s, easing the way for the normalisation of Sino–US relations. So after the two-decade-long freeze, the United States began to realise that it would have to recognise China.

Following Kissinger's visit in July 1971, which formally expressed Nixon's desire to meet Mao, the two leaders signed the first Shanghai Communiqué in 1972 in Beijing, and by December 1978 normal diplomatic relations were established. However, although the agreements enshrined the principles of respect for sovereignty and non-aggression, the United States was to retain a degree of ambiguity in the language of the communiqués as to whether or not it explicitly accepted Taiwan as a part of China.

Sino–US rapprochement is often attributed to the motivations on both sides to counter the growing influence of the USSR. China indeed had its own concerns about its deteriorated relationship with the USSR and the massive build-up of Soviet troops and nuclear weapons along its lengthy border. The restoration of relations with the United States certainly offered China a balance against this. However, to argue that China in effect became NATO's '16th ally', as some commentators claim, is to present the Sino–US agreement as a victory for Nixon, instead of, as it really was, a massive defeat. The United States had been seeking a way out from the Vietnam quagmire, its strategy to undo the Chinese revolution in tatters. China on the other hand emerged with substantial diplomatic gains: US recognition ended the years of damaging isolation and allowed China to gain access to capital and technology from the West largely on its own terms.

Engagement and Containment

Since the normalisation of Sino–US relations, engagement has become a feature of the US China strategy as successive administrations have sought to bring China into the framework of multilateral institutions under US direction. Nevertheless, while dialogue has been in play, containment has remained the ongoing process.

Debate on China in the United States is certainly more open than a complete Cold War freeze would allow. Nevertheless, anti-communism remains a core strand in a foreign policy whose idealism in promoting liberal principles in trade and politics is what gives the United States as a nation its sense of greatness. The missionary impulse to change China persists no matter which party is in power, with the 'doves' seeking ultimate regime change by 'peaceful evolution' through cultural and educational exchanges as well as foreign investment to help make China 'more like us'.

Since the early 1990s, the United States has launched a stream of bilateral disputes against China with little basis in evidence: repeated efforts to censure China's human rights record at the United Nations (which have all failed), opposition to its bid to host the 2000 Olympics (which was lost in 1993 by two votes); charges of weapons proliferation, as well as the constant ratcheting up of pressure on trade-related issues, whilst demanding tough conditions for China's World Trade Organization (WTO) membership. These attest to a containment approach within engagement, with economic threats, pressures and sanctions used in place of war brinkmanship to weaken the Chinese state and force changes in its domestic political and economic system if not to destabilise it completely.

Taiwan – The Make or Break Issue

With the end of the Cold War, the Taiwan issue, largely left dormant through the 1980s, was brought back into play by the United States. The importance of Taiwan not only for China's strategy but also for the US global hegemonic plans cannot be over-emphasised. In China's commitment to reunification and the United States' to military support for Taiwan, the two sides are potentially on a collision course.

From China's perspective, the Taiwan issue is a matter of the unfinished business of its national liberation, a legacy of its semi-colonial humiliation, when the island was taken over by Japan in 1895, as well as when the United States intervened in the civil war to back Chiang Kaishek. It is also a hangover from the Cold War when Chiang's Republic of China was installed on the UN Security Council. The barring of the PRC was a violation of the UN Charter: never before, or since, has a country's membership of the organisation been affected by a change in political power. The so-called 'true' Republic of China was itself essentially a creature of US protection. But for US backing, the military regime of Chiang Kaishek would not have survived for long and China would have been reunified. Meanwhile, it is over the Taiwan issue that China has been and remains subject to US nuclear threats.

Taiwan is also strategically vital for the United States. Never quite able to dominate regional security affairs across the Pacific as it has the Atlantic, the United States has relied on power politics in dealing with China. In the post-Cold War period, the United States has used a policy of dual deterrence – to both restrain Taiwan's independence and obstruct reunification – in order to 'maintain the status quo' by ensuring a 'dynamic balance' in military strength across the Strait. The United States has never given the green light completely to Taiwan's separatist politicians who began to emerge more strongly in the early 1990s. However, through continued arms sales and tinkering with its diplomacy in relation to the island, it continually sends signals to give them encouragement while maintaining leverage over China to secure its dominant position. A united China would leave the US military presence in East Asia without legitimacy, ending its claims to regional hegemony over the Pacific, and indeed, to global hegemony.

The Project for a New American Century and China

The question of the 'China threat' was first stirred up when the Wolfowitz document was leaked to the press in 1992, helping to support Bush senior's reversal of the pledge to reduce Taiwan arms sales. However, it was the crisis of 1995/6, when the United States and China were on the point of military conflict, that had the most profound implications not only for China's orientation and the acceleration of its partnership approach, but also for the US hegemonic strategy.

Amid the anti-China clamour that engulfed the US media at this time, the neocon think tank, the PNAC was officially formed, with key members Armitage, Wolfowitz, Cheney and Bolton, all linked to the pro-Taiwan lobby. It was in the PNAC statement of principle in 1997 that the idea that the United States was facing a 'window of opportunity' to establish its primacy was first declared.[28]

Together with Rumsfeld, these individuals, representing the right-wing view on containing China, looked to revive the Cold War in Asia. Through these members, the PNAC had considerable influence in the US defence establishment, and although Clinton agreed to a strategic partnership with China in 1997, the growing influence of the neocon think tank was clearly evident in the thinking on full-spectrum dominance. Fixated with China's military modernisation which was seen to directly challenge US interests, and determined to see China ringed by military bases, the PNAC pressed Clinton to revitalise US military cooperation with the South-East Asian states and pressure Japan to revise its 'peace constitution' in order to further strengthen the bilateral alliance. By 2000, the US Congress had started to institute an annual report on China's military from the Pentagon, just as had previously been done with regard to Soviet military capabilities in the 1980s.

PREPARING FOR WAR WITH CHINA?

Although since agreeing a strategic partnership in 2001, Sino–US relations have improved, with the United States promising for the first time that it does not support Taiwan's independence, the containment of China has remained the underlying thrust of US global strategy.

In its effort to 'shape the choices' of a rising China, the United States has been strengthening its geopolitical superiority in areas surrounding China, building up an extraordinary network of 'lily-pad' military bases across Asia, establishing military links in Central Asia, increasing its military deployments of long-range bombers, cruise missiles and nuclear attack submarines in the Asia-Pacific region, promoting Japan's remilitarisation within the US–Japan military alliance, establishing a pro-US government in Afghanistan, developing strategic cooperation with India, as well as continuing to sell arms to Taiwan.

As President Hu Jintao is reputed to have said at a meeting of senior Party leaders in 2003: 'They [the United States] have extended outposts and placed pressure points on us from the east, south and west. This makes a great change in our geopolitical environment.'[29]

While US attention has been focused to the west of Asia, the issue of China's rise has remained simmering just under the surface, emerging again into prominence in 2005. With the Pentagon loudly decrying China's military build-up, claiming it could pose a threat to peace and stability in the Asia-Pacific, a new military agreement was reached between the United States and Japan in June 2005 to cover major purchases of MD systems and co-production agreements. Alarmingly, it identified for the first time security in the Taiwan Strait as a common strategic objective of both powers.

Then in February 2006, following the annual Pentagon report to the US Congress on the Chinese military, the US Defense Department's *Quadrennial Defense Review* mentioned China by name for the first time. With China's military expansion seen as already such as to put the regional balance at risk, the QDR proposed a concrete strategy to strengthen US long-range strike capabilities in the Pacific. While China then was singled out as having the greatest potential of the major and emerging powers to compete militarily with the United States, in contrast, Russia was seen as 'unlikely to pose a military threat ... on the same scale or intensity as the USSR during the Cold War', whilst India was seen to be emerging 'as a great power' and a 'key strategic partner' for the United States given their 'shared values as multi-ethnic democracies'. China was to be encouraged to 'emerge as a responsible stakeholder' in the world, but it was also necessary to 'hedge against other possibilities' given the potential threat from rising Chinese nationalism.

As the QDR made clear, in the face of 'future strategic uncertainties' which may emerge over the next 20 years, the US intention was to maintain its ability to fight and win a nuclear war.[30]

The appointment of John Bolton, an avowed advocate of Taiwanese independence and once a paid consultant to the Taiwanese government, as the US representative at the United Nations, sent out a powerful anti-China signal. Then in October 2006, a National Space Policy was unveiled to assert the US right to deny access to space to anyone deemed 'hostile to its interests'.

The United States is now accelerating the realignment of its military deployment to enhance its capability in the Asia-Pacific region as it seeks to 'shape the choices of a rising China'.[31] It intends to deploy the greater proportion of its SSBNs – ballistic-missile-launching submarines – to the Pacific so that they can patrol near the Chinese coast. Six of its eleven nuclear-powered aircraft carriers are to be shifted under the operation of the 7th Fleet in the South China Sea by 2010 (China has none); its B52 bombers are on 'alert' status, equipped with nuclear-armed cruise missiles which, according to Leiber and Press, are probably invisible to Russian and Chinese air defence radar.[32]

The island of Guam in the western Pacific Ocean is being developed as a 'power projection hub' in this military build-up to serve as a base for Trident submarines. The United States is also building up its naval base in Singapore. Both of these facilities allow close access to the vital Malacca Strait. Meanwhile, in November 2007, the United States announced a $940 million missile deal with Taiwan.[33]

The 'sword' of US first-strike nuclear capacity will be covered by the 'shield' of the Aegis combat system, which the United States intends to base in Japan, South Korea, Taiwan and Australia, essentially surrounding the coast of China. Long-range interceptor missiles have been installed in underground silos in Alaska and California, although these have yet to be made ready for use, and a high-powered missile tracking radar is to be based in the Aleutian islands, long seen to serve as the US's northern bridge into Asia and China.

There are about 300,000 military personnel under the US Pacific Command and approximately 190 ships and 1,400 Navy and Marine Corps aircraft controlled by the US Pacific fleet. These forces were involved in around 1,700 exercises in 2005 and 2006.

By networking its bilateral military alliances and 'lily-pad' bases in the region through hi-tech joint military exercises as well as through the construction of MD, the United States is seeking to promote an integrated 'encirclement coalition' against China. The aim is to forge a NATO-like military mechanism across 'democratic' Asia under US command, ready to intervene in conflict over the Taiwan Strait. Essential to the plan is

Japan's ongoing remilitarisation, a matter not simply of expanded military budgets but also involving a commitment to join the MD system and to reform its constitution in order to legalise the sending of its military forces abroad. The deployment of Japanese warships far beyond its territorial waters in the Iraq war, albeit in a logistical role supporting US troops, was a move unprecedented since the Second World War.

The plan is to extend the US-led Asia-Pacific security network further to the Indian Ocean and Persian Gulf to join a southward and eastward-extending NATO, thereby establishing US global hegemonic control.[34] In Asia, Japan, South Korea, the Philippines, Thailand, Pakistan, Singapore and Taiwan all have non-NATO ally status and the aim is for India to gain this too.

India, and South Asia as a whole, is of crucial strategic importance. It lies at the hub of the US Eurasian, NATO and Pacific strategies, potentially linking all these in a single US-led global alliance to contain Russia and China. The neocons have long recognised the importance of a US–India alliance to secure US status as the world's sole superpower, advocating support of a rising India to serve as a counterbalance to China. Herein lies the real significance of the US–India nuclear deal which represents a de facto recognition of India as a nuclear weapons state.

CONCLUSION

In the post-Cold War period, regardless of who is in power in the United States, the strategic elements of encircling and containing China have continued. Western commentators tend to see US China policy as characterised by contradictions, ambiguities and inconsistencies, since it has to placate the contradictory demands of the free trade business lobby on the one hand and the neocons on the other.[35] But diplomacy is not strategy. The flexibility of the dual containment-cum-engagement approach not only allows for adjustment according to changes in the domestic political atmosphere but in particular reflects the need to adapt long-term strategy to the changing international context given fluctuations in unipolar–multipolar dynamics. It allows the two elements of military and economic means, including trade, both to be used in close coordination to slow China's economic growth, circumscribe its political influence and prevent the reunification of Taiwan with the mainland in order to hold back China's emergence as a world power.[36]

China's main goal after 1997 has been to prevent containment becoming the centrepiece of US China policy.[37] Although engagement itself has an element of containment, from China's perspective, its emphasis is obviously preferable to confrontation, allowing room for manoeuvre and negotiation. With a long-term view to transforming its relationship with the United States from one of subordination and potential rivalry to one of cooperation as well as competition, the Chinese government has continually endeavoured to cast its relations with the United States in a constructive light. It has gone out of its way to play down ideological difficulties in favour of good relations, stressing the wide range of common interests in trade, environmental protection, prevention of proliferation of WMD, tackling terrorism and so on between the two countries, even opening to dialogue on human rights.

A close and cooperative relationship is of primary importance for China not only for geopolitical reasons but also given China's need to develop its economy. Despite all its problems, the United States continues to lead other developed countries in terms of science, technology, education and productivity. Not only does China have much to lose from a confrontational stance, it has much to gain from an engagement which gives vital access to technology transfer and US markets.

Clinton's support for a 'constructive partnership' with China may have been at best lukewarm, but for China this paid off with US agreement on China's WTO entry in 1999 and Congress approval of permanent normal trade relations in 2000. These put an end to nearly 30 years of equivocation and placed Sino–US trade relations on a more secure basis.

However, positive developments towards partnership should not obscure the profound differences that exist between the United States and China, which, as Wang Jisi points out, are deeper than in any other relationship between major powers in the world today.[38]

Underlying the constant disputes between the United States and China over trade and human rights, and the periodic heightening of military tensions, lie differences far more fundamental than competition over oil or over economic interests, and beyond the question of competing geopolitical interests. As Kenneth Lieberthal argues, the United States and China exemplify different global development models – the Washington Consensus of open economies and financial systems premised on what is seen to be the superiority of democratic politics, and China's model positing more state intervention in the economy and a greater concern with political stability and strong government to guide the development process.[39]

But even more than this, the United States and China hold radically different international perspectives regarding the political and economic architecture of the post-Cold War order, concerning matters such as the role of the United Nations, the continued relevance of sovereignty, the legitimate use of force and the place of humanitarian interventionism in world politics as well as over global economic issues such as technology transfer, exchange rate management and the role of the financial sector.

The US–China contradiction is a structural one, rooted in imperialist history, and global in scope, with the United States struggling to maintain its hegemonic dominance while China is on the rise at the centre of a world multipolarisation trend. The heart of the matter concerns the future of the international order – a multipolar or a unipolar world.

3 HISTORICAL PERSPECTIVES ON MULTIPOLARISATION

The post-Second World War Cold War period is generally defined in terms of the hegemonic struggle between two superpowers. Instead it should essentially be seen as a period of transition from the old imperialist order of direct colonisation, with clashes between the Western powers partitioning the world, towards a new world of independent, if highly unequal, states. Revolutionary struggles of national liberation, of which China's was the first to succeed, were key drivers of this trend. Although the world situation was still dominated by the two superpowers during this period, and neocolonialism was prevalent, limiting the independence of the new states freed from direct colonial rule, the shift in effect was the first step towards a qualitatively new stage of world history, that of multipolarity.

Chinese analysts define a pole as representing the interests of a party which 'has the capacity to exert influence on international affairs and has certain control over other world forces'.[1] By this definition, not only states, but popular political movements – including revolutionary, anti-imperialist, anti-war, peace and social justice movements – can all serve as poles in a multipolar world, exerting strategic influence on world politics. As such, they stand in opposition to a hegemonic control of world affairs in the trend towards international democracy.

Employing this notion of polarity, it is possible to interpret world development since the Second World War in a new way to highlight how the bipolar world, and the US hegemonic order in particular, has been put under challenge by a series of emerging multipolar moments or turning points as a result not least of the rise of the Third World, the emergence of more independently minded second-order powers, especially in Europe, as well as the mobilisation of mass opposition around the world to the Vietnam War and the international peace movement.

This chapter seeks firstly to identify and analyse these moments of emerging multipolarity which began to form around the agendas for peace and development in the Cold War period. It then goes on to trace how China's gradual rise as an international player from isolation after 1949 fitted into this emerging multipolarity during the period.

THE ROOTS OF MULTIPOLARISATION

The Second World War is often regarded as a war of inter-imperialist rivalry with the rise of Germany and Japan challenging the empires of the British, the French and the United States. But to take this view of the war is to misunderstand it. Far more than a recurrence of the power rivalries that had culminated in the First World War, the Second World War was a war primarily to end a prolonged process of Axis aggression and, once it started, became a war against fascism. It was a war that came to be fought by a multipolarity of forces as the United States, Britain, the USSR and China together formed an anti-fascist united front – a cooperation driven from below by the forces of popular resistance and people's war.

China, as the main theatre of battle against Japan, played a key role in the World Anti-Fascist War. Resisting invasion, Chinese forces held down over 60 per cent of the Japanese armies.[2] This prevented Japan from opening up a second front against the USSR from the east and blocked any attempt to establish German–Japanese control across Eurasia. The USSR was then able to concentrate all its forces against Hitler.

Forced to acknowledge the importance of this resistance, the United States and Britain finally agreed to end the unequal treaty system imposed on China since the 1840s.[3] Then in 1945, when Japan surrendered its 50-year rule of Taiwan, China's semi-colonial status was at an end. Its war of resistance was to become the first war of national liberation to be won and the first victory of a weak, impoverished semi-colonial country, using the ingenious tactics of guerrilla warfare in a protracted people's war, to gain victory over a much stronger imperialist power.

As a war against imperialist aggression in fascist form, the Second World War was fought to establish a peaceful world in which countries could live in equality, free from foreign intervention. Victory was brought about by a unity of multipolar forces, whose aspirations to end war forever found expression in the United Nations' principles of non-aggression and non-intervention, respect for sovereignty and equality and mutual benefit among sovereign states.

The formation of the United Nations to establish a peaceful world order represents then the achievement of the first multipolar moment of modern history. China, having gained world recognition as an equal power, was one of the initiators of the United Nations, and included in its delegation to the San Francisco Conference in 1945 to set up the United Nations was a CPC representative from China's liberated areas.

The Second World War victory gained far more than a new balance between major world powers. The defeat of fascism, the most aggressive form of imperialism, unleashed progressive movements around the world to pose a wider challenge to imperialism in general. In China in particular, the momentum of people's resistance to Japanese aggression continued through into the struggle against the corrupt nationalist government of the Kuomintang (KMT), a struggle led by the CPC to prevent China falling under the influence of yet another dominant power – the United States.

The national liberation movements from Yugoslavia and Albania to Vietnam and Indonesia were all part of this continuous process of struggle for a more peaceful world free of intervention. As Hu Jintao pointed out in a speech marking the 60th anniversary of the victory of China's war of resistance against Japan:

> Victory [in the Second World War] expanded the world's progressive forces, hit hard the old era's international system characterized by the scramble of big powers for supremacy, undermined the foundations of world colonialism, promoted the struggle in the colonies and dependencies for independence and national liberation and opened a broad vista for the surging national liberation movements in Asia, Africa and Latin America.[4]

BIPOLARITY AND MULTIPOLARITY: OPPORTUNITIES LOST AND GAINED

Relationships of inter-imperialist rivalry clearly underwent fundamental changes with the end of the Second World War. The Bretton Woods Agreement (1944), which set up the IMF and the World Bank and later GATT (1947), the precursor of the WTO, indicated a new direction in cooperation among the major capitalist powers. Western debates on these post-Second World War developments have disputed whether the nature of this post-war imperialist order was one of 'suppressed rivalries' in which the old imperialist powers of Europe sought to rely on the military predominance of the rising US superpower against the challenge from the Soviet bloc, or whether rather it represented a Kautskian-type of ultra-imperialist economic coordination, as the dominant capitalist powers transcended rivalry to cooperatively secure for themselves the preconditions for capital accumulation.

Focused on the relationship between the imperialist powers, the debates have generally failed to really grasp the significance of the rise of the Third World, including China, as a growing strategic force of influence in world politics.

The breakdown of the colonial system brought about by the successful movements for national liberation and the gradual emergence of the Third World, as a group of states conscious of their common weakness in the global system, started to fundamentally transform the international order and its political and economic dynamics.[5]

The old order of imperialist division was no longer viable and a new international order of independent, though unequal, states was emerging. It was the rising radical currents of national liberation that should be seen as demanding the shift on the part of the imperialist powers from rivalry to unity behind the single hegemonic project of the United States. Faced with the surge in the independence movements together with their own declining abilities to resist this, Britain, France and the Netherlands as well as Japan, Germany and Italy, whose empires had already ended, looked to the superordinate power of the United States to organise and shape the new order from a position of dominance. The United States was to keep control of strategic territories and resources and shape, through military interventions if necessary, a neocolonial 'global empire' on their behalf.

Neocolonialism made the former colonies 'victims of an indirect and subtle form of domination by political, economic, social, military and technical forces',[6] such that, although the colonial powers had ceded political control, the political independence gained by the new states was only partial. The colonial international division of labour provided the structural foundation for continued global economic control. As Nkrumah saw it, international capital's control of the world market was a key to neocolonialism.[7] Whilst the powerful states maintained leverage through the processes of the terms of trade, aid, the repatriation of profits and technological dependency, they in addition used diplomatic pressure and military intervention to influence the internal affairs of the new states, to undermine their independence and exercise of national sovereignty and to continue to exploit the resources of their peoples.

In response, the focus of anti-imperialist struggle then began to shift from ending direct colonial rule to transforming the neocolonial relationship of domination and exploitation. As the new states of the Third World sought to use what little room they had for leverage through cooperation with each other, the coordination of international political economy was to become the new site of struggle between the advanced capitalist countries and the developing countries. While the leading capitalist countries sought, amidst their contention, to preserve and extend the colonial legacy of inequality and Western dominance by compradorising the newly independent elites, developing countries sought to resist this, aiming to end big power domination and to reshape North–South relations for peace and global equality

The Rise of the Third World and the Development Agenda

This recognition of the rise of the Third World as the motive force for change in the post-war world challenges the common view of the post-Second World War order as shaped primarily by Cold War division.

The division between the two camps of the United States and the USSR certainly dominated the international scene in the decades after the war. However, as Hobsbawm argues, whilst the threat of military confrontation with the USSR and an ever-more frenetic nuclear arms race between the superpowers was the most obvious face of the Cold War, this was not its major impact.[8] Despite Cold War rhetoric, the United States and USSR up until the mid-1970s 'worked on the assumption that long-term peaceful coexistence between them was possible'.[9] The two superpowers generally accepted the distribution of force between them, certainly in Europe, where their relationship was a stalemate of both confrontation and dialogue. It was in fact Asia that was the major zone of superpower friction.[10]

Bello suggests that when the Cold War first broke out in 1947, the Kennan doctrine of Soviet containment was viewed as a fairly flexible strategy to resist Soviet influence at certain points key to US interests, and that it was only after 1949 and the 'fall of China' that the Cold War hardened into a fully fledged ideological crusade.[11] The establishment of the People's Republic of China (PRC) meant in international terms that the fifth seat on the UN Security Council, with the power of veto over world affairs, would fall not into the hands of the West but into the communist camp. The intensification of the Cold War prevented this from happening.

The main impact of the Cold War was then, as Hobsbawm suggests, one of political polarisation.[12] In particular it meant the sidelining of the United Nations and the fragmentation of its multipolar promise, cemented not least by China's isolation.

For Marchand, the chief significance of the Cold War lay in the way it was used by the United States to define, wherever possible, North–South relations in terms of a battle against communism in order to expand its influence especially in the newly emerging Third World.[13] In fact, both superpowers intervened repeatedly during the Cold War to support opposing sides in regional conflicts in order to extend their global influence and expand the networks of their military alliances, but it was the United States that had the greater reach.[14]

The newly gained independence of the Third World was compromised by both the Cold War and the new neocolonial economic order. Against this background the Bandung Conference of 1955 should be seen as a major turning point, expressing the unity of the Third World not only in the aim to eliminate colonialism completely but also in its opposition to these new forms of imperialist pressure.[15] The Conference brought together those involved at the frontline of the Cold War, both East and West. Leaders from former colonies in Africa and Asia were able to share their common concerns about the threats of Cold War interventionism to their newly gained sovereignty, and to discuss how to tackle their problems of economic development, essential in consolidating their political independence.

Transcending Cold War divisions, the Bandung Conference was the first sign of an emergent independent Third World as a major world political force indicating a new step in world multipolarisation. The collective effort to transform the neocolonial relationship between the developed and developing world paved the way six years later for the formation of the non-aligned movement (NAM) which, as a counterweight to the rival Cold War blocs, sought to further limit superpower domination and contention.

Following the conference, decolonisation and Third World revolution accelerated, especially in Africa and the Caribbean, and as the numbers of newly independent nations increased, the movement towards a united Third World gathered momentum. The United Nations began to revive as more and more developing countries joined, and as they did so, they began to raise their own agenda for international economic coordination. The formation in 1964 of UNCTAD and the G77, which served as channels for these demands for greater equity, further helped to erode the two-pole Cold War structure, contributing to the world multipolar trend.

By the early 1970s, the United States was in serious trouble, facing defeat in the Vietnam War. The Vietnamese people were putting up a fierce resistance, and as the human cost of the war mounted and the anti-war protests escalated, the government risked serious unrest at home.

The war was fought at huge expense and led to the collapse of the dollar, breaking the whole dollar-based Bretton Woods system of economic coordination. With the United States unable to guarantee world economic stability any longer, Europe and Japan, which had only reluctantly supported the Vietnam War in the first place, began to lose confidence in their leading ally. These old imperialist powers were beginning to re-emerge internationally as powers of a second order following the collapse of colonialism. They looked to the United States to maintain and promote the capitalist world system but were becoming less willing to accept US leadership unconditionally as they themselves started to outpace US growth after their successful post-war reconstruction. The establishment of the Common Market in Western Europe, France's partial withdrawal from NATO and de Gaulle's independent stance, the reluctance to support US aggression in Indochina, the collapse of the dollar-based monetary system, and sharpening trade and currency conflicts between Europe and Japan on the one hand and the United States on the other – all by the mid-1970s marked a serious weakening in the imperialist camp headed by the United States.[16]

The Middle East war between Israel and Egypt was also weakening the

United States. European allies refused to allow US planes to use the US air bases on their soil to rush supplies to Israel,[17] and Japan, faced with the threat of the Arab oil embargo, also abandoned their support for the US pro-Israeli stance in favour of a pro-Arab position.[18]

The setback to US hegemonism at this time was clearly brought about by a rising multipolarisation of forces: the Vietnamese resistance, the upsurge in other national liberation movements, the anti-war movements in the United States and across the world, and the demands by Europe and Japan for a greater say in world affairs.

The moment of emerging multipolarity in the early 1970s provided developing countries with an opportunity to advance their cause. The move to 'go on the offensive' was led by OPEC, which raised oil prices in 1973. Then in 1974, the developing countries, in a move that has been described as the 'revolt of the Third World', were able to gain UN agreement for a New International Economic Order (NIEO) to restructure the global political economy to meet their needs.[19]

However, despite formal UN recognition, the demands for an NIEO failed to advance. Marchand argues that the problem was that 'OPEC did not seize the opportunity to capitalise on the growing rift between the US and other industrialised countries'.[20] It might have used its resources in a win–win deal, offering incentives to the second-order powers through for example special concessions with regard to oil price and supply, to encourage them to take a lead in addressing some of the key North–South conflicts. But what the OPEC leadership lacked, she argues, was 'a complete counter-hegemonic strategy to build alliances and for consolidating power throughout the world economy'.[21]

The failures in strategy and tactics in forging a counter-hegemonic bloc should not be seen to lie with the OPEC leadership alone. With US hegemonism struggling, the demands for an NIEO picked up momentum and Japan and Western Europe both responded with their own development agendas, the Fukuda Doctrine (1977) and the Brandt Report (1980). However, the opportunity to use this multipolar moment of US weakness to create a broader counter-hegemonic movement was not followed through. Instead, the USSR chose to launch a global strategic offensive, using the opportunity of a new wave of revolutions which it had supported to establish a string of military and naval bases in Africa and Asia as well as the Americas.[22] Whilst backing the Vietnamese invasion of Kampuchea, the USSR itself invaded Afghanistan.

This new expansionist drive by the USSR gave the United States the chance to reinforce Cold War divisions as once again other Western powers turned to the United States for leadership. At the same time a weakened United States was forced to accept the greater role of the European powers and Japan in coordinating the international capitalist economy through the

G7. However, these readjustments in relations between the major powers did not prevent the United States from embarking on a new hegemonic drive in the 1980s in the form of a nuclear arms race against the USSR, underwritten by a global economic and financial liberalisation drive. As high interest rates in the United States ensured that capital poured in from Europe and Japan and the developing world to support the huge spending on defence, the Third World advance went into reverse.

Multipolarisation in the 1980s: The Peace Agenda

The onset of world recession in 1980, the reduced demands for OPEC oil and the outbreak of the Third World debt crisis, all weakened the bargaining position of the developing South, which itself was becoming more diverse with widening divisions between the least developed and the rising new industrialising states in East Asia.

In relaunching the Cold War offensive and re-establishing the primacy of the East–West over the North–South conflict, US President Reagan aimed to roll back what were seen as Soviet gains in the Third World, for example, in Ethiopia and Nicaragua, while reasserting US leadership in relation to Japan and Europe to reverse the erosion of its alliance network.

Western Europe had agreed in 1979 to the rearmament of NATO, with both Britain and Germany accepting the siting of US cruise missiles in their countries from 1983.[23] Weaker in military power, Western Europe was still tied in to the United States in terms of defence for military balance against the USSR. But now the perspectives of the United States and Western Europe began to diverge even further. Not only did the latter have to bear heavy economic costs in the arms race, but there were strategic differences to consider. While the United States and the USSR, being roughly balanced, in effect held each other in check through mutually assured destruction, the Western Europeans faced the prospect of a 'limited nuclear war' on European soil.[24] Despite their dependence on the US alliance, they began to press for détente. Whereas the United States regarded Soviet rivalry to its hegemony as the strategic priority, Western Europe began to expand its political and economic exchange with the USSR in order to shift relations from Cold War freeze towards dialogue.

These differences in the strategic approaches of the United States and Western Europe were a new indication of the shift from the bipolar Cold War division towards a more multipolar direction as the EEC and Japan, both now surpassing the United States in economic terms, started to pursue a more independent approach in world affairs across a range of issues.

Western governments were also under pressure from the growing peace movements with the mobilisation of the biggest demonstrations against nuclear weapons in history and, in Europe, the biggest demonstrations since the Second World War.[25] Tensions rose, with the siting of US missiles on European soil in 1983, Reagan's announcement of the 'Star Wars' programme, followed by the breakdown in arms talks in 1984, all stoking the danger of escalation in the arms race. However, the international peace movements were to prove a key factor in bringing Reagan eventually to the negotiating table on arms control.[26] The Gorbachev–Reagan summit of 1985 saw the United States and USSR both declare their intent to cooperate to prevent a nuclear war and to begin the process of reducing their arms.

This further historic shift was brought about once again by a combination of multipolar forces: the mutual checking capacity of the United States and USSR able to annihilate each other many times over, the desire of Western European governments in particular for détente and dialogue, the pressure of economic costs and this time, in addition, the groundswell of public opposition to nuclear weapons which formed a new pole of resistance against hegemonism. In effect, the fundamental decisions about war and peace had been taken out of the hands of the two superpowers. The ability of the United States and the USSR to influence world events was beginning to decline.

Nevertheless, the moment of emerging multipolarity of the 1980s lacked its most essential component – pressure from developing countries to reform the international economic order.

The 1980s, a growth period for the peace movement, was a 'lost decade' for many as the global economy was plunged into recession. It was a decade of stagnation, debt crisis and increased impoverishment especially for the smaller developing nations, which bore a heavy burden in the global economic readjustment imposed by the United States in order to balance its budget. With the call for an NIEO pushed to one side, the United States was able to impose its own demands, exacerbating global economic inequality. In 1985 Europe and Japan were persuaded to revalue their currencies to reduce competitive pressures on the US economy, while steep devaluations in the developing world, as recommended by the IMF, promised ever cheaper exports to offset the losses to the developed world. Export orientation drove competition between developing countries, undermining South–South cooperation and hastening the fragmentation of the developing world.

In these ways, the United States was able to pass on the heavy costs of the arms race and to recover its strength by the end of the 1980s, whilst the USSR bankrupted itself, leaving the United States as the sole world superpower.

The end of the nuclear arms race, however, opened the way for a wider retreat from militarism. The Soviet withdrawal from Afghanistan, and the moves to resolve problems in southern Africa, were indicative of a general global shift in favour of finding political rather than military solutions for conflict.

The easing of Cold War tensions began to open more opportunities for political and economic exchange between states, allowing small states room for manoeuvre in their foreign policies. One indication of this was the formation of the New Agenda Coalition of smaller powers – Brazil, Egypt, Ireland, Mexico, New Zealand, South Africa and Sweden – which were able to carry the momentum against nuclear weapons forward to the 2000 Nuclear Non-Proliferation Treaty (NPT) review conference and gain international agreement on the '13 practical steps' to nuclear disarmament.[27] However, like the NIEO, this agreement was not to be delivered by the G7 powers.

Changing the World Order: The Roots of Multipolarisation

At one level, post-Second World War history appears as a continuous line of imperialist domination and oppression, reproducing nineteenth-century patterns. Neocolonialism seems in many ways to have been just a switch in the tactics of imperialism which, under the cover of giving independence, continued to devise 'innumerable ways to accomplish objectives formerly achieved by naked colonialism'.[28]

Nonetheless, the changes in the post-war world after 1945, the victory over fascism, the formation of the United Nations, the subsequent strengthening of world revolutionary forces, the ending of the colonial system with the ascendance of movements for independence and national liberation, all went together to transform the old international colonial order. While superpower hegemonism prevailed, and the legacy of global inequality meant that the problems of developing countries were far from ended, the new order of states contained the seeds of a qualitatively different stage, that of a more independent multipolarity with the potential to operate in a more democratic way to address new global agendas for development and for peace.

With decolonisation, the direct struggles of the oppressed peoples were no longer the main form of resistance against imperialism. Instead Third World states now shifted their energies towards reform of the unequal system of international economic coordination in order to strengthen their newly gained independence through development.

Although many developing countries experienced military interventions, destabilisation, coups and imposed dictatorships, instigated especially by the United States, an emerging South–South cooperation continued to propel both non-alignment and North–South dialogue. The demand for an NIEO can be seen to mark an historic watershed with a new stage in the struggle against imperialism and hegemonism, as the rise of the Third World and its reform agenda sought to put an end to the extra economic benefits and superprofits derived through imperialist power. This began to challenge the domination of international monopoly capital.

The post-war period then was not simply marked by the power politics of the Cold War. An emerging diversity of new forces, namely, the rise of the Third World together with the emergence of a more independent-minded Western Europe, driven further by the grass-roots peace movement in the 1980s, was starting to influence a shift in the international pattern from a superpower monopoly towards multipolarity.

Hegemonism nevertheless remained dominant as multipolarisation developed unevenly in a zigzag process, its diversity of forces remaining uncoordinated and politically directionless. The failure of the developing South in the 1970s to unite behind a win–win strategy which exploited the divisions within imperialism allowed US hegemonism to seize back the political initiative. This setback to the development agenda saw the economic balance shift back in favour of the United States, so that even though the European peace movement had exerted some influence in restraining US foreign policy, the United States remained standing as the sole superpower after the collapse of the USSR.

Nonetheless, the setbacks did not bring about a complete reversal of the multipolarisation process. European and Japanese responses to the NIEO were no doubt lip service and far from accepting the independence of the Third World, but they did indicate a compromise, opening the dialogue process. New agreements, not least to prolong the NPT indefinitely and adopt a set of time-bound and measurable Millennium Development Goals to reduce world poverty, laid down important principles. Although behind these lurked deep contests over the interpretation of the NPT and the role of free trade in poverty reduction, at least these established new agendas within which the issues of both peace and development could be pressed forward. Meanwhile, the institutions of South–South cooperation – the G77 and the NAM – and the networks for peace remained largely intact.

THE EVOLUTION OF CHINA'S STRATEGIC OUTLOOK

Emerging from Isolation

Since 1949, China has continued to identify its interests with those of the Third World, maintaining the view that the primary conflict in the world is between imperialism and anti-imperialism, rather than capitalism and socialism. Its stance is clearly evident in its own foreign policy, which has been followed consistently: to realise economic development; to build a politically united nation-state, bringing about unification with Taiwan; to maintain independence and to gain recognition as a world power.

China's perspective is rooted in its historical experiences in the nine-teenth and much of the twentieth centuries, when, following the Opium War of 1840, it was reduced to a helpless semi-colony. As imperialist powers fought each other on Chinese soil for spheres of influence, the country was weakened to the point where it became overrun by the armies of Japan. The Japanese occupation was exceptionally brutal: Chinese official estimates claim a staggering 35 million casualties, higher than those sustained by the USSR in the Second World War.

The 'century of shame and humiliation' from the Opium Wars to the founding of the People's Republic, when Mao declared that the Chinese people had finally 'stood up', is deeply ingrained in Chinese national identity.

In 1949, after decades of invasion, occupation and civil war, the Chinese economy was in a complete shambles. The new government had a huge task in rehabilitating the economy and tackling poverty, at the same time facing a hostile and confrontational United States, which imposed a long-term blockade and embargo on China while carrying out subversive activities.

The Chinese revolution had represented a massive extension of the international revolution, and as such it was the major focus of imperialist aggression. As has been seen, the Korean and Vietnam wars were both wars against China launched by the United States to stem the revolutionary trend in Asia. Hemmed in by the US–Japan military alliance, and faced, throughout the 1950s, with repeated threats of a nuclear weapons strike from the United States, the Chinese government was utterly focused on building up its ability to survive a massive surprise attack and on strengthening its position in the world in order to ensure respect for its territorial integrity. It is against this historical background of such heavy losses to the Chinese people that the nation's heightened sense of threat and stated aversion to war should be assessed.

The breakthrough against US encirclement came in 1954 with an agreement between India and China to set aside their ideological differences in the formulation of the Five Principles of Peaceful Coexistence. Proposed by Premier Zhou Enlai, these principles were then carried forward to provide the centrepiece of the 1955 Bandung Conference.

The Five Principles, based on non-interference and mutual respect in inter-state relations, provided for cooperation between developing countries with different social and political systems and values. At the Bandung Conference, they helped to sustain the UN spirit at a time when it was severely weakened by Cold War division. Sometimes criticised as vague, the principles were in fact of great value in indicating the intent and commitment among African and Asian countries to seek common ground and build consensus. As principles for unity between diverse developing countries, the ideas were influential in further shaping the non-aligned path and South–South cooperation.

The principles express China's desire neither to conduct foreign relations nor to determine its position on international affairs on the basis of ideological persuasion. As such, they set out China's understanding of peaceful coexistence as the active promotion of mutual exchange and economic cooperation to transform imperialism and hegemonism through Third World unity.

The seeds planted by Zhou Enlai at Bandung came to fruition when the votes of African, Asian and Latin American states succeeded in restoring China to its lawful seat in the United Nations as a permanent member of the Security Council (UNSC) in 1971. This recognition helped to pave the way for the normalisation of Sino–US relations, and the support it received from these countries has not been forgotten by the Chinese government.[29]

From its position as one of the five UNSC permanent members, the Chinese government began to lend its weight to progressive demands. In a speech to the United Nations in 1974, Deng Xiaoping, supporting the demand for an NIEO, issued a call for an international united front against hegemonism and superpower aggression.[30] This speech was to be elaborated in 1977 into a counter-hegemonic strategy in the *Theory of the Three Worlds*.[31]

The *Theory of the Three Worlds* presented an analysis of the world situation in which the major powers were colluding in the subordination of the developing countries and cooperating among themselves to make the rules of the global economy reflect their interests, while at the same time rivalling each other over the division of the rewards from uneven development. The CPC's analysis of the multipolar moment lent particular weight to the aspect of contention, given the emerging differences in the Western alliance, and the potential for Western Europe to develop as a counter-hegemonic force.

While Stalin had sought to avoid war by relying on the strength and might of the socialist camp, in Deng's view, the world situation was no longer one of straightforward imperialist–socialist confrontation. Instead it was shaped by power relations between the three worlds of the superpowers, the second-order powers and the Third World. These relations formed a complex web of interwoven layers and forces, and the politics of the rival blocs of imperialism and socialism only intensified tensions. From the perspective of the *Theory of the Three Worlds*, the Five Principles of Peaceful Coexistence were the best means to resolve the contradictions.

The strategy aimed to create the broadest possible front against superpower dominance and Cold War division. It sought to unite Third World states, regardless of their revolutionary or progressive stance, as the main force against imperialism and hegemonism, win over the capitalist Western Europe and utilise the capacity of the two Cold War superpower adversaries to balance and limit each other.

China's call to seize the multipolar moment was however complicated by the Sino–Soviet split. China had been resistant to pressure to join the Soviet bloc in the 1950s, and by the early 1960s relations had become acrimonious as Khrushchev sought détente with the United States, leaving China exposed at a time when US imperialism was entering a new stage of aggression in South-East Asia.

China's criticisms of the USSR have often been regarded within the world socialist movement as excessive if not damaging. Though distorted into dogmatic rantings by the domestic confusion of the Cultural Revolution, there was nevertheless an important kernel of truth at the heart of the Chinese critique of Soviet strategy insofar as it focused on the protection and extension of its socialist bloc under its nuclear umbrella rather than on forming a counter-hegemonic response to US expansionism. In China's view, the Sino–Soviet split, the Bandung Conference and France's partial defection from NATO, were all harbingers of the decay of Cold War bipolarity.[32] The *Theory of the Three Worlds* was then highly critical of the Soviet global strategic offensive of the late 1970s: it had abandoned Leninism and, instead of using to advantage the differences emerging between the major capitalist powers more widely, it only served to consolidate the Western alliances, closing off the multipolar moment. In subordinating multipolarity to its own leadership and seeking to extend the socialist bloc, the USSR was itself displaying hegemonic behaviour. The CPC's international influence was at this time too weak to make much of a difference to the situation. For the USSR, its mistaken emphasis on the socialist bloc and the need to defend it, rather than a political strategy of counter-hegemonism, was to lead it into the nuclear arms race of the 1980s and to ultimate collapse.

From 'War and Revolution' to 'Peace and Development'

In 1982, China's foreign policy underwent a fundamental shift in strategic direction. Its view that 'either revolution will prevent war or war will lead to revolution' was changed as it adopted an independent foreign policy of peace and development.

Chinese analysts considered that a qualitative shift had occurred in the world situation and its own situation within this. The post-Second World War era up to the early 1980s had been overwhelmingly dominated by imperialist wars to contain and control the anti-colonial movements, and revolutionary struggle was the only alternative to achieve peace. In this situation, China itself was constantly on the alert preparing for defence against war. Following its split with the USSR, China was able to use the situation of Cold War bipolarity to manoeuvre between the two superpowers, 'leaning to one side' to play one off against the other in order to strengthen its own position.

However, 1982 was a highly significant year for China, as relations with both superpowers eased. In a joint Sino–American Communiqué, the United States pledged to scale back arms sales to Taiwan.[33] Consultations also started on the normalisation of Sino–Soviet relations. No longer under pressure of imminent attack, China could afford to take a more non-aligned stance.[34]

This reduction in tensions created completely new policy options for China. The normalisation of Sino–US relations in 1979 opened the door for engagement in international economic exchange to support development. As China's strategic focus began to shift to the long-term objective of securing a peaceful international environment for development, a new debate on multipolarisation began to develop.[35] The improvements in China's relations with the two superpowers were seen to indicate a wider underlying change in the international situation. With the two superpowers more equitably balanced, and capable of checking each other, the danger of war, though not eliminated, was easing. The capabilities of the two superpowers to sustain Cold War divisions, and thereby dominate the world, were declining and their rivalry reaching a stalemate, making room for more voices to be heard on the world stage. Western European strategic thinking was increasingly opposing the superpower monopoly of world affairs,[36] and the peace movements in the West were growing stronger. These, Chinese strategists recognised, had become an essential force in checking the superpowers from launching an all-out war.[37]

Following the Reagan–Gorbachev arms control negotiations in 1985, by 1986 Deng Xiaoping declared that 'war was no longer inevitable'.[38] With its shift in strategic calculations from 'war and revolution' to 'peace and development', China began to integrate into the international rules-based system, seeking membership of international organisations and participating in the multilateral treaty system.

But China's apparent abandonment of the Leninist precept of the inevitability of war under imperialism, and its new willingness to work within 'the clubs of the rich and powerful', was far from a 'betrayal of world revolution'. In shifting towards a more cooperative stance in world affairs, China was essentially continuing, in changed international circumstances, its practice of neither basing its relations with other states nor determining its own position on international affairs according to ideology. While staying true to its own core values of independence, self-reliance and mutuality, with the grip of the two superpowers declining, China was starting to bring into play a more dynamic strategy adapted from the *Theory of the Three Worlds*, manoeuvring in opposition to hegemonism towards multipolarity.

In its support for arms control and disarmament, a strong United Nations and the demand for an NIEO, China was earning recognition as a different kind of world power. Its support for non-alignment and its 1982 proposal for a treaty to be signed by all nuclear weapons states committing to the 'no-first use' of nuclear weapons and their non-use against non-nuclear states was particularly appreciated by NAM.[39] Nevertheless, as it began to pursue its new plans for diplomacy, Deng cautioned through the 1980s that China should still 'keep a low profile', and 'bide its time, while building up strength'.

The development agenda had been forced onto the back burner and Western Europe was really only a 'semi-independent' voice. Nevertheless, overall the change from superpower domination represented a monumental shift in the international situation, and new opportunities were beginning to open for progressive forces to take initiatives, auguring a world of more egalitarian relations between states.

By the end of the 1980s, according to China's foreign minister, Qian Qichen, the trends towards the greater independence of smaller and medium-sized nations were making 'hegemonism and power politics run up against a wall' as they increasingly refused to bow to pressure, and in general there was a greater realisation that solving international disputes by military means was getting nowhere.[40] The heavy burden of military expense meant growth in the United States and USSR was at a standstill. Meanwhile without massive arms bills, Germany and Japan were able to invest more in industry, taking advantage of the revolutions in science and technology to accelerate their development and catch up with the United States. As Qian Qichen argued:

> In the world today, people can see on the one hand the increasingly important role in international affairs played by Western Europe, Japan and the developing countries, the regional politico-economic co-operative organizations in Asia, Africa and Latin America and the non-aligned movement, while on the other hand, there is the weakened position of the US and the USSR as superpowers. Although they are still overwhelmingly strong militarily, they are seriously challenged economically and their political influence dwindles. This is the so-called development of the multipolar tendency.[41]

Emerging from the Cold War

However, the end of the Cold War left the United States as the sole unrivalled superpower, and the Gulf War of 1991, a stunning reaffirmation of its military might, signalled its intention to establish a 'new empire'.

On the other hand, the relaxation in global tensions created conditions favourable to further multipolarisation.[42] Nations now had more scope to conduct their affairs independently. With the gap between US economic strength and that of the European Union and Japan narrowing further by the early 1990s, the United States was starting to find that its relations with its allies were proving more difficult to manage in a world without the 'Soviet threat'.[43]

China, on the one hand, was left more exposed to US hegemonism by the collapse of the USSR and the Eastern European communist states. The West had attempted to isolate China, imposing sanctions following the Tiananmen crackdown in 1989. Yet, in all, only about 20 countries reacted adversely against China.[44] Stepping up its multilateralist approach, China signed the NPT in 1991 and in that year was also admitted as an observer to NAM. In 1992 it issued a White Paper on Human Rights for the first time.

Adopting a more Asian-oriented foreign policy of good neighbourliness, China made major breakthroughs in restoring and normalising relations with Singapore, Indonesia, South Korea and Thailand. In 1991 China attended the ASEAN summit for the first time. Its assistance in brokering the peace accord in Cambodia that year had earned China a great deal of prestige in South-East Asia. Relations were also quickly established with the Russian Federation, and China was now able to form diplomatic links with the former Soviet republics. Improved relations with Vietnam after 1991 signalled an end to ten years of hostilities, and India too began to seek better relations with China.

In many ways, then, China was a beneficiary of the end of the Cold War.[45] By 1993, it had managed to end much of the diplomatic isolation imposed after June 1989, as Clinton adopted a softer approach, calling for an end to the trade restrictions. Nevertheless, the United States was bent on imposing its neoliberal agenda onto the developing world through the IMF and aid conditionality as well as sanctions, while seeking to expand its military influence.

As has been seen, the 1995/6 Taiwan Strait crisis threw into stark relief the potential for military conflict between the United States and China. For China, since it was far weaker than the United States by any measure of power, to have taken a confrontational stand would have been counterproductive. It would only have invoked further hostility from a vastly superior military adversary whilst jeopardising access to the international economy. It would have played into US hands, leaving it free to strengthen its links with Taiwan and construct a circle of containment around China.

Instead, the crisis was cause for a deep debate within China on the international situation and its own position within it as a basis for the development of a new more active multipolar diplomacy.

CONCLUSION

In the post-Second World War and Cold War periods, multipolarisation emerged as a zigzag, uncoordinated and unconscious process, its advance influenced by the relative strengths and weaknesses of the superpowers and the world progressive forces for peace and development.

The Chinese revolution was an integral part of world revolution and China's development since 1949 has been a central element in the world multipolarisation process. The CPC-led coalition came to power on the crest of a worldwide upsurge against imperialism, and in 1971, the PRC was able to regain its seat in the United Nations in a new wave of anti-imperialist opposition to the US invasion of Vietnam, with the rising confidence of the developing world.

China was able then, through cautious diplomacy and balancing between superpower rivalries, to escape from the isolation imposed by the United States and rise gradually as an independent pole towards the end of the Cold War period.

Since 1982, the multipolar strategy has been at the core of China's foreign policy as it has actively pursued North–South dialogue as well as the expansion of South–South cooperation as a form of collective Third World self-reliance. With superpower contention declining, China began to change its strategic calculations although, throughout the 1980s, it tended to keep a low profile.

The end of Cold War bipolarity raised some hope for the development of a multipolar world, and China began to take a more proactive role. However, the United States was set on putting into place a unipolar strategy to prevent the rise of regional powers which might challenge its hegemonism.

The Taiwan Strait crisis put China to the test. How was it to manage its rise and promote multipolarity in a world dominated by a single superpower which was not only vastly superior militarily but was also taking an adversarial stance? Had its vision of a new multipolar world structure emerging in the post-Cold War period overanticipated the decline of US influence?

4 MANOEUVRING TOWARDS MULTIPOLARITY

The mid-1990s marked a turning point in China's diplomacy, as, following the Taiwan Strait crisis of 1995/6, strategists sought to re-evaluate the world order and China's place within it, in order to decide on what approach to take in the face of US primacy.

China's new diplomacy, with its greater commitments to multilateralism and the pursuit of cooperative partnerships with major powers, including the United States, has been widely viewed as 'acquiescing' to the United States. Instead of seeking the revolutionary overthrow of imperialism, it is argued, China aims to become a 'status quo' player, accepting the existing global rules. At best, China is seen to be pursuing 'pragmatism over principle'.

However, China's new approach was based on a shrewd assessment of the existing international trends of unipolarity and multipolarity given the relative comprehensive national power (CNP) of the major powers.

China's adaptations in the post-Cold War period in response to the situation in which US power was preponderant are, in fact, a continuation of the counter-hegemonic strategy to promote multipolarisation and create the most favourable conditions, in unpromising circumstances, to further the agendas of peace and development.

This chapter sets out in the first place to examine China's strategic assessment of the post-Cold War world situation as shaped by a unipolar–multipolar dynamic. It moves on to examine how, with the United States putting into place its hegemonic strategy to prevent the rise of regional challengers, China responded by cultivating partnerships with all the major powers aimed at placing its key international relationships on a completely new footing of cooperative security, equality and common development in line with a New Security Concept (NSC).

Countering the claims of China's acquiescence to US primacy, the discussion aims to highlight the ways in which the counter-hegemonic role of the NSC contrasts with, and provides an alternative to, the 'Bush doctrine'.

ASSESSING THE POST-COLD WAR ORDER: THE
UNIPOLAR–MULTIPOLAR BALANCE

Although the United States clearly emerged as the sole superpower at the end of the Cold War, Chinese analysts, debating their country's options in the mid-1990s, saw the world order configured not simply as a unipolar one but rather as a unipolar–multipolar dynamic. This was characterised as a five-pointed star pattern: one superpower – the United States; and four major powers – Europe, Japan, Russia and China.[1] The other developing countries which ultimately, with China, are regarded as the decisive factor in multipolarisation, were still largely in a condition of weakness and disunity. This meant that multipolarisation would mainly be facilitated in the foreseeable future through mutual checking and balancing among the major powers.[2]

The unipolar–multipolar balance was seen to depend on the competition between the five major powers as determined by their relative CNP. The exact measure of CNP has been a topic of debate among Chinese analysts but is generally understood to centre on the development of science and technology, military strength and increasing economic power.[3]

The 'five-pointed star' pattern was seen not as a static arrangement but one of constant adjustment between unipolarity, in which the United States was dominant, and multipolarity, in which it was balanced by the four other powers. Shifts occurred as on the one hand, all the different powers cooperated to keep the world stable, but at the same time they checked each other, competing for strategic advantage at the margins of the international order.[4]

The zigzags of the unipolar–multipolar dynamic were evident throughout the 1990s. The United States had put on a dramatic display of overwhelming military superiority in the first Gulf War, but its economy was plagued by deficit. To Chinese strategists it appeared that the dream of a unipolar world was one that the United States could not afford. US relations with its chief allies, Europe and Japan, were also proving more difficult to manage.[5] The deadlocked situation of the Uruguay round of GATT in the early 1990s was seen to indicate that neither of these two major powers were so keen to remain junior partners of the United States but wanted greater equality. Russia meanwhile was still regarded as a major military power with strategic nuclear clout and a certain scientific, technological and economic potential.[6]

In 1995 the world was seen to be moving 'at a dizzying pace' towards multipolarity and at the same time, it was recognised that the United States was moving towards a preventive strategy of containment in dealing with China, which it regarded as a potential rival.[7] From the Chinese strategic viewpoint, the US pursuit of global 'democratisation' was in reality a bid for unipolarity. This ideological drive had escalated rather than abated since the end of the Cold War, directed towards confrontation not only with China but with developing countries generally, over issues of neoliberal economic policy as well as 'human rights and democracy'.[8] The imposition of US values and mode of development on other countries constituted an attack on sovereignty, which, as Third World consciousness revived, was bound to trigger further conflicts.[9]

Towards the end of the 1990s, the United States was beginning to recoup its strength and the unipolar–multipolar dynamic intensified.[10] Economic rivalries between the United States, Japan and the European Union sharpened, precipitating the Asian financial crisis. More than a war of currencies triggered by hedge funds, it was a struggle between United States, European and Japanese monopoly capital for financial power.[11] China, by resisting devaluation had helped significantly to stabilise the situation, gained credit not only in the East Asian region but also in the eyes of other major powers, an improvement which from China's perspective, helped to accelerate the multipolarisation trend.[12]

But by the end of the 1990s the multipolar trend overall was clearly ebbing. As Yong Deng pointed out, neither Europe nor Japan had really made a credible attempt to become independent poles.[13] Their economies were in the doldrums, Russia was mired in economic stagnation and China was absorbed in its own economic restructuring. The US economy on the other hand was beginning to revive. Capitalising on advantages in technical innovation, especially in hi-tech weaponry, as well as its cultural influence, the United States was re-establishing its power superiority. By reviving both NATO and its military alliance with Japan, the United States was able to reincorporate Europe and Japan as junior partners and rein in their growing assertiveness, and to contain Russia as well as China, so weakening the multipolar trend.[14]

This serious imbalance between the unipolar and multipolar trends meant that US foreign policy could go ahead virtually unchallenged as it proceeded to launch an offensive against Yugoslavia. For Chinese analysts this war marked a new phase of US neo-imperialist interventionism and expansionism – a bid to create a 'new empire' which presaged new rounds of aggression and which would be seriously damaging for the sovereignty and developmental interests of many countries.[15] The United States was stepping up its global strategic deployment, preparing to 'contain, besiege and even launch pre-emptive military strikes against any country which dares to defy [its] world hegemony'.[16]

However the Chinese formula of the 'one superpower; four major powers' global pattern captured the inherent contradiction in the US global strategy. Although the United States was the only truly global power with the capacity to intervene in every part of the world, 'as powerful as America may be today, it cannot prevail without the help of others'.[17] The United States could not simply dictate the global agenda. It had had to rely on

NATO to launch a collective attack on Yugoslavia, and its failure to gain agreement on economic sanctions against Cuba and Iran and on the extra-territoriality of the Iran–Libya Sanctions Act, as well as on censuring China's human rights record at the United Nations, were all evidence that although the United States was able to maintain its leading position in the world, there were limits to its ability to impose its will on other nations.[18]

So, in order to achieve its strategic objective of unipolar hegemony, the United States had to contain potential rivals but at the same time it could only act in conjunction with other major powers to maintain its dominance. This meant that rather than confront them, the United States had to network and collaborate with other players on many international issues, thereby promoting a cooperation which conversely was conducive to improving the overall strength and international influence of its potential rivals.[19]

Although the United States was able to strengthen its military alliances and undermine the multipolar trend, the space for autonomous action by nation-states had not been so completely shrunk as during the Cold War period. As Chinese strategists recognised, there were numerous countries not willing to accept US hegemony.[20]

With the North–South gap widening, South–South cooperation was reviving as developing countries sought to resist Western pressures of polit-ical conditionality and economic liberalisation. Latin American countries had joined together to form their own regional organisation, Mercosur, in 1994, and ASEAN, in many ways a Cold War creation, began to expand in a new direction extending its membership to include the countries of Indochina. Meanwhile, the success of the ANC in South Africa in 1994 had also marked a turning point in the revival of the developing world.

The Asian financial crisis brought about a further significant change in the East Asian region. When basking in success in the 1980s and early 1990s, the export-oriented economies of East Asia had looked to the United States as the world economic leader to maintain global financial stability. However, under pressure to open their financial markets, their over-hasty financial reforms left hedge funds free to launch aggressive attacks on their currencies, bringing down governments. Their trust shat-tered, as these countries painfully sought to rebuild their economies, they began to look for new ways to reduce their dependence and vulnerability through Asian cooperation.

Nevertheless, most developing countries still wanted to keep good and stable diplomatic relations with the United States despite their disillusion-ment with the neoliberal model. So although there was potential for more and more widespread opposition to US hegemonism, Chinese strategists recognised that the majority of countries were not yet willing to come forward and organise a unified and lasting counter-hegemonic movement.[21]

China's strategy in these circumstances was to continue to 'bide its time'.

Meanwhile, the constant adjustment of relations between the major powers created room for diplomatic manoeuvre, and while avoiding taking a leading position, China could still advance in a roundabout way, adding its weight to augment the initiatives of others to make a meaningful impact.

THE COOPERATIVE SECURITY APPROACH

From the mid-1990s, and especially after the 15th CPC Congress in 1997, China began to pursue a new diplomatic track, developing its good neighbour relations in Asia into regional initiatives, embarking on partnership building to establish relations of equality with the other major powers, and becoming more and more active in international institutions.

The various elements of this diplomacy were drawn together into a New Security Concept (NSC) which was initially presented by President Jiang Zemin at meetings in 1997 with the Russian Duma and with ASEAN, and then in 1999, at the UN Conference on Disarmament. Each venue provided an opportunity to highlight a different key aspect of the approach – as a model of cooperation on traditional security issues without 'targeting a third party' (Russia); as a model for economic cooperation (ASEAN); and as a model for arms control and disarmament. The NSC was incorporated into China's National Security Strategy in 2000 and formally launched at the inauguration of the Shanghai Cooperation Organisation in 2001.[22]

The NSC can be summed up as 'four no's': no hegemonism, no power politics, no arms races and no military alliances.[23] Put positively, it sets out to establish principles of international relations based on 'mutual trust, mutual benefit, equality and coordination'. These principles present a view of security which is cooperative, in which countries endeavour to work together to foster a shared sense of security. As such, they frame an agenda of peaceful coexistence and world development which translates into the following guidelines:

- to give full play to the leading role of the United Nations
- to resolve disputes peacefully, through dialogue and negotiation
- to reform the existing international economic and financial organisations in order to promote common prosperity and common development
- to address both non-traditional (terrorism and transnational crimes) and traditional (preventing foreign invasion) security issues
- to conduct effective disarmament and refrain from an arms race.[24]

China's leaders were clearly concerned about the United States' strengthened alliances in the Asian neighbourhood as well as its plans for missile defence. China's firmer assertions of its claims in areas of contested ownership around islands and reefs in the South China Seas,[25] together with the

PLA's shelling of the Taiwan Strait, were being taken by its critics as evidence of growing expansionism.

In this context, the NSC can be seen as an exercise in good neighbourliness presenting an image of China as a responsible, peaceful and cooperative power, aimed at allaying the anxieties of the South-East Asian countries about its growing power. As an immediate measure, then, the NSC appears to be an effort on China's part to prevent its smaller neighbours from being over-influenced by US views of the 'China threat' and to 'warproof' its own environment by dissuading them from participating in US containment.[26]

However, whilst the NSC was certainly aimed to make it difficult for the United States to follow a strategy of encirclement, it represents, according to Roy, a far broader statement of the kind of international political environment in which China would feel secure and in which it could then concentrate on its own battles against poverty and for development.[27]

Yet the NSC is still more than this: beyond simply a guidance for China's bilateral relations and multilateral participation following the Five Principles of Peaceful Coexistence, it addresses US interventionism and the doctrine of preventive strike in the widest context. As a response to the 'Cold War' mentality of the US 'China threat' stance, it represents a Chinese proposal for a completely different kind of international order. (See Table 4.1.)

Drawing together the various strands of China's diplomacy developed since the end of the Cold War, the NSC represents a more coherent approach towards China's part in promoting multipolarity, focusing on minimising US unilateralism with the intention of fostering international democracy through a strengthening of international institutions, the United Nations in particular, in order to stabilise the world situation while developing North–South dialogue and South–South cooperation.

The NSC offers an alternative system for managing relations between countries which differ in their social systems, values and development levels. Where the United States stands for an ideologically driven international security environment shaped by military power and military alliance, the NSC seeks international relations based on dialogue and win–win economic cooperation, to build trust and institutionalised multilateralism in which the views of diverse countries should carry equal weight. As such it provides a long-term basis for the active shaping of multipolarisation.

The NSC is designed to promote multipolarisation in circumstances in which unipolarity was by far the more dominant aspect in the world situation. In effect it constitutes a blueprint for a worldwide counter-hegemonic response to contain US unilateralism and hegemonism, offering a concrete agenda to bring about the greater democratisation of international relations and a shift towards an alternative international political and economic order.

Van Ness argues that the core of the Chinese alternative lies in a

Table 4.1 China's cooperative security model versus the US hegemonic order

China's co-operative security model	US hegemonic order
*Multilateralism	*Unilateralism/ coalitional multilateralism
Promoting multipolarity	Maintaining and extending US dominance
Security based on development	Security based on military power
*Common security through cooperation; seeking to work with potential adversaries rather than making war on them	*Absolute security for the United States
*Conflict resolution diplomacy and rules-based collective action	*Preventive war and regime change
Constructive and cooperative partnerships based on equality and shared interests	Military alliances and power politics based on shared values (ideological stereotypes)
Sovereignty of nations as cornerstone of international order	Values of 'freedom and democracy' as cornerstone of international order
Non-interventionism	Humanitarian intervention
*Negotiations to achieve win-win outcomes	*Zero-sum strategic games
*Builds international institutions to strengthen leading role of the United Nations	*Disdain for international law and treaties
Coordinated world development to reduce global inequalities	Neoliberal 'free market' policies benefiting the strongest MNCs
Recognition of diverse paths of development	Pursues 'one size fits all' pattern of neoliberal globalisation
Harmony in diversity	Universality of liberal values/clash of civilisations

This table is adapted from a list devised by Peter Van Ness in the Conclusion to *Confronting the Bush Doctrine: Critical views from the Asia-Pacific*, ed. Mel Gurtov and Peter Van Ness (London and New York: Routledge Curzon, 2005). p.266. The asterisk* marks points drawn from this original list.

cooperative security response to Bush's unilateralist, preventive war strategy.[28] As China's *National Defense White Paper* for 1998 states:

> Security cannot be guaranteed by an increase in arms, or by military alliances. Security should be based on mutual trust and common interests. We should promote trust through dialogue, seek

security through cooperation, respect each other's sovereignty, solve disputes through peaceful means and strive for common development.[29]

According to Ye Ru'an, the NSC means that:

> ... all countries, big or small, rich or poor, strong or weak, should have an equal right to security. No country should unilaterally seek absolute security by persisting in strengthening its both [sic] offensive and defensive military capabilities at the expense of the security of other countries.[30]

The US goal of achieving absolute security through overwhelming military power, preventive strike and the threat of nuclear attack, is a search for security beyond challenge which is only to be gained at the expense of others and which tends to undermine international security overall. In direct contrast, cooperative security advocates that, in seeking its own security interests, a nation should also ensure the conditions of other nations' security, respecting their sovereignty, in order to create conditions for the security of all parties concerned.[31]

As opposed to Bush's method of targeting specific countries as 'rogue states' or potential adversaries, the cooperative security approach is inclusive. Where the United States bases its relations with other countries on 'shared values of freedom and democracy', that is, on ideological stereotypes, invariably reinforced by military alliances and links, China, according to the NSC, seeks to cooperate in a friendly way over common issues and to build on common interests, no matter how limited.

Cooperative security is to be sought through negotiation and can be built through economic, trade, scientific and technological exchange and interaction. Co-prosperity is then an integral part of cooperative security, based on win–win exchange in place of a Cold War zero-sum approach of winners and losers.

As China's then president, Jiang Zemin, stated at an informal meeting of East Asian leaders in 1997:

> ... it is imperative to adhere to the principle of mutual respect, participation on an equal footing, mutual benefit and common development so as to form a model of economic cooperation which is not exclusive and discriminatory in nature and which balances the interests of participants and gives full play to the advantages of each participant in the interest of all. It is also imperative to enhance trust, expand common ground, set aside differences, settle

disputes in a proper way and ensure regional peace and stability through friendly dialogue and consultation.[32]

Inevitably smaller and weaker powers feel threatened and suspicious in their relations with bigger powers. But power asymmetries do not mean that big and small powers cannot treat each other as equals. From the NSC perspective, all countries, big and small, have an equal right to security in that their security sensitivities are to be acknowledged and addressed. Equality in this sense, the respect for sovereignty, involves recognising the other party's 'red line' in order to negotiate win–win agreements.

The NSC is concerned to address not only traditional threats such as territorial disputes between nations but also non-traditional threats such as the spread of disease (SARS, bird flu), natural disasters (the Asian tsunami), trans-border crime, the proliferation of WMD, terrorism, financial instability, environmental degradation, and grave disparities in North–South economic development.[33] It is clearly in the common interest of differing nations to cooperate in tackling these wide-ranging threats.

Cooperative security then is about achieving common security for the world as a whole and is not just something for countries with similar or identical views and modes of development:

> Differences exist between states and nations in areas of social system, values, road to development, historical tradition, religious belief and cultural background...Differences in history, culture and economic and social systems should not become the reason for estrangement, hostility and conflict.[34]

Given the world's diversity, China advocates 'setting aside differences and seeking common ground'. This flexible and diversified approach to negotiation seeks to avoid conflict and achieve accommodation. Within Asia, China has sought 'consensus through consultation, gradual progress and proceeding at a pace comfortable to all'.[35]

For China, issues of difference and diversity are to be approached through frequent, and if necessary, over particularly intractable issues, protracted dialogue. Cold War suspicions may be dispelled through 'getting to know each other' exchanges helping to ease tensions and improve mutual understanding, and win–win agreements help to build trust and confidence, before broaching discussion of controversial issues and disputes.

The promotion of 'inter civilisation harmony and coexistence' is seen as integral to the achievement of common security and development in the world.[36] A spirit of 'harmony with diversity' is central in China's conception of peaceful development, going beyond a neutral stance of tolerance to offer opportunities for mutual learning as 'different civilisations can draw on the strong points of others to make up for their own weak points'. Differences then are not seen as barriers to cooperation but rather as providing an important basis for mutual emulation and common progress.[37] The diversity of civilisations and development patterns is something to be preserved as conducive to the development of human civilisation as a whole and the realisation of common development.[38]

This perspective contrasts sharply both with the US 'one size fits all' development model, and with Samuel Huntington's view of the 'clash of civilisations' in which he takes differences in a diverse world to be the most important aspect.

BUILDING PARTNERSHIPS WITH MAJOR POWERS

From 1996, China stepped up its efforts in international cooperation. By signing the Comprehensive Test Ban Treaty (CTBT) in 1996,[39] it signalled its further commitment to multilateralism and a negotiated world order, a move which helped support new efforts to foster strategic partnerships with all the major powers, including the United States, as a means to stabilise the world order.

The partnership approach marked a new phase for China's international relations, placing greater emphasis on building strong relationships with the major powers on an equal basis.

The 1996 Sino–Russian agreement was the first partnership to be arranged – a strategic cooperative partnership which marked a qualitatively new departure for exchange between China and Russia after centuries of frequently tumultuous relations between the two countries. An agreement followed with the United States in 1997, in which both partners committed to work towards a constructive strategic partnership. There then followed a raft of partnership arrangements with France, Britain and Germany (1997 and 1998). Chinese and Indian leaders reached a consensus on the establishment of a partnership of constructive cooperation in December 1997, and in 1998 China and Japan agreed to make efforts in developing an 'amicable and cooperative partnership for peace and development in the Asian region'.

For Medieros and Taylor Fravel, the partnership approach marks a fundamental shift in China's priorities, in which relations with major powers take top priority as 'Chinese strategists increasingly see their interests as more akin to major powers and less associated with those of developing nations, which have been downgraded to a lesser priority'.[40] Was China abandoning its vow to 'stay forever on the side of the Third World' in order to gain acceptance and enhance its own international standing?

China's efforts to build a partnership with the United States are seen in particular as acquiescing to US supremacy. But why would China not choose a good or normal relationship with the United States rather than confrontation with Washington? As Goldstein argues, while the United States remains relatively more powerful than the other major powers, at least for the foreseeable future, a cooperative partnership is the only feasible approach.[41]

China clearly lacks the capability to take on the United States. As has been pointed out previously, the costs of confrontation could be catastrophic: if China did directly challenge the United States, its regional security environment would almost certainly be destabilised. Confrontation would achieve precisely what China seeks to avoid, creating an opening for the United States to extend its alliances of encirclement around China and deepen its commitment to Taiwan's defence.[42]

Through partnership, on the other hand, China gains access to US markets, loans, investment and advanced technology. Its economic interdependence with the United States, even if asymmetric, means that were China to be seriously threatened in its modernisation by the United States, as Wang Jisi points out, it would not be the only one to suffer.[43] Many US enterprises in China would lose the returns on their investment, and the American people would no longer be able to buy inexpensive Chinese products of relatively good quality for their price. On the other hand, although US motives for developing economic and trade ties with China are undoubtedly self-interested, these ties have also helped China, spurring its economic prosperity and technological advancement.

As Goldstein puts it, a partnership with the United States which affords a certain, if limited, leverage may simply be 'the best of a bad lot of options available to a relatively weak China trying to cope with life in a unipolar world the US dominates'.[44]

From a critical viewpoint, partnership arrangements seem to promise much but lack substance. China's initial agreement with the United States to build a 'constructive strategic partnership' stood on very shaky ground and began to fall apart soon after it was signed, to be ditched by Bush in 2001. Although he then altered his position of targeting China as a 'strategic competitor' to one of working towards a 'constructive and cooperative partnership' with China in 2002, this was a case of 'same bed, different dreams',[45] as evidenced in the uncertain status of President Hu Jintao's visit to the United States in 2006, which fell short of the US protocol for an official state visit.

In the case of India, in the year following agreement on forming a partnership, its foreign minister declared China to be a threat at the time that his country carried out its nuclear weapons test.

Progress in the Sino–Japanese partnership has also been extremely difficult. China failed to gain from Japan an assurance that it would not become involved in any conflict in the Taiwan Strait: instead in 2005 a joint

US–Japanese statement was issued identifying security in the Taiwan Strait as a 'common strategic objective'.

The United States has also succeeded for the time being in driving a wedge between the European Union and China, persuading the European Union not to lift its arms embargo on China.

The Sino–Russian relationship has been held up as the model partnership. Much has been made of the military dimensions of the Sino–Russian partnership – the sale of Russian fighters to China and the more recent joint military exercises. But continued difficulties between the two countries appear to weaken the partnership's effectiveness. In 2002, it proved to be no insurance against Russian accommodation of the United States, which left China isolated when the United States withdrew from the ABM Treaty. By 2005, even the Chinese media was regarding Sino–Russian relations as 'hot on top but cold underneath'. With Moscow's machinations over whether to pipe oil from its east Siberian fields to China or to a port near Japan, China's main goals of secure energy from Russia seemed to be falling short of success, while Russia on its part wants to export machinery to China for which the latter had little use.[46] Too weak then to provide a counterweight to the United States, the partnership is considered by Western commentators to be a failure.[47]

Clearly, it is easier for political leaders to proclaim a strategic partnership than to build one in practice. However, although China's efforts have undoubtedly encountered numerous setbacks, its leaders have persisted in seeking to cultivate cooperative relations, making a certain if variable progress in all cases. Before the approach can be deemed a failure, it is necessary to consider precisely what it is intended to achieve.

China's partnerships are not designed to create counter-balancing alliances targeted against the United States and should not be defined in terms of 'anti-Americanism'. The idea of non-confrontation is in fact fundamental to the partnership approach – the agreements state that they are 'not directed at third parties'.

The Sino–Russian strategic cooperative partnership, which progressed initially from the settlement of border disputes, developed into an agreement based on common interests. Clearly Russia and China have shared security concerns especially since the 1990s with regard to the US expansion of its military alliances, missile defence and the US-led wars. However, the partners' opposition to US hegemonism was expressed in the Joint Declaration of 1997, not as an anti-US alliance but as an agreement between themselves to pursue dialogue and consultation with each other to promote their mutual understanding and build confidence. Their declared aim is to work together to promote disarmament, strengthen the United Nations and the Security Council, foster multipolarisation and seek the establishment of a just and equitable international order. Both sides also recognise developing countries and the NAM as important forces in promoting world multipolarisation and building a new international order.[48]

In this way, the Sino–Russian strategic partnership can be said to set a pattern for a new type of international relationship of non-alliance and non-confrontation, one based not on power politics but on equality and trust.

This was made clear in the speech of China's then president Jiang Zemin to the Russian Duma in 1997, a keynote address in launching China's new approach to diplomacy:

> Under the new international order, each country has the right to choose independently its road of development in the light of its own national conditions .... The world is a colorful place, where countries differ from each other in terms of historical background, social system, development level and cultural tradition and values. These differences, instead of posing barriers to the development of normal State-to-State relations, should serve as driving forces behind closer exchanges and cooperation of countries and greater common development and progress. Imposing one's own social system and ideology on other countries in international relations is absolutely unacceptable, and trying to do so will go nowhere.[49]

Saunders points out that for Chinese analysts, a constructive partnership is not an accomplished result but a 'possibility that may be realised', a process as well as a goal.[50] As recognised by its leaders, China's emergence as a new international power is bound to give rise to tensions and strains in its relations with other powers. The partnership pattern aims to involve both potential adversaries as well as non-adversaries with the long-term purpose of providing a workable framework within which to handle differences and to manage often difficult relations, in order to address and resolve disputes and potential conflicts in difficult circumstances through dialogue.[51]

By setting aside ideological considerations, limiting disagreements and focusing on shared interests and concerns, the aim for China is to promote trade and economic cooperation with the other major powers and to establish frequent dialogue and build trust in order to create more effective cooperative mechanisms and eliminate barriers to the growth of bilateral relations.[52]

With the focus on common ground, partnerships provide China with an opportunity not only to allay fears of a 'China threat' but also to demonstrate to others the advantages provided by its development and hence also the costs in terms of loss of mutual benefits should relations deteriorate. At the same time, they form a mechanism within which China can also raise its own security concerns without unduly heightening the security concerns of others.[53]

As has been seen, China's partnerships are not immune from US pressure. The point however is their flexibility: unlike alliances they do not commit partners to come to each other's defence. Nor do they preclude military relations with other partners. The growing military dimension of its partnership with Russia has not prevented China from seeking improved relations with the US military, as demonstrated when Rumsfeld visited China at the end of 2005.

Flexibility in the Sino–Russian partnership allows for the fact that, for the time being at any rate, close ties with the United States carry greater weight for both sides in their economic development than their partnership with each other, since their mutual trade is as yet limited and far exceeded by their individual trade with the United States. This flexibility has meant that the partnership remained intact despite Putin's acquiescence, under US inducements and pressures, to US withdrawal from the ABM Treaty. Since then, close collaboration between Russia and China is to be seen in their continuing coordination at the UN Security Council over a number of issues, not least in endeavouring to limit the imposition of stringent sanctions on Iran, which has clearly been a bane to US efforts to set the global agenda.

What makes the partnership approach workable is the fact that whilst the United States is not strong enough to act alone, it cannot sustain a unilateral position for long, and since it cannot dictate how other powers conduct their relations with each other, this leaves a certain room for manoeuvre.

By adopting a flexible approach then, China has been able to build good relations with other powers despite their military alliances and ties with the United States, thereby deflecting the US encirclement strategy.

Take the case of Australia, which next to Japan is the key US ally in the Asia-Pacific region. As Denny Roy has observed, China, which buys huge amounts of resources from Australia, is in a position to use its economic leverage to demand that Australia downgrades its security cooperation with the United States. This could be crucial since Australia's Pine Gap space-tracking facility is a part of the US missile defence system. As Roy argues, Australians might conclude that the gains from close collaboration with the United States, chiefly, access to advanced military technology, are no longer worth the cost of incurring Chinese displeasure.[54]

At the same time, a reasonably good or at least a reasonably stable relationship with the United States is of crucial importance to China in developing a wide range of partnerships. If China is able to reduce its own conflict with the United States, this means other powers – in the European Union and ASEAN as well as Australia and Japan – will not feel that they would have to choose between Beijing and Washington. Equally, stable relations with other major and neighbouring powers help to limit the possibility of breakdown in Sino–US relations, making it harder for the United States to treat China as an enemy.

Uyanayev, tackling the question of the cooperation of India, Russia and China with the United States after 9/11 over terrorism, takes the argument further, putting forward the view that the closer relations with the United States, rather than limiting Russia–China–India cooperation, on the contrary potentially created 'a more favourable atmosphere for tripartite cooperation'.[55] While all three countries faced the common challenge of US hegemonism, they were reluctant to form an opposition bloc given the importance of their individual trade with the United States. On the other hand, a non-confrontational cooperative stance increased their chances of overcoming US Cold War suspicions that their coalition would serve as an anti-US bloc. Cooperation with the United States against terrorism made clearer the peacemaking potential of the Russia–China–India relationship, increasing the possibility of gaining US recognition of their need to access state-of-the-art technologies and investments for their internal development. At the same time, though, Uyanayev stresses, the trio's views on anti-terrorism also differed from those of the United States, since this was seen as 'a valuable part of, but not the basis of, the resolution of the challenges of globalisation, the North–South confrontation and a multipolar fair world construction'.[56]

Although it might seem contradictory, improving relations with capitalist powers, especially with the United States, is vital for China in maintaining an overall peaceful international trend, which allows it to focus on its own economic development while manoeuvring into a more advantageous position.

While China has certainly had to give ground to the United States on many occasions, by promoting partnerships with other major powers, it is also seeking to avoid over-dependence on the United States. The aim in the longer term is to strengthen its position by diversifying trading partners and sources of foreign investment and technology. By creating a wide network of beneficial economic relations, China will be able to maximise its leverage in relation to any one partner.[57]

TOWARDS A NEW POLARITY?

The pursuit of partnerships with the other major powers was a significant step in implementing China's new approach to security, complementing regional and international multilateral initiatives. Rather than bowing to US primacy, these efforts were a key part of a coordinated response to the US assertion of its sole superpower status, in the context of the international power dynamics as they unfolded from the mid-1990s.

China's aim was, in the manner of Sun Zi, to 'win without fighting', to limit, without overtly challenging the United States, so as not to have to forgo the opportunities to promote its own economic interests. On the one hand, the United States was growing increasingly aggressive and indeed by the end of the decade, as one Chinese analyst put it, China found itself 'trying hard to avoid becoming another USSR'.[58] On the other hand, there was still potential for the multipolarisation trend to strengthen. The challenge facing Chinese strategists was to devise a means, adapted to the international five-polar dynamics of cooperation and conflict, to promote multipolarisation in circumstances in which unipolarity was by far the more dominant aspect without provoking a new Cold War contention and the break-up of the world order into rival ideological blocs.

Pursuing stable, if often tenuous and fragile, relations with the major Western powers on the one hand, China was at the same time able to strengthen its relationships more widely with its Asian neighbours and develop a qualitatively new relationship with Russia. These developments, as shall be seen in more detail in Chapter 6, paved the way for China to introduce a series of Asian regional initiatives. The Sino–Russian partnership laid the ground for a wider Central Asian regional networking leading to the formation of the Shanghai Cooperation Organisation in 2001. Improved relations with both Russia and South Korea helped to place China in a position to initiate six-party talks on Korean denuclearisation in 2002. Meanwhile, stable relations with the United States also greatly assisted China in gaining WTO accession in 2001, subsequently smoothing the way for the rapid development of China's economic relations with South-East Asia.

In other words, in adapting to US primacy, China was able to create a certain space to pursue a counter-hegemonic strategy, not through anti-US alliances but by using its new diplomacy to 'loosen the coils' of the US 'python strategy' and speed up the multipolar process, strengthening its own position in this whilst staving off US containment.

Bush's adoption of an absolute security approach and the unilateralist pre-emptive strike on Iraq were aimed at reversing the multipolar trend advancing not least as a result of China's diplomacy. As one Chinese strategist saw it:

> ... the US, flaunting the banner of counter-terrorism and, taking Afghanistan and Iraq as breaches, attempts to control the Middle East and proceed to control the Eurasian continent and establish a 21st century global empire.[59]

China's calculation, however, was that in unleashing a new round of powerful expansion on a global scale, the United States, especially under the influence of the neocons, was liable to overestimate its strength and overreach.[60] Indeed, the US-led invasion of Iraq produced precisely the opposite of what was intended, spurring the development of world multipolarisation yet further. According to a key article in *People's Daily* at this time:

> The multipolarization of the world is a reflection of the diversity of the world. The world is colorful and varied in posture, and the mode of development is diversified, it should not and cannot be such a phenomenon that when 'my flowers blossom, a hundred other flowers will wither away'. The ultimate aim of the advocacy of unipolarity is to popularize US-styled democracy, freedom and the concept of value world wide by the use of both soft and hard tactics. Imposing a country's concept of value and mode of development on other countries and pushing this through by force is bound to trigger conflicts with other countries or other civilizations. This can only be the way of causing disorder. The fact is that world multipolarization … has brought to view its contour: A unified Europe is rising; the fallen Russia is regaining its vital energy; the ASEAN countries are forging ahead hand-in-hand; India and China are undergoing rapid development; Africa has also begun to take off and march toward unity and self-improvement, only this is the balance favourable to peace and the democratization of international relations, and is the development trend of history.[61]

For China, the fact that France, Germany, Russia and India had all joined to oppose the Iraq War, despite the fact that they attached great importance to their relations with the United States, signified a substantive development in multipolarisation. Although these powers had been unable to stop the United States from launching the Iraq war, they could provide a certain restraint on its unilateralism.[62] So long as the United States was unable to sustain its global hegemonic drive on its own but depended on continued international support and cooperation from other major powers to get things done, its interventionist tendency might be limited.

In addition, new forces were emerging on the international stage:

> from the Gulf War to the Iraq War, many new characters have [emerged onto] the international political stage, they have gradually 'reached the hall and entered the chamber', playing a noticeable role on the international political stage. The anti-economic globalization, anti-terrorism, antiwar movements, organizations and religious groups and other forces will play roles together with the forces of traditional big countries in the future international pattern. The future international pattern will be far from an arena of rivalry among big powers, but rather it will be a stage for the joint performance by various characters.[63]

As large-scale global anti-war protests spread on an unprecedented scale, for Chinese strategists this all went to demonstrate that 'peace has become the common will of people worldwide'.[64]

Of great significance from the Chinese strategic viewpoint, the overall position of developing countries was also growing in strength. After 9/11, these countries had started to push forward their development agenda, and with the G77 also opposing the Iraq war, the developing countries were seen to be playing an important role again in peace and development. According to China's National Security Strategy for 2004, although the tendencies of hegemonism and unilateralism had 'gained new ground' and the North-South gap had continued to widen, developing countries had become 'important players in promoting a multipolar world and democratised international relations'.[65]

CONCLUSION

Despite the new phase of US unilateral aggressive expansionism, Chinese leaders have maintained their position that 'peace and development' are the dominant world trend, persevering with initiatives to strengthen the multipolar trend by multilateral means.[66]

Multipolarisation in the post-Cold War period has continued to develop in zigzag fashion, with the major powers adjusting and readjusting their positions in the five-pole pattern as the unipolar–multipolar dynamic has intensified. In seeking to minimise US hegemonism, China's foreign policy has had to be flexible and adaptable in its tactics in response to this constant shifting in international relations which both opens up and closes off opportunities for initiatives.

The new imperialist drive of the United States has been less about the acquisition of territories and more about the spread of US cultural, political and economic as well as military influence, employing also tactics of divide and rule. However, since other states have generally sought to pursue more independent policies, 'hegemonism today', according to Shen Jiru, 'needs submission to its domination of the world order and its formulation of international regulations. Therefore today's hegemony often uses ideology (democracy, human rights and other value concepts) as weapons.'[67]

The US hegemonic drive is a particular threat to the sovereignty of developing countries, through its imposition of the neoliberal 'one size fits all' ideology and economic pattern of globalisation, backed by power politics and Bush's doctrine of preventive war. China's new diplomacy has been variously interpreted by critics as rhetoric, image creation and defensive reaction. However, while its initiatives are certainly self-serving, its need to create a peaceful rules-based environment in which it can pursue its own development is also conducive to both the security and the development of the Third World.

The multipolar moments of the 1970s and 1980s lacked political guidelines for developing a more just and equitable international political and economic order. Now the NSC offers just such a framework, providing the essential ingredient for an overall peaceful process of evolution towards a multipolar order.

As it promotes cooperative security through its new diplomacy, China is gradually building up a network of international relationships of a new type as a basis for a multipolar world aimed to promote interdependence through coordination for a new international political and economic order.

A developing power as well as an emerging major power, China has the potential to take on a very distinctive role within the five-power dynamic to shape this multipolarisation. Its partnership approach to establish equal relations with the major powers is intended to work in tandem with its multilateral agenda for peace and development, exercising a positive influence on the operations of regional and international organisations. The bilateral agreements form part of a phased approach which allows China to stabilise its key international relationships, situating itself to advantage in the readjustments between the major powers. By increasing its own ability to network, its aim is to strengthen the multipolar check on US unilateralism, creating spaces to foster regional arrangements and South–South cooperation allowing developing countries to also strengthen their position overall.

From this positioning, China was ready, when the US-led attack on Iraq intensified the unipolar–multipolar tensions thereby opening up new prospects for South–South cooperation, to take its strategy to a new level through expanding links in Asia and reaching out to Africa and Latin America with new initiatives.

5 GLOBALISATION, IMPERIALISM AND MULTIPOLARISATION

From the Chinese perspective, economic globalisation is a major driver of political multipolarisation since it promotes the diversification of centres of industrial production and accumulation with economic integration mainly on a regional basis.[1] At the same time it leads to new relationships of inter-dependence between nations, widening their common interests and opening new avenues for cooperation.

Nevertheless, globalisation is recognised as a contradictory process – a double-edged sword – that has widened the gap between North and South, creating risks that China regards as a major security challenge.[2] Despite this problem, China actively engages with the globalisation process, partic-ipating in international economic institutions such as the World Trade Organization (WTO).

Anti-globalisers and anti-imperialists in the West regard globalisation as the process of capitalist expansion, driven by the multinational companies (MNCs) whose search for profits is aided by international economic insti-tutions such as the WTO. But where these perspectives advocate resistance, Chinese strategists favour multilateralism, seeing within the contradictions of globalisation the potential for multipolarity shaping a new kind of inter-national political economy. For them globalisation is a process that needs to be managed better, and the WTO and other international institutions provide a possible means through which China, together with other developing countries, may influence the global economy to promote a fairer and more democratised order.

These contrasting outlooks reflect differing assessments of the inter-national situation that has emerged in the post-Cold War period, of the problems of globalisation and the nature of global capitalism, and of how change might be affected.

As has been noted previously, China's advocacy of multilateral engage-ment, emphasising North–South dialogue, was based on the adjustment of its strategic vision of the dominant world trend towards one of 'peace and development' in the 1980s, a shift which has been taken by numbers of China's left-wing critics around the world as the abandonment of the Leninist tenet according to which imperialism as a system of domination is intrinsically linked to war.

The post-Cold War situation however has seen some new developments: the end of the bipolar nuclear arms race which reduced the relative influence of military over economic factors in world development, and the consequent acceleration of globalisation promoting both interdependence and regionalism. All these have to be taken into account in strategic analysis.

This chapter takes a more theoretical and conceptual approach in examining China's multipolar strategy. The overall aim is to show how China has assessed these new developments in relation to their influence on the constantly changing unipolar–multipolar dynamic, and why they are seen to create new opportunities to effect change through multilateralism and diplomacy.

The discussion further aims to show how China's strategic approach continues to operate within the Leninist framework of analysis of imperialism adapted to the new conditions of the post-Cold War world.

To do so, the chapter starts with a brief review of Western debates on imperialism and hegemonism and on the nature of the post-Cold War period in order to provide the background context for discussion. It then sets out Chinese debates on the contradictions of globalisation, which took place around the time of the country's accession to the WTO in 2001. It goes on to discuss the different elements of China's multipolar strategy in the light of the developments in global interdependence and regionalism. Finally the various strands of discussion are drawn together to highlight the ways in which the Chinese approach as a whole represents Leninism for the twenty-first century.

WESTERN DEBATES ON GLOBALISATION AND IMPERIALISM

The 1990s saw the unprecedented internationalisation of finance, markets and production, a process driven by capitalist tendencies towards concentration and monopoly, and one which is continuing to develop apace. The process is however contradictory: at the same time there has been a growing regionalisation with the emergence of the so-called Triad – the European Union, the United States and Japan – which have been extending their regional economic bases.

Relationships between the Triad members have on the one hand been competing and conflictual, particularly in the area of trade, as regional organisations have served to strengthen the position of these leading states and their multinational companies, extending their global influence. On the other hand, the Triad have increasingly coordinated their policies and activities through the G7[3] and with the formation in 1995 of the WTO. Growing internationalisation has enhanced the role both of international institutions and of regional organisations.

From the beginning of the decade, the uncertainty of the post-Cold War situation and the new developments of globalisation, interdependence and regionalism have given rise to some intense controversies among those in the West concerned to make 'another world possible'.

From a neo-Keynesian perspective, as governments around the world emerged from the grip of Cold War division and began to shift their attention from military to economic affairs, the prospects for reform of the international economic institutions to produce a new form of cooperative regulation were seen to brighten.

Progressive voices such as Stiglitz argue that while the current institutions of global governance are dominated by the commercial and financial interests of the wealthiest countries, making globalisation an unmitigated disaster in much of the world, were it to be properly and fairly run, with all countries having a voice, it in fact has great potential to benefit the developing world.[4]

At the same time, the increasingly close economic cooperation between the major capitalist powers in the G7 has given rise to a new form of Leftist opposition in the anti-globalisation movement, with its focus on corporate power – the MNCs – and the WTO.

From this perspective, globalisation is rooted in capitalism which, through agendas of liberalisation and privatisation, furthers the global reach of the MNCs, creating a new transnationalised form of capital. The formation of the WTO is seen as a defining moment in ending the era of nation-based capitalism: traditional imperialism is dead, replaced now by an indivisible world of capital with an internationally organised division of labour.[5] Opposition to this requires an entirely new form of globalised resistance.

For many on the Western Left, however, the debate on globalisation obscures the reality of power politics: globalisation is about imperialism, and violence organised by the state remains its central feature. At the end of the 1990s, as the United States set upon its path of aggressive intervention, sections in the anti-war movement started to call for anti-globalisers to shift to an anti-imperialist direction.[6]

Anti-imperialist perspectives, focusing on the central role of the state, also take issue with neo-Keynesian reformism: war and imperialism in their view is not a policy or a case of the United States straying from its proper course as a benign superpower, but rather a matter of power and exploitation. Critical of the anti-globalisation movement's focus on corporate power, they argue that the persistence of inequality and poverty ultimately depends on coercive power relations both within and between states.

From the anti-imperialist perspective, the error in the anti-globalisation view is the error of Kautsky's ultra-imperialism. Kautsky argued that the increasing scale of capitalist firms and economic integration of the major capitalist powers necessitated the stable coordination of the capitalist world economy in order to guarantee the preconditions for capital accumulation, allowing firms and states to compete peacefully for a share of the profits. However, where Kautsky saw a peaceful 'alliance of imperialists' as therefore permanent, for Lenin, since the world was divided by the imperialist powers on the basis of strength, and since strength was relative and constantly changing, war between imperialist powers was inevitable. Ultra-imperialism, as Lenin saw it, was an abstraction from the realities of inter-imperialist rivalries and the struggle for hegemonism rooted in capitalism's uneven development.

The key question then for anti-imperialists is that of political order, that is, how the inequalities of capitalism and imperialism are maintained. Yet within the anti-imperialist perspective, opinions are divided and diverse on the nature of the post-Cold War political order. Was US expansionism extending the capitalist system as a whole or was it simply a pursuit of particular hegemonic interests to secure its own predominance within the system? In whose interests was the US-led war on Iraq and what was the nature of the 'fracture across the Atlantic'? Which political forces would make 'another world possible'?

Anderson has been dismissive of the idea that Europe might serve as a counterbalance to the United States, in effect seeing their differences as those of tactics not principles, as a temporary blip in their partnership which would be restored as the European Union eventually realigned again behind the renewed US imperialist drive.[7]

It is a common view among anti-imperialists that conflicts between the United States and its capitalist allies have essentially been pacified by the overwhelming military power of the United States. Anderson's argument sees the United States as a superimperialist power, performing a dual role in serving the interests of big capital in general while pursuing its own predominance to open up the far corners of the globe to exploitation by extra-economic pressure and force.[8] Globalisation represents a new stage of imperialism, achieving greater levels of monopolisation such that European and Japanese interests coalesce increasingly with those of the US super-power to form a grand alliance in the G8 and the WTO. US hegemonism, as Anderson puts it, represents 'a general unification of the field of capital', with the United States taking on the role of coordinator for the monopoly capitalist system as a whole,[9] that is, in effect, substituting for Kautsky's ultra-imperialist federation. The role of ideology is key for Anderson, with the United States leading its partnerships and alliances by consent to create an international community based on a mutual sharing of moral as well as economic values in a 'free market and free elections' agenda.

On the other hand, for Rees, Harman and Callinicos,[10] despite the formation of the WTO and the G8, the modern imperialist world order is inherently one of rivalry. For them, the notion of US super-imperialism leads to an overestimation of US power, presenting a monolithic view of imperialism – a Kautskyite-type error. With the United States in fact in decline, the rise of Europe and Japan, followed by Russia and China,[11] is leading to a new, increasingly unstable, imperialist order with rivalries between these imperialisms intensifying as the increasing internationalisation of capital comes into conflict with the national basis of corporate organisation. Whilst direct conflict between the advanced capitalist countries is held in check by the interpenetration of their economies, they seek to settle their differences in the less industrialised parts of the world.[12]

Both the perspectives so far discussed share the view that Europe is an imperialist bloc, and oppose calls for a stronger and more united Europe to counterbalance the United States.[13] Yet where the United-States-as-super-imperialist view sees the opposition to imperialism as a whole as coming from the worldwide social movements – the anti-war, mass democratic and anti-imperialist movements both within the imperialist heartland and especially across the developing world – for Harman, the main action against imperialism – that is, internationalised capital – is seen as taking place in the centres of capitalist accumulation and exploitation, with the mobilisation of the international working-class movement.[14] Although nations' rights to self-determination against imperialist interventions must be defended, anti-war and anti-imperialist movements in the advanced countries should be turned against capitalism through the mobilisation of the working class.[15]

Differing from both the above, Gowan sees Europe as the main possible new challenger to the US hegemony. Where Anderson emphasises the role of ideology and political values in US hegemony and sees the dual aspects of the US power as compatible, serving its own as well as the interests of capitalism in general, Gowan regards the US pursuit of its own economic hegemonism as leading to conflicts with the economic interests of its partners. This gives rise to more complex relationships between the core capitalist states, ones which are conflictual as well as consensual, shaped by both partnership and rivalry.[16]

Gowan sees globalisation as a particular project of the United States. Rather than a general neoliberal agenda serving the interests of capitalism overall, it represents a new form of US economic domination to uphold the international primacy of the dollar. This Dollar–Wall Street Regime (DWSR) focuses specifically on the international expansion of US finance through the liberalisation of international financial markets and the operations of the International Monetary Fund (IMF) and World Bank.[17]

Dollar primacy, as Gowan notes, allows the United States to manipulate its exchange rate unilaterally and to run up huge current account deficits without facing the kind of constraints that other states have to do. Exposing the US bias within the neoliberal approach, he argues:

> Multilateral steps eliminating trade barriers make no sense as a level playing field if a leading state can then manipulate exchange rates at will and free itself from the payments disciplines applying to other states. And when that leading state is also the producer of the world's main international currency, you have something like an imperial economic framework facing other capitalisms.[18]

So while all other states in the world face the rule that deficit countries must adjust internally, the United States applies the reverse to itself: its deficits require that everybody else pay the costs of adjustment, via exchange rate swings.

For Gowan, the main threat to the DWSR comes from the euro. The US strike upon Iraq should be seen as a strike on Europe to restrain any further development of the European regional project.[19] Taking the North-South divide as the main problem for capitalism, he regards a New-Deal Keynesian social democratic type response as the solution. However, he argues, West Europeans, together with the East Asians, who might possibly organise a further competing yen-centred bloc, are too weak to push this through. Ultimately, the future lies with emergence of a global left centred on international labour movements to oppose the global capitalist programme of the United States. But for the moment it is 'the old story of chaos, wars, imperialist exploitation'.[20]

Articulating the voice from the developing South, Amin's analysis generates a qualitatively different view of hegemonism. Where other theorists of imperialism have been concerned to examine the structure of capitalist relations, Amin, arguing for the primacy of the political, points out that hegemonism is 'always relative, vulnerable and provisional'. His focus then is on the strategies of seeking hegemony as well as the challenges to these strategies.[21]

Amin sees the United States–European Union–Japan Triad as a form of collective imperialism, which, with the increasing parasitism of the North on the South exacerbating North–South conflicts, is driven to rely on the United States as the only power capable of leading the militarisation of the North's intervention to 'make the peoples of the South accept the dictatorship of transnational capital'.[22]

On the one hand, collective imperialism, as Amin argues, is replacing the old patterns of rivalry between the dominant powers, as a result of the emergence of a genuinely new element – transnational capital – which is arising out of the changed conditions of globalised competition. Where once a country's strength as a world power depended on the strength of its national economy, now it is its global presence that determines national power: since the size of the market necessary for gaining the upper hand, even in their own national markets, is vastly increased, the competitive battle between large firms 'must be launched straightaway on the global market and won on this ground'. It is the common interest that transnational firms therefore have in the management of the world market that provides the basis of the new collective imperialism.[23]

On the other hand, frictions and cracks appear in Triad relations, since, rather than sharing equitably the profits of its leadership, the United States relies on capital flows from Europe and Japan to support over-consumptionist habits.

However, although the United States reduces its allies to 'vassals' and is only ready to make minor concessions to its Triad partners, cooperation and complicity override conflict: Europe and Japan accept US leadership since the advantages in terms of the management of global markets outweigh the disadvantages – the price or tribute to be paid to Washington to ensure permanence of the system of global inequality.[24]

While inter-Triad conflicts then 'unfold in a minor tone: it is conflicts between the Triad and the rest of the world which set the major tone'.[25] Different from Gowan, although Amin also focuses on the problem of US hegemonism, he locates the main force of opposition as coming less from the other major powers than from the Third World, states as well as peoples, which challenges the imperialist system itself.

From this perspective, Amin saw the widespread opposition to the war on Iraq as raising an entirely new prospect:

> [With] an authentic cohesion between Europe, Russia, China, the whole of Asia and the entire Africa will constitute the foundation on which will be constructed a multi-centrist, democratic and pacific world.[26]

Bello too recognises a role not only for popular movements but also for progressive states, not only in the developing world, to oppose the unequal world order maintained by US hegemonism. For him, the split between the United States and Europe was:

> a positive step for most of the world. It opens the possibility that Europeans will begin to grapple in a positive way with the problems of injustice and poverty in the developing world by

addressing the structures of Western domination largely responsible for it. It paves the way for innovative global alliances that can be beneficial for most of the world, including the eventual formation of a Europe-Africa-Latin America-Asia alliance against US hegemony.[27]

CHINESE STRATEGISTS ANALYSE GLOBALISATION

Chinese analysts and policy makers began to discuss issues of the internationalisation of production and global economic integration from the time of adoption of the Open Door policy in the early 1980s. However, the major debates about globalisation did not occur until the latter part the 1990s. At this time, the Chinese leaders were seeking to speed up WTO entry, and negotiations with the United States over the conditions of China's accession were reaching a critical point.

At the same time, the financial crisis broke in East Asia, exposing the vulnerability of those countries whose industrial growth had been integrated into a globalised production system to fluctuations in a trade and finance system geared to the needs of the developed countries.

This development caused considerable controversy within China, with voices both pro- and anti-globalisation.[28] Although divisions of opinion remain, the debates reached a certain consensus tilting towards the positive aspects of globalisation and therefore in support of China's WTO entry, deepening China's cooperation with the global economy. According to China's then president Jiang Zemin: 'Economic globalisation will not only bring about new opportunities for various countries and regions, but will also promote the peace and stability in the world.'[29]

China's multilateralism, especially in joining up to the WTO, has been seen by Leftist critics in the West as an opportunistic reformism, serving the interests of a compradorised elite. On the other hand, also from a critical viewpoint, Jiang's statement might seem to represent an ultra-imperialist vision of globalisation as a system of peaceful economic competition. However, further consideration reveals that the decision to speed up WTO accession amid debates on globalisation was made to expand China's scope for win–win economic diplomacy so as to accelerate its multipolarisation drive. Insofar as it promotes interdependencies, globalisation was seen to provide an essential basis for China's New Security Concept (NSC).

To understand the links here between China's participation in the global economy and its pursuit of multipolarisation, it is necessary to appreciate the contradictions within the globalisation process as seen by Chinese analysts – the opportunities for development as well as the threats; the trends of cooperation as well as competition; and the generation of regional trends.

The Contradictions of Globalisation 1: Opportunities and Threats

Chinese analysts have focused in the first place on globalisation as a technological revolution which has transformed production processes to permit the organisation of an integrated international system of production. The global economy is becoming integrated in a qualitatively new way, not just through trade and investment, but through the use of new information, communication and transport technologies; innovation and scientific research; and intra-industry specialisation. Globalisation therefore marks a higher phase in the international development of capitalism and imperialism. Following the first stage of the internationalisation of markets driven by colonialism, and the second phase of imperialism marked by the internationalisation of capital, the current phase, since the 1980s, involves the internationalisation of the production process itself.[30]

New technologies enable new forms of economic coordination on an international basis, opening far greater opportunities for developing countries to realise gains from trade. As Yuan and colleagues argue, in exchange for the export of low-cost manufactures, developing countries are able to import more advanced products at a cost much less than if they produced them themselves, making huge savings for domestic investment.[31]

Rong Ying suggests:

> Developing countries could make full use of international markets, technologies, capital and management experience of developed countries to cut the cost of learning and leap forward by transcending the limits of their domestic markets and primitive accumulation.[32]

The huge developments in technology and science demonstrate a positive side to globalisation, a potential to increase productive capacity on a huge scale, opening up world economic growth through revolutionising the international division of labour, promoting intra-industry specialisation and the more efficient allocation of resources.[33]

However, globalisation is recognised to be a 'two-edged sword' which in fact is widening the gaps between developed and developing countries in economic, technical and scientific levels. As Yuan and colleagues have argued, the international division of labour is not based on the principles of equality and mutual benefit but rather has been shaped by capitalist relations of exploitation in order to increase profits and alleviate economic stagnation in the core economies of the developed world.[34]

Long Yongtu, the deputy foreign trade minister responsible for negotiating China's WTO entry, recognised economic globalisation as 'a worldwide industrial restructuring in which the developed countries dominate and the multinational companies are the main motive force'.[35] With the globally integrated production systems controlled by the big US, European and Japanese MNCs, developing countries, in joining these chains, put their industrial sectors in a subordinate position, and place the lifelines of their economies into the hands of others.[36]

The internationalisation of production requires a framework of international rules of conduct and international organisation but developed countries, with their strong comprehensive national power (CNP), are able to structure these to suit their needs. Thus the rules of the IMF, World Bank and WTO are basically set by the G7 to allow developed countries to capitalise on their advantages in technology, finance, hi-tech products and management expertise.[37]

Developed countries use their monopoly position to preserve an unfair pricing system in the world market. With the prices of low-end products so low, the development of industries in the South has been hindered and developing countries have not been able to obtain the modern technology and expertise necessary to upgrade their industry and harness their natural resources.[38]

Under US leadership, the rules of the global economy have aimed to support a massive increase in the transnational flow of international capital.[39] In the first place this assists the MNCs which require huge amounts of funding to support R&D. Given the enormous profits to be made through the international production chains, competition in R&D is severe.[40] But it also allows the United States, as the main financial power that controls the international economic and financial organisations, to utilise the 'soft hegemony' of this power in continuously attacking competitive opponents and plundering developing countries.[41] Financial globalisation, whilst causing a boom in international financial markets, generates enormous amounts of 'hot money' which have made developing countries with weaker regulation systems even more vulnerable to international financial turmoil and crisis.[42] Numbers of Chinese analysts noted at the time that the losses caused to Indonesia and Thailand by unchecked speculation in the Asian financial crisis were no less destructive than the NATO war on Yugoslavia.[43] Economic globalisation is seen to have further negative effects in accelerating the 'brain drain' as well as the transfer of more and more polluting industries to developing countries.[44]

While the international system then bestows greater freedoms on developed countries, developing countries face increasing marginalisation and insecurity.[45] Forced to participate in rules not of their making, encroached upon by MNCs, exposed to unrestricted flows of capital and rendered passive by the advanced countries' domination of science and technology, developing countries have increasingly surrendered control over their national economies, their sovereignty eroded. Many of the poorest countries in the world are again 'plunging into a colonized state'.[46]

Globalisation also affects the cultural traditions and value judgments of developing countries which are then in danger of being colonised in a spiritual way.[47] Putting 'human rights above sovereignty', developed countries cover their real intentions to intervene in developing countries' internal affairs to further their own interests.[48] The United States in particular, pursuing its 'one size fits all' model to promote its own political system, values and ideology, seeks to dictate the direction of world development.[49]

The roots of the problems of globalisation mainly originate from the nature of capital as a system for the maximisation of profit. As Yu Zhou puts it:

> The advancement of the globalization process is mainly due to capital's eagerness to seek a vast and unified international market to reallocate global resources ... as the internal market profit rate keeps falling. Only by this can capital acquire maximum profit.

The result is that 'if unrestricted capital is allowed to freely lead the globalization process, inequality and unjustness [sic] between countries, individuals and regions will further worsen.'[50] As Chinese analysts see it, then, globalisation is an unequal and unjust hegemonic system, its potential to hugely enhance the capacities for common progress and prosperity trapped within the capitalist system of exploitation.[51]

However, despite all the negative aspects, and although it is inevitable that Western countries gain more, Chinese leaders argue that developing countries can make use of economic globalisation and should take an active part in the process, undertaking reform and opening up in accordance with their own national conditions.[52] As developed countries increasingly focus on the hi-tech and high-value-added parts of production in view of efficiency and cost, they no longer try to dominate a whole industry. This creates substantial opportunities for developing countries as production links within a given industry shift across borders.[53] Such arrangements, which were not available to Japan and South Korea in their post-Second World War industrialisation, allow China and other developing countries to accelerate their industrial transformation.

As Chinese Foreign Minister Li Zhaoxing argued:

> We need co-operation to realize common development. The ongoing economic globalization has increased the level of economic interdependence on the one hand, and aggravated the unevenness of development on the other, reducing some countries to a precarious position of being marginalized. A globalized economy calls

for globalized cooperation. It is only through co-operation that we can gradually redress the imbalance in global development, efficiently ward off economic and financial risks, and enable countries to seize the opportunities brought by globalization to realize common development.[54]

However, in contrast with the US over-emphasis on financial and trade liberalisation, Jiang Zemin pointed out that globalisation should give stress to 'the popularization of scientific and technological knowledge'.[55] Technological sharing is seen by China as key to a globalisation that is fair to developing countries.

The Contradictions of Globalisation 2: Conflict and Cooperation

The Chinese view regards economic globalisation and the accompanying progress in science and technology as changing the parameters of great power politics through deepening global interdependence. Inter-imperialist wars are basically now in the past and world war avoidable.[56]

The argument here draws on three key points.[57] In the first place, as a result of developments in technology, mutual investment among major powers has multiplied and with closer economic links, the costs of large-scale military conflict escalate.

Second, through macroeconomic controls, using financial mechanisms, interest rates and taxation to regulate economic activities as well as engaging in constant technological upgrading, the major powers are more able to manage world economic recession. Through the IMF, the World Bank and GATT as well as the G7, the major powers have sought to reconcile their economic contradictions so that trade frictions have not run out of control as they did in the 1930s.

Third, wars between the imperialist powers were in the past sparked by territorial expansion as the major capitalist countries made a grab for colonies in order to reap profits worldwide. Now that they can gain huge profits from the rise in productivity, big business relies more on the enormous economic strength formed by scientific and technological progress.

Major powers now tend to compete in terms of comprehensive national power (CNP). Since advantages in R&D and information are key to controlling the organisation of production chains, competition has become increasingly focused on gaining the technological lead.[58] As Yan Xuetong argues, 'world powers are more likely to defend their interests through financial strength and scientific advantage rather than through military means'.[59]

In fact, the vastly increased productive capacity and the expansion in gains from trade means that competition can be transformed from win–lose to win–win outcomes. Globalisation, then, can change imperialist relations by contributing to conditions of peaceful competition rather than hostile rivalries.

At the same time, closer economic links have meant that upheavals in one part of the world economy will impact on other parts in unpredictable ways, a globalisation of risks which increases incentives to manage global imbalances and maintain stability in the world economy.

Other non-traditional security issues have also risen up international agendas, calling for greater international cooperation in managing threats for example to the environment, global warming, ecological degradation, energy shortages, financial crises, nuclear proliferation, international terrorism, the spread of infectious diseases such as SARS, the drugs trade and so on. Since these problems cannot be solved without joint efforts from the international community, they are a driving force of global cooperation and multipolarisation, demanding democratisation in international relations.[60]

Chinese strategists nevertheless recognise that globalisation also stokes conflict. As pointed out in *China's National Defense White Paper* for 1998, despite increasing economic contact between nations, geopolitical, military security and ideological factors still play a role that cannot be ignored.[61]

Putting this more strongly, Pan Tao argues that, since globalisation also accelerates the polarisation between rich and poor and developed and developing countries, generally weakening the political and economic strength of the developing countries, 'hegemonism and power politics will intensify for a considerable period of time and new interventionism will likely run wild'.[62]

Chinese perspectives therefore highlight the contradictions within the globalisation process. On the one hand, globalisation creates the possibility and necessity for cooperation among the major powers 'amid their confrontation'.[63] As a result, the international system in the post-Cold War period has remained relatively stable. However, in conditions of increasingly uneven development, big power politics persist, as major powers seek to maintain and extend their dominance, both cooperating together to subordinate the developing countries to the rules of the global economy, and also competing amongst themselves over the division of the benefits from uneven development. Because of the imbalances of globalisation, the cooperation required to fully realise its benefits for the world as a whole remains trapped by inter-imperialist frictions.

These mutually reinforcing trends of 'hegemonism and big power politics' on the one hand, and imbalanced development on the other, are, however, from the Chinese perspective, not something that is intrinsic to globalisation. Rather it is a question of how it is managed.

China's view that 'peace and development' are the main trend internationally, and hence its advocacy of the NSC, rests at least in part, on the calculation that the cooperative currents of economic interdependence have the capacity to transform big power politics, in Deng and Moore's words, 'from the unmitigated struggle for supremacy to a more cooperative form of interstate relations'.[64] But for hostile zero-sum competition to be replaced by peacefully contested change ultimately depends on 'the emergence of a new type of international relationship formed by a multiplicity of voices seeking win–win outcomes'.

THE ASPECTS OF MULTIPOLARITY

In China's view, the multipolar trend incorporates an increasingly determining role for a rising Third World, but also includes all forces capable of exercising a restraining influence on hegemonic behaviours. This involves a recognition of the duality of the second order of major powers, such as the European powers, which benefit from an unequal world order yet are themselves constrained in taking initiatives by superpower domination, as well as of a whole range of middle powers including Canada, New Zealand and Australia – developed countries which have often found their interests at variance with superpower pursuits and which have to varying degrees sought to express their own points of view, resisting hegemonic constraints.

Chinese strategists also attach great weight to the new regionalist trend, recognising a further contradiction in economic globalisation which operates not only as a centralising process, promoting monopoly, but also as a reactive and competitive process, promoting regionalisation. Globalisation and multipolarisation then are seen to reinforce each other.[65]

The recent proliferation of regional organisations has become a key feature in shaping North–North and North–South relations in the post-Cold War international order. From the Chinese viewpoint, organisations such as the European Union, OPEC, the Asia–Europe Meeting (ASEM), ASEAN and the Shanghai Cooperation Organisation (SCO) as well as the G77 and the United Nations are regarded as significant accelerators of multipolarisation.[66]

China's multipolar strategy makes use of the new developments of regionalism, as well as increasing global interdependence, to constrain the US hegemonic tendency and open up new opportunities for South–South cooperation and North–South dialogue.

Engaging with the Hegemon: US Duality

The Iraq War not only demonstrated divisions in the transatlantic relationship but also, as Harris notes, highlighted splits within the US ruling class itself between the anti-war inclinations of transnational capitalism and the pro-war nationalist military–industrial complex.[67]

For Bello and Malig, the adjustments between the different fractions within the US ruling elite explain shifting dollar policies, with the nationalist-oriented hegemonist fraction favouring a weak dollar to ensure the supremacy of US corporate interests at the expense of competitors, while the more globalist fraction, which lays more emphasis on the common interest of the global capitalist class, favours a strong dollar to support a growing world economy.[68] As they argue further, these differing perspectives within the ruling elite also help to explain the shifts in US position towards China. While the global capitalist fraction seeks engagement with China, seeing its economy as an investment area and market for US capital, the nationalist-oriented hegemonist fraction regards China as a threat.[69]

China has used this duality within the US ruling elite to play the globalist elements against hegemonic militarism. As Saunders has argued, successful engagement of the US business community has been very important in preventing the consolidation of anti-China sentiments in Washington.[70] As the volume of US exports to China increased, a growing network of businesses dependent on Chinese imports emerged. The US business lobby involves powerful interests committed to doing business with China and since the early 1990s, it has been able to play a significant role in limiting protectionist restrictions on trade with China, helping to reduce China's vulnerability to US pressure despite the increased dependence on the US market. China then has so far been able to exploit these divisions to its advantage, steering its relations with the United States sufficiently to keep the militarists at bay by gaining support from the more transnational elements.

Second-Order Powers

Regionalism and the European Union

China attaches considerable significance to the role of the European Union in promoting multipolarisation. But to what extent does this new regionalism provide the basis for a real anti-hegemonist project? Do these regional trends reflect a new inter-imperialist rivalry, presaging an even more dangerous world?

Regional trade organisations such as the European Union and the US-led North American Free Trade Agreement (NAFTA), as Cohn points out, are more open than such organisations have been in the past.[71] Although there is a certain element of protectionism, on the whole they are quite unlike the closed protectionism of the 1930s and not aimed at regional self-sufficiency. Rather than forming rival economic blocs, regional trade agreements have been sought by the advanced industrial countries to promote their own economic growth and strengthen their position in the global economy as competitors. So, for example, the United States formed NAFTA as a means of gaining concessions from the European Union in the negotiations leading up to the 1995 WTO agreement.[72] Equally, the European Union was not set up as a rival separate bloc to the United States but to improve the bargaining power of European countries in negotiations to set up the WTO. It is more by default than by design that the euro has offered an alternative to the dollar.

What drives the new regionalism then is globalisation. Within the US-dominated system of economic coordination, new regional centres of capital accumulation have emerged as economic integration takes place on a regional basis. Both MNCs and states, facing increasingly intense competition, have sought to reorganise the division of labour on a regional basis so creating a wider and more integrated economic base in order to compete more successfully on global markets.

While these competing regions operate within the global economic system, they have their own interests and configure differently in the international political order. In the case of Europe, although its alliance with the United States is clearly underpinned by shared goals in the spread of liberalism, real differences exist over not so much whether but how to promote these values. The European Union has developed its own style. It tends not to favour the dogmatic assertion of a one-size-fits-all model; nor does it agree with the United States' bottom-up approach to the pursuit of freedom by regime change. EU support for interventionism is much more limited. As Kopstein argues, the Europeans have a preference for order over freedom and favour a top-down approach which gives more emphasis to stability through building institutional capacity.[73]

Undoubtedly the EU agenda aims to increase its own global influence, but its different positioning in the world political order is of great significance. Lacking the military capacity for global domination, it seeks not to replace the United States as world leader but rather to counterbalance US dominance to achieve stability. As Gowan points out, the EU aim in constraining the use of US military aggression within the framework of international law is to create the basis for a more equal partnership so that it might have greater influence in coordination of the global structure.[74] The rifts in the transatlantic partnership are then not of the same order as the inter-imperialist rivalries of the past.

Sino–EU Relations

The transatlantic rift over the Iraq war was seen as a particular opportunity for China to expand its engagement with the European Union with some success, following a 2005 agreement to forge a Sino–EU strategic partnership, when it was agreed China should join the Galileo satellite tracking system.[75]

Europeans are far less concerned than the United States with the 'threat' of China's 'hard' power and instead see China as a large developing country in the process of transition, a process which the European Union seeks to assist.[76]

However, there are clearly considerable differences between China and Europe, first and foremost since the European Union does not share China's adherence to the doctrine of non-interference in other states' internal affairs. They have different understandings of human rights and of free trade, with the European Union pursuing issues of labour standards and favouring more rapid liberalisation, which for China could have a negative impact on development.[77] In common with the US engagement approach, the European Union shares a basic interest in 'socialising' China into the established international order. Although China's NSC recognises that NGOs can play an important role, the European Union's pursuit of a 'soft' line to promote civil society in China tends to be viewed askance by Chinese critics as displaying a tendency to 'Westernise and divide China'.[78]

Following the attack on Iraq, the tone of the European Union towards China became more muted, indicating a greater willingness to accommodate China's gradualist approach towards political reform.[79]

From China's point of view, the European Union's 'soft' liberal internationalism is far less threatening than the Bush administration's unilateral impulses.[80] Europe has no military forces stationed in East Asia, and EU members adhere to the one-China principle. Lacking the hegemonic reach and ambition of the United States, Europe has to get what it wants through negotiation and is more prepared to treat China as an equal. In the absence of any fundamental conflicts of interest between the two sides in terms of geopolitics and strategic intention, whatever differences there may be can be resolved through dialogue.[81]

The rise of the European Union has, then, been viewed by China not as a threat but as providing more options and more room for manoeuvre.[82] Direct relations with the European Union may offer a buffer between China and the United States,[83] and especially when it has improved its relations with Russia and China, the European Union can be seen as promoting multi-polarisation within the UN framework.[84]

While it is true, as Anderson predicted, that transatlantic commonalities have reasserted themselves over the differences, Chinese analysts note that there is considerable potential for new rifts to emerge. Differences over the US missile defence system, the Kyoto Protocol to curb global warming as well as the war on Iraq, mean that the rifts between the European Union and United States cannot be easily repaired.[85] This is so not least since the differences are fundamentally rooted in the drive to redivide the world's strategic resources among the major powers.[86] Europeans, according to Qian Qichen, should 'give up the illusion that Europeans and Americans are living in the same world'.[87]

The Middle Powers

The non-militarist leanings of increasing numbers of middle-range powers such as New Zealand, Canada, Belgium and other European powers are also seen to help strengthen global trends towards peaceful economic competition. These powers have a certain influence within regional and multilateral organisations as a curb on US aggressive unilateralism, and as such are an important element in advancing the multipolarisation process.

Canada, for example, has been resistant to US plans for missile defence (MD),[88] and Australia too has expressed its reluctance to become involved in a China containment policy despite heavy US pressure.[89]

Japan

In the case of Japan, despite its status as the world's second economic superpower, its role in political multipolarisation has been much more limited than that of the European Union, which has its own political as well as economic project. Japan's regional economic hegemonism in East Asia has taken shape under US political and military leadership. Unable or unwilling to initiate any formal organisation in the region, Japan has actively encouraged its companies to regionalise their trade and investment, setting itself up as an economic rather than political role model to its developing neighbours. Projecting an image of lead goose in a 'flying geese' formation, Japan has presented its own rapid industrialisation and fast ascent into advanced technological development as providing lift-off for the rest of the region.

However, Japanese-led economic regionalisation has been decidedly unbalanced, with the 'flying geese-style' industrialisation structured around the import of Japanese intermediate capital goods and the export of finished products to the United States, leaving many countries in trade surplus with the United States but with a matching trade deficit with Japan. In this way, much of developing East Asia has been integrated via Japanese investment into the US-led global economic system. Meanwhile, East Asia's economic regionalisation, based on Japan's one-sided approach to globalisation, has left a political vacuum in which a number of regional projects are beginning to emerge. This is creating room for China to take initiatives in promoting a new agenda for a more balanced regional growth.

The Developing South: Regional Organisation and North–South dialogue

China's aim is to break through the ideologically driven 'one-size-fits-all' neoliberal orthodoxy that divides North and South by appealing to the economic interests of the North in the development of the South, in so far as their own economic growth cannot be achieved without the rich resources, vast markets and economic prosperity of the developing world. However, for the South to also benefit, its own negotiating powers must be strengthened. In this regard, from China's multipolar perspective, the most significant development in the international order has been the rise of organisations involving developing countries independent of the United States.

In the late 1980s and early 1990s, many developing countries, driven to near-paralysis by the demands of the IMF, began to look increasingly towards their own regional cooperation for economic security. This new development in regionalism in the developing world can be seen as a form of reactive defence against US economic hegemony. For example, Mercosur, the trade organisation of a number of Latin American states including Brazil and Argentina, was formed in 1991 to loosen their ties with the United States by diversifying trade on a regional basis. In East Asia, regional organisation was hastened in the wake of the Asian financial crisis after 1997/8 as countries sought to insulate themselves from the instabilities of the global financial system and currency markets.

However, critics such as Harman see Mercosur as an attempt by sections of Brazilian big business to hegemonise the other economies in the region.[90] The same might equally be argued in the case of India in the South Asia Association for Regional Cooperation (SAARC) and Singapore in ASEAN.

Certainly tensions exist among regional neighbours in the developing world, arising in conditions of uneven regional economic development as well as from the ambitions of the stronger members. US global strategic plans may also lend support to such regional ambitions to foster divisions.

Nonetheless, South–South cooperation gained new momentum at a global level at the Cancun meeting of the WTO in 2003, when Brazil, South Africa, India and China joined forces to form the G20 bloc of countries to demand that the United States and European Union open more widely to trade flows from the South. Noting this ability to limit the imposition of neoliberalism, Wallerstein goes on to argue that regional organisation in the developing world has had some effect in obstructing US economic hegemonism.[91]

For Chinese strategists South–South relations also represent international cooperation of a different kind. Chen Zuming argues that cooperative relations between China, India and Russia, which had similarly experienced many negative effects of globalisation since 1990, are not aimed purely towards geopolitical goals but are rather driven by 'a great motivation of interest: first to reduce the damage caused by unreasonable regulations; second to provide an alternative for economic development; and third to look for a buffer … to avoid economic crises'.[92]

Regional organisations of developing countries, argues Nesadurai, can be used by governments as a 'developmental tool' to build up domestic firms amid global market competition.[93] Pulling together on a regional basis, developing states can create new opportunities for themselves by making regional agreements on market regulation to support state-centred development strategies. Regional coordination and horizontal trade links provide opportunities to generate economic development and technical innovation beyond the capacities of the nation state. In other words, regional organisation offers a frame – a developmental regionalism – within which countries can nurture their domestic industries to eventually become competitive internationally.

From the Chinese strategic perspective, South–South regional economic organisation assumes particular significance as a means for developing countries to grasp the opportunities as well as cope with the challenges of globalisation. Regional cooperation helps to improve the survival capacities of developing countries offering better risk-resistance ability.[94] But beyond reactive defence, it is a means of enhancing their bargaining position in dealing with Western countries, allowing them to strengthen their voice in world affairs, and so realise greater independence.[95] The more that regions can unite, 'the more they can determine their own destiny in the global order'.[96] To strengthen themselves through unity requires that these regional organisations generally apply equalising measures to assist the integration of less developed members.

Although the incorporation of developing countries into a global economy dominated by the developed countries takes place on an unequal basis, their participation can be turned to advantage given growing economic interdependence, as Chinese strategists perceive. In the event of a war on the Korean peninsula, as Lynn points out, half the global production of D-RAM chips would be at risk which could cause massive disruption in the electronics industry; and if a major uprising were to occur for example in India, this could mean that banks would be unable to process information because their back-office operations have been relocated to the region.[97]

Such conditions demand then that MNCs and developed states be concerned about stability at the more distant ends of the supply and production chains, so providing developing countries with new opportunities to participate in global dialogue.

Taken together, interdependence and regionalism create new opportunities for pursuing the world development agenda, increasing the bargaining power and scope for participation by developing countries to shape the international economic order. Given this context of increased leverage, the Chinese government has urged developing countries to adopt a more open and pragmatic attitude to globalisation and to engage fully in formulating international trade and investment rules, and, while seeking to deepen North–South dialogue, also to enhance South–South cooperation to maximise their policy coordination in 'countering the rules of the game' and ensuring that decisions governing the global economy reflect their own interests.[98]

At the same time China urges the North to recognise that developing countries require flexibility in adopting economic strategies that suit them so that they can adapt to globalisation at their own pace.[99]

For its part, China has pledged 'to promote the development of economic globalisation in a direction conducive to common prosperity, [to] draw on its advantages and avoid its disadvantages so that all countries, particularly developing ones, can benefit from the process'.[100]

Inter-Regionalism and Multipolarisation

Regional organisations in the post-Cold War period represent a complex and variable geometry of conflict and cooperation in North–North, North–South and South–South relations. The United States and the European Union both use regional organisation to increase their penetration into the developing world, promoting free trade policies and liberal values in order to consolidate and extend their own positions and those of their corporations. However, as Chen Zhimin points out, the differences in their approach has significant implications for inter-regional dynamics.[101]

For the United States, regional organisations are a means to pre-empt other core regions from becoming real challengers to its supremacy: for example, NATO is used to constrain the European Union from developing its own independent military; Asia-Pacific Economic Cooperation (APEC) is used to subsume East Asia's economic organisation; and the Free Trade Area of the Americas (FTAA) is used to compete against Mercosur. The European Union on the other hand practices a 'soft expansionism' promoting cooperation through dialogue with other regional groups, which helps to strengthen regional trends. The Asia–Europe Meeting (ASEM), he argues, has opened an inter-regional Eurasian dialogue to which the United States is not a party:

> interregionalism, as the ASEM process indicates, also serves the other relatively weaker regions to strengthen themselves. By reaching out to each other, and by cooperating on political and economic issues, Europe and East Asia could both boost their bargaining position when they face the United States respectively. Moreover ... the ASEM process also promotes regionalism in Europe and in East Asia. It allows EU [sic] to project collective power to defend Europe's values and interests in the world, and establish Europe as a cornerstone of a multipolar world order. It also prompts East Asia to join the global trend of

'racing to regionalism', viewing regionalism as about pooling sovereignty to enhance sovereignty.[102]

So although individual countries such as Britain and France are not averse to interventionism and interference in the affairs of developing countries, and the European Union's dialogue process is promoted as a means of extending European influence globally, its initiatives nevertheless provide a stimulus for other regions to organise.

Although the new regionalism of both North and South may reflect certain hegemonic aspirations, it also is being used to enhance inter-regional interactions and cooperation to promote multipolarisation.

CHINA'S MULTIPOLAR STRATEGY: LENINISM FOR THE TWENTY-FIRST CENTURY

By Chinese calculations, as has been seen, although, the United States is the world's most powerful state, its hegemonism is incomplete. This creates room for multipolar manoeuvre to strengthen South–South cooperation and to use to advantage any divisions within the North to isolate the United States, the linchpin of the existing unequal international order, and to set the agenda for a world that is more fair and just.

This strategy derives from the application of Lenin's analysis, as set out in *Imperialism, the Highest Stage of Capitalism*, to current world conditions: it is Leninism for the twenty-first century.

Crucially, Lenin understood imperialism not as a monolithic system but as developing unevenly, such that different states occupied different positions in the international economy. The internationalisation of capital, driven by the search for profit, is then articulated through power relations between nation states. The international political order is not a fixed structure but in a state of constant flux, its dynamics shaped both by the contention between imperialist rivals as they seek to maintain and advance their position in the international order, and by the struggle between the oppressor and oppressed nations. Chinese Leninism takes uneven development as the starting point of its strategic analysis, seeing this as the soil in which hegemonism and imperialism are rooted, thus placing the Third World struggle for development at the centre of world transformation.

Progressive movements in the West have often tended to ignore or underestimate the transformative potential within Third World nationalism, including the developmental energies of the national capitalist classes, which under certain conditions will oppose the tendency of foreign capital to monopolise markets. Third World states are generally seen as reduced by the neoliberal orthodoxy to dependence on global capitalism. For example, from an anti-imperialist perspective, Harman argues against what he sees as a redefining of imperialism to refer to the exploitation of the Third World. However, in placing the emphasis instead on Lenin's other point about inter-imperialist rivalry and the drive to war, he ends up viewing the marginalised peripheries of the South as no longer of significance – their ruling classes only interested in exploitation, constrained by imperialism to act 'as collectors of debt repayments for the Western banks, royalty payments for MNCs and profits for Western investors'.[103] Anti-globalisers generally assume that domestically rooted capitalism in the developing world is subsumed unproblematically into the global circuits of accumulation. However, as Nesadurai's discussion of developmental regionalism suggests, the processes of such integration are rather more complex since markets are politically constructed and may be governed in different ways.

At variance with these views on the compradorisation of Third World elites, and more consonant with the arguments of Amin, Bello and Wallerstein, who all note the increasingly assertive behaviour among Third World states, Freeman and Kagarlitsky point to specific examples: Argentina's robust response to its IMF creditors, Malaysia's response to the Asian financial crisis, Cuba's dogged independence, as well as Russia's debt default. The point they make is that since Third World governments are politically independent and can, if they so choose, set their own policies in defiance of the strictures laid down by international institutions, the endeavour of the dominant developed countries is constantly focused towards the political division of the Third World.[104]

Although developing countries have become increasingly fragmented with diverging rates of growth, organisations such as the G77 and the Non-Aligned Movement (NAM) continue to express their united 'voice' and common concerns with widening global divisions of wealth.

As Amin has pointed out, Southern countries are awakening to the fact that 'the neoliberal globalised management has nothing to offer them' with the '[Non-Aligned] Movement ... becoming ... that of non-alignment with liberal globalisation and US hegemony'.[105] If this awakening strengthens South–South cooperation, equally South–South cooperation offers a way to counteract the trends of compradorisation amongst Third World elites.

Significantly, Harris sees in the formation of the G20 a qualitatively new phenomenon of Third World globalism. Here the vision for national development as he recognises goes beyond the 1960s idea of state-backed industrialisation to demand a different kind of globalisation, one of the full and equal integration of developing countries into the global economy but with a cautious approach to privatisation and capital mobility to balance growth and welfare.[106]

From the Chinese perspective, the world multipolarisation process is understood to involve two dimensions: not only the rise of developing countries but also the interactions and readjustments of relations between the major powers. In this, the strategy uses Lenin's approach, basing itself on an appraisal of the overall balance of world forces. Key to Lenin's analysis was the recognition that uneven development opened up differences between imperialist powers. This he saw to be critical from a tactical point of view, arguing that, while partnerships or cooperative relations with the intermediate sector of imperialism were not to be relied upon, it was not only possible but necessary under given conditions to '[make] use without fail of every, even the smallest, rift' between the imperialist powers and to '[take] advantage of every, even the smallest, opportunity of gaining [an] … ally, even though this ally be temporary, vacillating, unreliable and conditional', in order to succeed against a more powerful adversary.[107]

The CPC had learned the value of this lesson in its own war of resistance against Japanese aggression. With Japan threatening the entire basis of the Chinese nation, the CPC sought to end the civil war with the KMT and form a united front. At the same time, the CPC also drew a distinguishing line between Japanese imperialism and its allies, and the other imperialist powers, particularly when Britain and the United States reopened the Burma Road in October 1940 to allow support to get through to the resistance forces in the west of China.[108] Without these adjustments in strategy it is doubtful that the CPC would have been able to lead China through war to emerge after 1949 as a more stable society.

Equally, Stalin's recognition of the political division in the Second World War between the fascist and anti-fascist camps and his strategic shift in 1941 towards alliance with Britain, France and the United States against the axis powers was critical to the Second World War victory.[109]

In the 1970s China's strategy, as has been seen, lent particular weight to the emerging differences in the Western alliance, and China has subsequently continued to look to the European Union as a force capable of restraining US hegemonism. According to the *Three Worlds Theory,* secondary powers especially in Europe, although tied to US power, might, in their struggle against hegemonism for equal partnership, remain neutral or even be prepared to make concessions to Third World countries.[110] According to Ding Yuanhong, writing in the 1980s, since the Third World is the base to which the West European economy owes its existence and development, it may also be viewed as a 'strategic supplementary force' in Western Europe's countermove against hegemony. He goes on:

As the contradictions between Western Europe and the US intensify, the tendency of the former to make the third world a new key link in its diplomatic and strategic moves will become all the more evident. To improve its strategic security, it will energetically promote North–South dialogue, European–Arab dialogue and other similar activities.[111]

China's new diplomacy of the 1990s, its multilateralism and partnership approaches, therefore have a Leninist and an historical foundation. China's strategy, however, has not sought to rely on these cooperative relations and partnerships: the European Union is not seen as a counterbalance to the United States as such, but only as a part of a counter-hegemonic movement driven by trends towards Third World unity.

It was precisely the unevenness of capitalist development that Lenin took as the basis of conflictual and war-prone relations between imperialist states. However, his view of the inevitability of war is not one to be elevated to a timeless applicability. Lenin's analysis was a materialist one grounded in the contradictory trends of the early twentieth century. Chinese Leninism, whilst absorbing the logic of the analytical approach, similarly concerns itself with what is new about imperialism in the post-colonial period and the post-Cold War era. While hegemonism continues to trigger rivalry and conflict, the emergence of the new world order of independent, though unequal, states, with a resulting unipolar–multipolar dynamic shaped by regionalism and economic globalisation, although not ruling out conflict and war completely, make major war less likely.[112]

Globalisation is not simply 'the same old imperialism' since, as the operations of transnational firms become more globalised, increasingly larger fractions of the capitalist elites have a vested interest in seeing a stable growth of the world economy over the instabilities generated by the US drive for financial and military domination.

The extent of global interdependence and the implications of unmanaged globalisation were brought home by the Asian financial crisis, which was driven in large part by rivalries between US, EU and Japanese banks for a share of East Asia's rapid economic growth. While it was most devastating for South-East Asia itself, the crisis reached beyond the region, not only affecting the economies of Russia and Argentina, but also threatening pension funds in the West, causing panic amongst the world's financiers.

The financial crisis heightened recognition worldwide of the need for international joint efforts to regulate the process of interdependence in order to manage the risks as well as realise the potential of globalisation. So, as has been seen, although the imbalances of globalisation tend to perpetuate contention between the major capitalist powers, providing a limit to their international cooperation, growing interdependence broadens and deepens their shared interests, placing a limit on their rivalry. This situation is one that favours stability and peaceful competition, creating new incentives as well as scope for North–South dialogue.

From a strategic viewpoint, the contradiction within the US ruling elite between the hegemonic fraction pushing for global domination and the demands by the transnationalised fractions for stability, leaves it caught in its dual role between the demand to stabilise the capitalist system as a whole and its own destabilising drive for predominance. This leaves Europe simi-larly trapped between its role as US partner in manipulating the rules of the world economy and competing with the United States for a share of the benefits.

There is clearly a strong ideological and consensual dimension to US relations with partners and allies, but while there are commonalities of values, there are also calculations of interest. The success of the US hege-monic drive is ultimately contingent on its ability to fulfil both aspects of its dual role: ensuring capitalist expansion in general as well as the continued dominance of US capitalism within this. As Freeman and Kagarlitsky suggest, the problem for US hegemonism results from the fact that it is too weak to do both.[113] For Bello and Malig, the extent to which the United States shares the benefits of its domination with its partners is contingent upon the capitalist cycles of boom and crisis. So Clinton's strong dollar policy during the mid-1990s boom helped to boost growth in Europe and Japan, while the onset of capitalist crisis and a weakening dollar contributed to the tensions and ultimate division between the European Union and the United States over the Iraq war.[114]

Applying this to Amin's argument, namely, that what America's partners may lose as 'vassals' is outweighed by the benefits they receive as its allies, it is clear that the equation is not absolute. The relationships underpinning US hegemonism are not fixtures but unstable and contingent, always in the balance with the potential to tip either way.

From the Chinese perspective, developing countries on the one hand have a stake in globalisation, in gains from trade and benefits from the appli-cation of new technologies, as well as in the avoidance of large-scale global confrontations and the promotion of peaceful economic competition in order to have a chance to develop. Looking at Amin's equation in reverse, the developing South also has leverage here to influence the balance of conflict and cooperation between the United States and its partners and intensify the tensions inherent in its dual hegemonic role. Which way the trends go cannot be answered in the abstract.

For China, economic interdependence is the most significant incentive to influence calculations of interest and tip the balance in favour of coopera-tion in both multilateral and bilateral negotiations. The emergence of glob-alist or transnationalised sections of the elite in developed countries seeking stable conditions for competition creates openings to negotiate win–win agreements. By developing mutually beneficial economic contact it is possi-ble to shift perceptions of national interest in the developed world and diminish the reliance of the globalising fractions of their elites on the impe-rialist gains to be made by US hegemonic elements through the exercise of military influence. This then reduces the influence of geopolitical and ideological factors in international relations and strengthens partnerships.

As Chinese strategists have recognised, this places developing countries in a position to gain leverage in negotiations in multilateral forums such as the WTO and the United Nations where the major powers seek to manage their differences.

Developing countries hold the balance between the options of friction or peaceful competition between the major capitalist powers, since they may intervene as these powers adjust their relations to offer incentives and thereby unleash the potential for cooperation trapped by big power political contention.

Whilst interdependence creates common ground conducive to North–South dialogue, regionalist trends expand the scope for developing countries to negotiate, enhancing their ability to speak collectively while manoeuvring within the shifting relations among the major powers. Although hegemonism and power politics complicate the process of multipolarisation, the trend nevertheless creates a real basis for a counter-hegemonic strategy to realise the peaceful potential in world relations, paving the way for a greater democratisation of international relations and the advancement of the development agenda so weakening the foundation of imperialism.

China's position on achieving a fairer and more democratic international order through participation in multilateral negotiation, however, is quite distinct from the reformism of neo-Keynesians such as Stiglitz. The uneven development that the reformist agenda seeks to tackle, in fact constantly generates a power field of conflictual and unequal relations which obstruct and undermine reform negotiations. On the other hand, what China advocates is no mere listing of measures for improvement, not just new policies but a strategy for fundamental change through the promotion of multipolarisation. It is a concrete strategy to eliminate uneven development by addressing the realities of the international situation, weighing up the conjunctures of power relations, seeking to isolate the hegemonic tendencies of the United States, which generate frictions and conflict, by engaging with and changing the relations between diverse power centres in the world through win–win negotiation and South–South cooperation.

China's vision of a new order of peaceful economic competition sees the realisation of a system of regulation, not as envisaged by Kautsky, coordinated by the major capitalist powers – something which Lenin pointed out was impossible in conditions of uneven development – but through the inclusion of developing countries, that is, the creation of a post-imperialist order, by the application of a Leninist analysis and strategy.

6 PROMOTING MULTIPOLARISATION: REGIONAL ORGANISATION IN ASIA

In aiming to strengthen the multipolarisation trend, China has become an active promoter of regional multilateralism in Asia – in the Shanghai Cooperation Organisation (SCO); in the ASEAN+1 (ASEAN plus China) and the ASEAN+3 (ASEAN plus China, Japan and South Korea) processes and, since 2003, playing a key role in brokering the six-party talks on Korean denuclearisation. The foundation for these initiatives were laid by China's practices of good neighbourliness in the 1990s and especially through its willingness to sign border agreements often on terms beneficial to others.[1]

These initiatives represent the new thinking in China's diplomacy in the twenty-first century. A study of China's role in these three regions of Central, North and South-East Asia demonstrates not only how it is going about the task of managing a neighbourhood without conflict essential for its own development but also thereby constructing a new security order region by region.

In contrast with the EU model of a closed, identity-based community grounded ideologically in liberal democratic values, these initiatives aim to bring countries together on the basis of common interests in trade and security, with each case a test of the potential of China's 'harmony in diversity' philosophy to foster cooperation between diverse powers on the basis of equality and trust.

The countries involved not only differ in their political systems and levels of development but also have long histories of conflict. The groupings all involve a combination of major and smaller powers:

- Russia and China and four of the Central Asian states in the SCO
- China and the ten smaller South-East Asian states in an ASEAN+1 process embedded in ASEAN+3, which itself is evolving into the East

Asian Summit to include Australia, New Zealand and India (but excluding the United States)

- The six-party talks on the denuclearisation of the Korean peninsula which involve the United States alongside three other major world powers – Russia, China and Japan.

The importance of these initiatives extends beyond their respective regions, having the potential to influence the wider field of international relations through a 'demonstration effect' as they serve as new examples in the formation of regional models and international partnerships as well as in approaches to resolving deep-seated international conflicts.

The SCO provides the most advanced model of cooperative security: its vision, captured in the idea of the 'Shanghai spirit' set out by Jiang Zemin at the organisation's inaugural meeting in 2001, is based on mutual trust and good neighbourliness, respect for sovereignty and territorial integrity, settlement of disputes by dialogue, equality between member states and a new international political and economic order (NIPEO).[2] The China–ASEAN developmental regionalism represents the most advanced form of China's economic cooperation with other developing countries, of relevance as it extends its diplomacy and economic activity from Africa and the Middle East to Latin American and the Caribbean.

In setting up the six-party talks on the denuclearisation of the Korean peninsula, China initiated a new model of conflict resolution in which bilateral negotiations between two hostile parties are embedded within a multilateral framework. This model has possible application not only for the US–Iran nuclear dispute but also the very fragile relationship between the nuclear powers of India and Pakistan.

THE SHANGHAI COOPERATION ORGANISATION

The SCO covers a region which occupies a key geopolitical position as the meeting point for Russia, China and India as well as Iran, and one which has its own very complex and intricate history of religious and ethnic conflict. The organisation sets out to provide a working mechanism for discussion and decision making, to allow the very different states involved with their diverse interests, to settle their disputes through dialogue in order to manage the extremely difficult affairs of the region more effectively.

With the Sino–Russian strategic partnership lying at its heart, the organisation originated in the formation of the Shanghai Five – China, Russia, Tajikistan, Kyrgyzstan and Kazakhstan – which came together in 1996 to resolve their border disputes.

In 2001, as membership expanded to include Uzbekistan, the group became formally constituted as the Shanghai Cooperation Organisation.

Against the background of rising Islamic militancy in Afghanistan the organisation took as its main objective the 'fight against terrorism, separatism and extremism'. With armed oppositionist terrorist groups in these states seeking refuge in neighbouring territories, the aim of the SCO was to bring the states together to cooperate in anti-terrorism.

China's key concern in helping to initiate the SCO has been to strengthen its control over its own Central Asian territory of Xinjiang, where terrorist Uighur separatists are in operation. The autonomous province is of vital interest to China both as the base of its nuclear weapons installations and as a route to the energy-rich Central Asian states. These Islamicist groups, using Kyrgyzstan and Kazakhstan as a safe haven and Afghanistan as their training ground, have carried out numbers of attacks against unarmed civilians in China.[3]

In particular, China's fears have been that the United States would seek to consolidate its strategic interests in the region by sponsoring these separatist terrorist groups in a policy of 'containment by proxy', just as they used the activities of the Kosovo Liberation Army to justify NATO intervention in Yugoslavia.[4] However, in 2002, the Chinese government succeeded in gaining the agreement of the United Nations, and also the United States, to formally include the 'East Turkistan Islamic Movement' on the lists of terrorist organisations.

Since 2001 the SCO has sought to reduce the threat of 'humanitarian intervention' as well as prevent the Afghan conflict from spilling over into neighbouring states. Through the development of a regional approach to tackling separatism and terrorism, it has been taking progressive steps towards the formation of a region-wide peacekeeping force and a regional conflict prevention mechanism. The ultimate aim is to create a nuclear weapons-free regional cooperative security architecture under the United Nations, which could take responsibility for Central Asian stability.

The key steps have been:

- A series of joint cross-border peacekeeping and counter-terror military exercises carried out within the framework of the SCO. The first was a China–Kyrgyzstan joint exercise in 2002. A joint Sino-Russian military exercise took place in 2005.
- Gaining international recognition as a regional body with the formation of an official secretariat in 2004. The SCO was granted official observer status at the United Nations in 2004 and agreed to form partnerships with the Commonwealth of Independent States (CIS) and ASEAN in 2005.
- Forging a closer partnership with Afghanistan, which, along with India, Iran, Mongolia, and Pakistan has been granted SCO observer status and attended the 2005 summit. Cooperation focuses on anti-drug trafficking

work, which has been made a priority, but the clear intention is for the SCO to play a role in the peaceful reconstruction of Afghanistan.

- The 2005 summit announcement that the SCO would take the main responsibility for safeguarding security in Central Asia with the call for a timetable of withdrawal of the US-led coalition forces from Afghanistan as well as from the Uzbek and Kyrgyz airbases.
- The declaration of a Central Asian nuclear weapons-free zone (NWFZ) in September 2006. Although these negotiations have been carried out independently of the SCO, progress has been made possible by the earlier Sino–Russian agreement on the mutual non-targeting of nuclear weapons. The Central Asian NWFZ aims to make the region off-limits to US tactical nuclear weapons and to place this highly risky area, surrounded by Russian, Chinese, Pakistani, Indian and Israeli as well as US nuclear weapons, beyond the danger of involvement in a nuclear arms race. It serves as a powerful example of nonproliferation, and was welcomed by anti-nuclear activists as 'a remarkable, unbelievable moment ... not just for Central Asia, but for the whole world'.[5]

Economic and Energy Development

At the same time the SCO started to make progress on an agenda of economic cooperation at its 2006 Summit.[6] Of particular significance are the developments on energy cooperation. The admission of Iran and India as SCO observers widened opportunities, and in 2007 the SCO formed an Energy Club to start to work towards a common regional energy strategy. The club brings together large producers, (Russia, Kazakhstan, Uzbekistan and Iran), and the significant consumers (China and India), as well as transit countries, with the aim of increasing energy security for all.[7] The premise here is that, whether as producers or consumers, all share concerns in the security, stability and sustainability of energy supplies, and all share the need for economic development as the key to poverty eradication.

The grand aim is to build an Asian Energy Community, coordinating the energy strategies of producers and consumers through the integration of joint pipeline projects. The key to achieving this interdependent trade lies in mutual investment in the oil and gas sectors. China has been particularly active here, with substantial direct assistance to the major SCO projects including low-interest loans to promote economic development in different countries to facilitate cooperation.[8] Path-breaking deals with Kazakhstan for an oil pipeline in 2004 and with Uzbekistan for oil and gas exploration in 2006 helped to lay the basis for the Energy Club. Most recently, the SCO has formed a business council and has set up an inter-bank association as a preliminary step towards a regional bank, to facilitate the funding and management of joint projects.[9]

Russia has finally signalled approval for a pipeline to carry its oil exports direct to China. According to one senior energy executive, 'Little by little Russia and China are breaking down barriers of mutual distrust with cooperation from the SCO playing a facilitating role.'[10]

These developments bring closer agreement on a regional free trade area (FTA), although the details are yet to be worked out.

A Pioneer in International Democratisation?

The weakness of democracy within its member states is seen by some critics to be the Achilles' heel of the organisation, throwing doubt over its claim to be pioneering international democracy. From a Western liberal perspective the SCO is seen as 'a club for autocrats and dictators' bound only by a shared lack of respect for human rights and democracy.[11] At any rate, reliance on repressive methods alone, which is liable to generate opposition, is likely to make Central Asian states more rather than less fragile.[12] Clashes between the Uzbek army and rioters in the Ferghana valley drew international condemnation in 2005.

Yet clearly, the continuing war in Afghanistan, the resurgence of the Taliban, and in particular, the failure of NATO's counter-narcotics policy, with poppy cultivation rising after the end of Taliban rule, contribute in a major way to the grim security situation in Central Asia.[13] Kyrgyzstan in particular is too weak to police its border with Afghanistan and is thus falling prey to insurgents and drug traffickers.[14]

China too has been criticised by Amnesty International for methods used in its 'strike hard' campaigns to deal with armed terrorist Uighur separatist groups.[15] Excessive methods to crack down on terrorism are not to be condoned wherever they occur. Nevertheless, China and the SCO seek to actively cooperate with the Counter Terrorist Committee of the United Nations. They regard the problem of terrorism not as one of religion or a 'conflict of civilisations' to be defeated by reliance on military means, but one that must be addressed by eradicating its root cause in poverty, and by strengthening international cooperation to solve the problems of development and regional conflicts.[16] With most of the radical separatists operating in the poorest areas of Xinjiang, clearly more needs to be done to address the province's uneven development. However, according to Zhu and Blatchford,[17] the Chinese government has been able to maintain stability in its minority regions and keep separatist forces subdued largely by persuasion, only using coercion when necessary.

There is no quick fix to the deep-seated security problems in the region. Yet as Alison Bailes, director of the highly respected Stockholm

International Peace Research Institute (SIPRI), admits, the SCO 'makes some real impact on the security of the wide territories it covers and ... has real potential for further development'.[18]

For centuries the region has been fraught with conflict and instability, a 'cauldron of ethnic conflicts' which, according to Brzezinski, risked becoming a centre for a new 'great game' of big power rivalries at the end of the 1990s.[19] Thus the progress made by the SCO in uniting states with considerably diverging agendas in a matter of just a few years is a rare case in the history of international relations, a turning point for the region.

By shifting the region away from economic rivalry towards economic cooperation, the SCO is beginning to address its people's greatest concerns in battling poverty and the need for stability in a way that Kyrgyzstan's 'Tulip revolution' has not. Despite the change of government, Kyrgyzstan's political problems remain, only now, according to a recent report, its capital city Bishkek 'reeks of bitter democratic disenchantment'.[20]

A New Type of Regional Organisation

Although prompted by NATO's eastward expansion, and with it the encroaching threat of 'humanitarian intervention', neither the Sino–Russian strategic partnership nor the SCO are aimed at constructing an anti-US alliance to confront the projection of US power. The organisation's own agenda is essentially driven by the domestic concerns of its member states, seeking to tackle their common problems in relation to stability and economic development. Rather than opposing any third party, then, the SCO seeks to create a substitute security framework under the United Nations to replace NATO's activities in the region.

By confronting the power politics of energy competition and providing a means for Russia and China to manage their tensions, the SCO embodies an unprecedented model of international relations, one of peaceful coexistence between major powers. According to Bailes and Dunay, the power of Russia and China are well balanced within the group, and they grant that, although the Central Asian states face a highly asymmetric position in relation to both Russia and China, arguably the organisation helps these smaller states in their policies of balancing.[21]

Equality in partnership, and a commitment to consensus, ensure that the interests and concerns of smaller states are not ignored. With a tightly focused agenda addressed at conflict avoidance, confidence building and peaceful dialogue, SCO operations are characterised by common initiatives developed jointly by large and small states together. It is sometimes claimed that the SCO is used one-sidedly by either Russia or China as a means to extend their control and military influence over Central Asia, but quite distinct from a Cold War-type organisation under the leadership of a single power, the SCO aims to uphold the UN principle of respect for sovereignty.

Unlike a bloc or military alliance, the SCO is an open mechanism with a flexibility that allows it to adapt to the changing circumstances in this unstable region. Taking a non-confrontational approach, the SCO does not obstruct its member states in developing links with the West, and whether large or small, these continue to conduct their own individual foreign policies. Kazakhstan, for example, hosted simultaneous exercises with NATO and under the SCO framework in different parts of the country in 2003.[22] Nor did Kyrgyzstan's Tulip revolution see the country split from the SCO: indeed the new president endorsed the organisation's call for a timeline on US withdrawal from the Manas airbase. In fact, within the framework of the SCO, individual member states may actually be freer to develop links with the West, operating from a stronger footing.

If the erosion of the SCO was a part of the military objective of the United States in its intervention in Afghanistan, this has not succeeded. US presence in Central Asia has not made the SCO redundant: on the contrary, the organisation has shown a remarkable speed of evolution, taking an increasingly more active role in developing a cooperative security framework for the region. By helping to diminish the power politics that feed into local ethnic and religious rivalries, the organisation offers completely new opportunities to tackle regional conflicts. For Afghanistan, the SCO's alternative anti-terror agenda opens up a choice as to whether its long-term needs would be better met by NATO or by the 'Shanghai spirit'.

The aim of the SCO according to Troitsky is to create an arc of stability in the north of Eurasia to contain the arc of instability along the SCO's southern rim which has resulted from the United States' flawed intervention in Afghanistan.[23] Engdahl claims the successes of the SCO as potentially the greatest strategic defeat for the US power projection of the post-Second World War period, thwarting US plans for the reordering of Central Asia.[24] Pan Guang highlights the importance of the SCO as a demonstration of China's new diplomacy which has the potential to assist in China–India relations;[25] while for Varadarajan, the group's potential lies in playing a pivotal role in fashioning new security architectures for Asia.[26] Clearly for Russia and China, cooperation in the SCO has enhanced their ability to coordinate their policies and collaborate more widely on the world stage to uphold UN principles.

The weakness of the democratic systems within individual SCO member-states is problematic, but the organisation itself may be regarded as a pioneer in the democratisation of the international political economy in the sense that it operates on principles of equality and consensus, respecting the independence of its members, thus enabling these states themselves to make collective decisions about the future of their region. China takes the stance that the genuine development of human rights protection is to be achieved gradually through the promotion of conditions of peace and development. From this perspective, insofar as the SCO stands for democratisation against US hegemony, strengthening the implementation of UN principles in the region and addressing the inequitable aspects of economic globalisation, it has the potential to provide a framework for the improvement of human rights, including social and economic rights, over the longer term.

THE SIX-PARTY TALKS ON KOREAN DENUCLEARISATION

It is more than anything in hosting the six-party talks on the denuclearisation of the Korean peninsula that China has moved to centre stage as a world power since 2003. The threat of North Korea developing nuclear weapons has provided an opportunity for China to engage the United States in negotiations over cooperative security within a framework involving not only North and South Korea but also Russia and Japan. The talks have enormous international significance as a test of the extent to which major world powers can cooperate and move beyond relations of power rivalry.

Situated at the centre of North-East Asia, Korea is of key geostrategic significance as the meeting point of four of the world's five biggest powers.[27] Still divided by the Cold War legacy, the region lacks any mechanism for security consultation between these powers, three of which are nuclear weapons states while the fourth, Japan, has singularly large plutonium stockpiles.[28] No peace agreement was ever signed at the end of the Korean War in 1953, and with the United States and North Korea still technically in a state of war, the region teeters on crisis which could easily trigger a dangerous nuclear arms race in the region.

With Bush threatening a pre-emptive strike, North Korea withdrew from the Non-Proliferation Treaty (NPT) in 2002. This was seen as a highly destabilising move, but then from the North Korean's point of view, their inclusion in Bush's 'axis of evil' and even more in a list of possible targets for an actual nuclear strike in the US 2002 Nuclear Posture Review, was a bewildering turnabout in US policy. Although talks on North Korea's nuclear facilities had dragged on since an agreement in 1994, Clinton had been preparing to visit Pyongyang to meet Kim Jong Il just before the 2000 US presidential election.

North Korea, it must be remembered, has faced nuclear intimidation longer than any other country on earth. The United States has prepared for and explicitly threatened the use of nuclear weapons against North Korea on several occasions both during the Korean War and since.[29] Today, as Goldstein points out, this country of 25 million people, and an economy undermined by half a century of US sanctions, with a GDP of a mere US$16 billion, faces the hostility of the world's superpower with its US$10 trillion economy and is surrounded by an armoury of nuclear bombers, nuclear-armed submarines, aircraft carriers and destroyer fleets.[30]

After the situation came to a head in 2002, to prevent further deterioration, China convened the talks, involving North and South Korea together with the four major powers. Since the 1994 agreement had made little progress, with both parties continually blaming each other for creating difficulties as a pretext for failing to deliver on their own commitments, the six-party talks aims to involve other powers to serve as witnesses and guarantors of the process in order to keep any fresh negotiations on track.

The Talks So Far

The United States set out to stack the agenda with a long list of demands covering not only the 'the complete, verifiable and irreversible' dismantling of North Korean nuclear facilities but also human rights, money laundering and counterfeiting, drug smuggling and missile proliferation issues. North Korean security concerns were not a topic for discussion and North Korea was expected to yield unconditionally.[31] The US aim was evidently to use the talks to establish its own right to determine which countries do or do not have the right to nuclear technology, as a means of embedding its global primacy, regardless of the NPT. The talks were also an opportunity to pressurise China into accepting US hegemony in the region or to force it into an error. China's willingness to lean on North Korea was seen as a test by US hardliners spoiling for a confrontation.

China meanwhile has stuck doggedly to the cooperative security approach in which the security concerns of both parties are treated equally to achieve at the same time the denuclearisation of the Korean peninsula and a permanent peace settlement to normalise US–North Korean relations.

In September 2005, there was a major breakthrough when an agreement in principle and on an equal basis was reached. North Korea pledged to 'abandon all nuclear weapons and existing nuclear programmes' and both sides agreed to 'respect each other's sovereignty, exist peacefully together and take steps to normalise their relations'. The deal however was not sustainable. The US neocons were outraged at having gained so little. Four days later, the US Treasury department, accusing North Korea of money laundering, imposed sweeping financial sanctions in the form of a freeze on North Korean bank accounts, designed to cut off the country's access to the international banking system. The crisis escalated to new heights as, in the face of the continuing hostile policy of the United States, North Korea threatened and then ultimately carried out the explosion of a nuclear device in October 2006.

At the same time, the North Korean government reiterated its position, stated previously when it withdrew from the NPT, that it had no intention of seeking permanent nuclear weapons status, and that '[i]f the US drops all their hostility ... then we will not feel any threat from the US side and we will not need our nuclear weapons'.[32] Its actions are essentially negotiating ploys to press the case for the removal of intimidation.

Despite the test, North Korea was still far from developing an offensive nuclear capacity. Nevertheless the move left the United Nations with little choice other than to act to support the NPT. However, Russia and China succeeded in heading off the United States and Japan when they pressed for drastically punitive sanctions so averting a further reckless escalation of the crisis. With agreement on much milder UN sanctions, China redoubled its efforts to undo the deadlock and kick start fresh negotiations.

In February 2007, a second historic breakthrough came with consensus on the timing and sequencing in implementing the agreed principles through a phased approach of 'commitment for commitment, action for action'. This set out a series of coordinated steps of reciprocal actions with clear pledges on both sides linking denuclearisation to concrete benefits including security assurances and normalisation.

North Korea would first shut down and seal the Yongbyon heavy water nuclear reprocessing facility in exchange for an initial shipment of oil. It would discuss a list of all its nuclear programmes, and in exchange North Korea and the United States would start bilateral talks aimed at moving towards the establishment of full diplomatic relations. Then, in return for completely dismantling the Yongbyon facility, declaring all its nuclear programmes and rejoining the NPT, North Korea would receive the rest of the oil deliveries to a total equivalent to 1 million tonnes, as the United States moved towards recognition. This sequencing would allow a peace deal to be signed on the day of North Korea's complete denuclearisation.[33] Meanwhile, with both Russia and China insisting on North Korea's sovereign right to develop nuclear power for peaceful purposes under the NPT, the agreement reached a compromise confirming that the 'other parties expressed their respect for North Korea to regain its sovereign right to acquire Light Water Reactor technology and agreed to discuss the subject of the provision at an appropriate time'.[34]

Bush, it appeared, was at last engaging in serious negotiations. The neocon strategy had achieved precisely the opposite of its intended goal of preventing North Korea from developing nuclear weapons. The US position had worsened; meanwhile Kim Jong Il had retained a firm grip on power.

Bogged down in the Iraq war, Bush was clearly in desperate need of a win for his foreign policy with elections starting to loom. Calculating on this, China had encouraged North Korea to 'seize the time'[35] and return to the negotiations. Sanctions had put a certain pressure on the North Koreans, but essentially they were getting what they wanted from the deal, namely a return to one-to-one negotiations, with the initial oil shipments a positive gesture of US recognition. Both parties met to end the freeze on North Korea's bank accounts and, with this show of willingness on the part of United States to adjust its hostile stance, North Korea proceeded swiftly to shutdown the Yongbyon plant in exchange for the first shipment of oil.

Looking Ahead

The six-party talks are a demonstration of how to achieve cooperative security in practice. They set out to tackle the entrenched distrust dividing the United States and North Korea through the implementation of consensus in simultaneous steps aimed at a win–win goal. The key is that the security concerns of both parties should be mutually respected and treated equally. In this, the talks have succeeded, setting in motion direct one-to-one negotiations with a view to normalisation of relations. On the basis of 'seeking common ground, whilst reserving differences', the talks first achieved agreement in principle and then moved ahead by looking to small gains as 'big gains mean big losses to the other side' in order to resolve matters that are most urgent and easiest to tackle first, leaving aside more difficult issues to be dealt with later. Frequent meetings, avoiding blame, building trust through deeds, keeping focused on achievable goals, all aid in keeping up momentum, making constant progress bit by bit.

So far, the United States has not been able to dictate the agenda: on the contrary, China is succeeding in pressuring the United States to accept consensus and equal treatment. As Mohanty argues, China has altered the US policy of unilateralism and pre-emptive strike.[36] But to what extent does the progress in the talks so far represent a long-term adjustment in the US hegemonic strategy as opposed to a short-term tactic of 'playing for time'? It is entirely possible that the talks may drag on for years or even break down yet again. As of the time of writing, whilst the agreement has advanced through its easiest stages, the most difficult stage is yet to make progress.[37]

Considering the US strategic interests at play here, Shi Yongming argues that after the collapse of the USSR, the United States cited the North Korean threat to justify the enhancement of its military presence in the region and the strengthening its alliance system. However, now that this build-up is almost complete, the United States is likely to be more prepared to adjust its position.[38] If the United States were to accept full diplomatic relations with North Korea, this would still leave it as the overwhelmingly dominant military power in the Pacific.

On the other hand, the six-party talks look towards expanding into a permanent institutionalised security arrangement for the whole of North-East Asia and have set up a working group, chaired by Russia, to look at this. Such arrangements could ultimately take responsibility for security in the region.

A settlement of the Korean issue would very likely ease the way for further historical reconciliation within the region, allowing a series of mutually stabilising regional relationships to emerge, not least between Japan and North Korea, and Japan and China. Released from the constraints of the Second World War and Cold War legacies, the economic dynamism of North-East Asia would be fully unleashed. This in turn could give rise to demands for SCO-type multilayered cooperative security networks for East Asia covering economic integration, energy cooperation, joint military exercises as well as discussion on averting a regional nuclear arms race. Indeed, within the framework of the six-party talks, civil society groups, including the Chinese People's Association for Peace and Disarmament are calling for the creation of a North-East Asian NWFZ once the Korean issue is settled.[39]

In the face of its encirclement, China has used the North Korean situation in a finger lock with the United States to prevent 'an American fist forming around it'.[40] In order to unravel one of the world's most intractable and polarised situations, China has, without losing patience, been quietly conducting protracted negotiations through the six-party talks to counter the US unipolar strategy and edge instead towards multilateral cooperation based on equal treatment and mutual constraint. The talks have provided a platform for China to lay out an alternative vision for effective and equitable multilateral cooperation to achieve peaceful coexistence and common development in North-East Asia.

A successful outcome of the talks, with the United States accepting the legitimate existence of the North Korean state, would not merely be a defeat for US unilateralism and a significant win for China's strategy of 'harmony in diversity' in a region with some of the largest economies in the world. As Mohanty puts it, the message from the six-party talks is that 'patient negotiations aimed at an equitable, win–win outcome will facilitate movement to a just world order'.[41]

CHINA AND SOUTH-EAST ASIA: A NEW ECONOMIC REGIONALISATION

In ASEAN, China has a partner that is itself a diverse organisation of member states differing in cultures, religions, political systems and levels of economic development, operating on the basis of consensus and mutual respect for sovereignty to achieve its own 'harmony in diversity'. However, the South-East Asian states harbour some serious reservations over China's regional role, not least given their overlapping claims to islands in the South China Sea. While these islands are minuscule, their value is in the potential resources that lie beneath and around them as well as their geostrategic positioning on the key sea lanes, currently patrolled by the US navy, linking the oil-poor North-East Asia with the Middle East.

China's firmer assertion of its claims in this area in the mid-1990s triggered fears rooted in the history of the aggressive expansion of the Mongol Empire (the Yuan Dynasty, 1206–1259 AD) into South-East Asia. However, in 1996 China ratified the UN Convention on the Law of the Sea, and later put forward proposals to 'shelve disputes and go for joint development' to demonstrate its intentions to solve the disputes peacefully.

Then, when during the Asian financial crisis of 1997/8, China resisted currency devaluation, it began to establish itself as a stabilising influence in the region's economic development. The crisis gave strong impetus to a regional cooperative security process bringing Japan, China and ASEAN (ASEAN+3) together to set up the Chiang Mai Initiative creating a regional financial swap mechanism aimed at staving off future speculative attacks on currencies and providing a degree of stability for the region's weak financial structures.

Cooperation and Competition: China and East Asian Economic Integration

When China joined the World Trade Organization (WTO) it was widely predicted that this would adversely affect its South-East Asian neighbours, heightening competition for foreign direct investment (FDI) and export sales to the United States, European Union and Japan. Meanwhile the outflow of cheap Chinese goods was expected to flood Asian markets, harming local producers.

To allay these fears, Premier Zhu Rongji proposed a China–ASEAN Free Trade Agreement (ACFTA) in 2000. The underlying idea was to expand opportunities for specialisation on a regional basis in a coordinated way such that individual countries could compensate for each other's economic weaknesses. ACFTA would allow ASEAN to gain better access to China's growing market, and it was forecast that it would add one percentage point to the annual economic growth in ASEAN countries and 0.3 per cent in China.[42]

According to the framework agreement signed in 2002, ACFTA is to be based on a two-tier division to take into account the different levels of development in ASEAN. The FTA will take effect in 2010 for the six most developed members of ASEAN, while less developed members are given more time until 2015 to adjust, with the assistance of measures prioritising tariff reductions on primary commodities of export interest to South-East Asian countries. To support this two-tier commitment, China proceeded to slash tariffs in favour of other countries, on the principle of 'give more, take less',[43] giving their companies wider access to China's market and offering an 'early harvest' of benefits for agricultural traders. This win–win approach to regionalisation stands in contrast with Japan, which has been concerned to protect its own rural economy, limiting the benefit of trade for its less developed partners.

Most ASEAN members now enjoy healthy surpluses in their China trade, as the fast-growing economy imports their primary commodities and high-tech components in increasingly large quantities. In fact, three years after China joined the WTO, ASEAN exports had increased 51.7 per cent.[44] Far from cutting the ground beneath the export-oriented countries of East Asia, the development of manufacturing in China has been the engine of regional economic growth. After 2001, with the United States in recession and the Japanese economy still stagnating, China's growth was key to reflating the regional economy still shaky after the 1997 crisis.

In 2005, inward investment to ASEAN exceeded the boom years of the 1990s at $38 billion.[45] Fears of competition are giving way to new hopes in some business sectors as China absorbs hi-tech exports from the rest of the region and promotes technological cooperation. The burgeoning electronics industry in the Philippines, for example, has been one such beneficiary.[46] Where regional businesses face increased competition, China's low-cost intermediate products help to maintain profit margins. Now capital and expertise from China also offer a fresh impetus to regional economic development.

Critical of the win–win scenario, Hart-Landsberg and Burkett, in an essentially anti-globalisation argument, see China's increasing regional economic integration as accelerating a 'race to the bottom'.[47] The argument is that regional economic integration is essentially shaped by the broad dynamics of transnational capital. With more and more FDI attracted to the region to exploit China's cheap labour economy as the final production platform for the region's exports, and the further increase in export competition, China is seen to be driving the region more and more deeply into cross-border production networks of competing transnational corporations. This, it is argued, will lead to competitive wage cuts which suppress domestic consumption and so intensify ever-greater dependence on export markets. For Hart-Landsberg and Burkett, the growth in intra-regional trade reflects not a growing regional independence but an increasing dependence on US markets, with China's new role in the global capitalist production chains, far from generating regional stability, only increasing the risks from unstable capital flows and excess export production.

Rajan, on the other hand, pointing out that China's sustained trade surplus with Western economies, the United States and the European Union, is matched by a deficit of roughly the same magnitude with the rest of East Asia, argues that China could provide a 'cushion to smaller southeast Asia countries against gyrations in the industrial country economic environment'.[48]

Hart-Landsberg and Burkett are right to emphasise the fragility of export-led growth geared to US markets, and indeed China is seeking to diversify its export markets as well as to gradually expand its own domestic market. Clearly there are also areas of friction in regional economic relations as well as complementarities, not least with China's low-cost exports displacing local products.

However, China's rise poses not so much a threat as a challenge and an opportunity to East Asia. Competition will certainly intensify as China's production rises up the value-added chain, altering the regional division of labour. This will involve some degree of economic dislocation for other countries. Governments will need to strengthen policies to help industries upgrade, but here cooperation with China, given its growing demand, opens new opportunities to mitigate the pains of adjustment and seek a more balanced regional development through a carefully coordinated approach.

The weakness of the anti-globalisation argument, quite apart from all the evidence that the regional economy is flourishing, lies in its analytical approach which discounts the role that states play in regulating markets. As Nesadurai has pointed out, cooperation in ASEAN displays a type of developmental regionalism that is quite distinct from the neoliberal agenda pursued by the United States through APEC.[49] While the former aims to foster the competitiveness of indigenous firms at the same time as attracting foreign investment, the latter, driven exclusively by the regional strategies of the transnational corporations operating in East Asia, imposes considerable adjustment costs on its developing countries.

Regional regulation may cover coordination on a range of policies appropriate to regional needs including for example, industrial and investment policies, restrictions on the use of anti-dumping, the elimination of export subsidies, as well as reaching beyond trade and investment to cover cooperation in science and technology, human resource development, the treatment of smaller and poorer economies, and dispute resolution.[50]

In the case of the Chiang Mai Initiative in particular, Stiglitz sees this as taking a definite step towards a new type of regional macro-economic coordination aimed at protecting economies from volatile currency fluctuations and stabilising the market framework of East Asian development.[51]

Towards an East Asian Community

While the SCO has developed from cooperation over shared security concerns into trade and economic exchange, in South-East Asia security dialogue and military exchange with China has emerged out of a common interest in development and shared concerns over economic globalisation and financial instability.

In 2002 alongside ACFTA, China and ASEAN in a landmark agreement established a Code of Conduct in the South China Sea to avoid armed clashes over the disputed territories. In 2003, with ASEAN strengthening its own commitment to the self-management of security matters, China acceded to ASEAN's non-aggression pact, the Treaty of Amity and Cooperation, the first country outside South-East Asia to do so, and the China–ASEAN Strategic Partnership for Peace and Prosperity was forged. This helped to improve dialogue on defence issues, paving the way for wide-ranging security interaction on non-traditional threats as well as joint military exercises.[52] Then in 2002 China announced it would sign a treaty establishing an NWFZ in South-East Asia.[53]

Regional organisation took a further turn in December 2005 with the first East Asian Summit including Australia, New Zealand and India. It is thought that the United States was pushing for the participation of countries sharing 'democratic values' in order to support a Japanese bid for regional leadership. This would have provoked Sino–Japanese tensions and slowed the process of East Asian community development. Nevertheless, it was agreed at the meeting that the grouping should not replace ASEAN+3 and that ASEAN should remain the driving force of regional integration.[54]

For the ASEAN+3 and the East Asia Summit to develop any further necessitates reconciliation between China and Japan. A big move in this direction came with former Japanese prime minister Abe's 'icebreaking tour' to China in October 2006. With the prospects for regional cooperation now on more solid political ground, a further step was taken in 2007 when the second East Asia Summit issued a declaration on energy efficiency. This achieved agreement on reducing dependence on fossil fuels through the expansion of renewable energy sources and ensuring stable energy supplies through investment in an ASEAN power grid and a trans-ASEAN pipeline.[55]

Although the course of East Asian regional development continues to be heavily influenced by the United States as its largest investor, China is emerging as a catalyst for economic integration and cooperation. When the United States sought to strengthen its military and naval presence in South-East Asia, this alarmed the Muslim-majority states of Indonesia and Malaysia in particular. Their calls for 'regional solutions for regional problems' created openings for China to propose joint military exercises in the South China Sea.[56] Meanwhile, fears of a 'China threat' have diminished, as many of the East Asian economies have found ways of cooperating rather than competing with Chinese producers. As the Thai foreign minister, speaking of China's win—win approach, commented, 'China has no intention of taking advantage of ASEAN ... A wealthy China creates stability for South-East Asia.'[57]

China's increasing involvement is opening the way for a fundamental readjustment in the existing pattern of East Asian growth, driven by Japanese investment, dependent on Western markets and tied to the US dollar, and a new vision for an East Asian community is beginning to take shape through the development of an alternative form of regional governance for trade and investment aimed at closing the gap between the developed and developing parts of the region.

CONCLUSION

China's view of security is inextricably linked to development: security cannot be established in conditions of uneven development. Region by region, it is helping to drive a multidimensional agenda to address the long-term needs of Asia's peoples for stability and development. In this, since it is primarily concerned with its own domestic political and economic affairs, China tries to act as a promoter rather than regional leader, favouring a partnership approach.[58]

The focus in region building is on the creation of long-term regional relationships to address common problems, looking at how these might be tackled through collaborative efforts. The first step is agreement on the principle of equal treatment: this provides the political foundation for cooperation. Once political differences have been set to one side, it is important to keep momentum going. Free trade agreements which address problems of uneven development; the creation of energy partnerships and joint military exercises; cooperative activities covering disaster relief; exchanges in science and technology, education and training, healthcare, culture and media, sports and tourism and so on, all provide clear follow-up goals. They help to create a sense of community before tackling the most difficult decisions, namely how regional relations with the United States are to be defined and the question of its military presence in the regions. The essential element in a regional peace mechanism is an NWFZ agreement.

On the other hand, critics see China as seeking to use regional organisations as a means for economic penetration into the rest of Asia in the pursuit of oil and markets. The Bush administration in its 2006 National Security Strategy accused China in this respect of 'acting as if they can somehow "lock up" energy supplies around the world'.[59] 'China threat' theorists blame the escalating price of oil on China's rising demands.[60] OPEC on the other hand has made clear its views that oil price rises are caused by speculation, the weakness of the dollar and geopolitical instability.[61]

Oil imports by China are in fact relatively small, as little as 3.4 per cent of total world imports in 2004 by some estimates.[62] On a per capita basis, imports of oil by Japan and the United States are 20 times those of China, which still meets about 90 per cent of its own energy needs, a much greater percentage than the OECD average.[63] Although China's growth is a factor behind higher oil prices, the effects of its increasing demands have been minimised since as oil prices have risen, China has reduced imports and fallen back on its own reserves, while investing in oil facilities around to world to increase supplies.

With oil prices at US$120 per barrel in April 2008, having risen 80 per cent over twelve months, it is hardly surprising that both producers and consumers gravitate towards China's proposals for a more stable energy regime.[64] For its part, as Wu and Shen point out, China is concerned that its energy imports are overly dependent on sea lanes which from the Persian Gulf to Shanghai are controlled by the US Navy. The real fear is that if the 'cold war' between the United States and China should turn hot, the United States would likely move to cut off China's oil lifelines in order to destabilise the country.[65]

Given the circumstances, China has unarguably sought to enhance its own strategic position within its neighbourhood. In the event of a crisis with the United States, especially over Taiwan, it now has the guaranteed support of the SCO which is explicitly committed to countering separatism, and is working to keep South-East Asia neutral whilst maintaining the Korean talks on a separate track.

China is without doubt pursuing its own strategic and domestic agenda within the Asian regional organisations, but this is precisely the point of interest-based organisations – to provide a vehicle for multilateral relations which each member can harness to their own needs so that they can pursue their own national goals but without creating friction with their neighbours.[66]

Rather than seeking to turn its Asian neighbours into its appendages, China is finding ways to strengthen the position of smaller powers in regional organisations. Through measures for example of zero-tariff treatment, preferential loans, debt cancellation and support for development projects, China seeks to reduce regional inequalities.[67] The Mekong river basin provides one such example as a mega-project to improve navigability of the river as well as road and rail links between China and Vietnam which will promote economic growth in the area, and reduce the development gap among South-East Asian countries.[68]

At the same time, China seeks to draw other major powers into regional networks in such a way as to balance out power relations. Just as the success of China–ASEAN relations helped to draw Japan further into the East Asian regional process, China's bilateral energy deals in Central Asia increased Russia's commitment to the SCO. A link up between the SCO and the East Asia Summit might offer a way to encourage India's engagement. Such moves help to alleviate the pressures of overt competition between major powers for influence over smaller countries, strengthening equality and promoting consensus in region-building.

China is also taking a multilayered approach to multipolarisation through cooperative partnerships and networks geared towards specific purposes such as SCO–Afghanistan cooperation to combat drug trafficking. This helps to provide the means of engaging with other powers such as India, Iran, Pakistan, Australia and New Zealand, in a variety of ways beyond the organisation itself without the risk of weakening its existing cooperation processes.[69]

Meanwhile the flexible approach to region building in Asia is well-adapted to shifts in the international environment that occur given the zigzag dynamics of the unipolar–multipolar balance. It allows the various powers to adjust their bilateral relations with the United States at different speeds. In this way it has been possible to make headway, despite instabilities within many Asian nations and their foreign policy shifts.

However, although there have been some substantial breakthroughs, these organisations have still to demonstrate their ability to respond swiftly to crises, such as the tsunami in South-East Asia and the Ferghana valley riots in the case of the SCO. This remains their weakness: they are yet to be fully established. On the other hand, China's active participation in regional multilateralism is helping to infuse a new sense of shared growth and community in Asia.

Working within existing regional trends, China then is creating a new international security order region by region, promoting and building a network of mutually supportive security communities across Asia.[70] As then premier Zhu Rongji noted, the development of linkages between the regional groupings provides a means to explore pan-Asian cooperation.[71] This raises the longer-term prospect of a new multipolar Asian cooperative security order. In this way, China's development is becoming part of a wider pattern of Asian development, in which its own rise is a part of Asia's rise.

The US aim to encircle China through networking the hub-and-spokes pattern of its bilateral military alliances into an Asian NATO based on the conditions of its own absolute security, is therefore being thwarted as China, region by region, seeks to foster an alternative model of cooperative security. With Asians themselves advocating 'regional solutions to regional problems', China is working to build a series of multipolar pillars to underpin the United Nations. With the democratic characteristics of respect for independence and sovereignty, agreement on settling all disputes through dialogue and the gradual reduction in development gaps, these pillars will strengthen the implementation of UN principles on a regional basis against US unilateralism and its unipolar strategy.

PART 2

CHINA'S DEVELOPMENT TRAJECTORY

7 MAINTAINING SELF-RELIANCE IN AN INTERDEPENDENT WORLD

China's ability to operate successfully within international networks of interdependence, to initiate win–win agreements and to bargain over the rules of the global economy depends on its own self-reliance. Self-reliance is the anchor of the multipolarisation strategy for cooperative security.

In China, self-reliance, understood not as autarky but as depending on one's own efforts, emphasising the primacy of internally generated development, has been the continuing guiding principle of its socialist path. Resting upon the basic system of socialist ownership set up during the Mao era, it has been strengthened by subsequent reforms as China's development path has adapted under changing circumstances.

However, across a wide spectrum of views among the Western Left, China's gradual path of economic reform since the later 1970s has been regarded as a 'creeping privatisation' undermining self-reliance bit by bit, with foreign investment steadily encroaching on the country's economic sovereignty. Its 2001 WTO accession is thus seen as the outcome of a gradual process of capitalist restoration – a final step in sweeping away the last obstacle in the way of China's transition from socialism.[1]

On the contrary, this chapter argues that China's 'embrace of globalisation' is in fact a rather audacious move to strengthen its own national security. Responding to changing conditions in the international order, China is reaching towards a new stage of modernisation involving deeper reforms. The goal is not to transform the entire system into a capitalist one but to improve and strengthen the socialist system and develop the Chinese economy as quickly as possible within the framework of socialism.[2] In what ways can these new directions be seen as an evolution from the developments under Mao and Deng? In what ways do the new reforms aim to strengthen China's CNP? How is China to manage the challenge from the giant global corporations and succeed in playing a determining role to shape a developmental world order?

SELF-RELIANCE: THE EARLY STAGES – FROM MAO
TO DENG

The Mao period accomplished a 'Great Leap' in transforming China from a semi-feudal and semi-colonial country into a major independent industrial power of global significance.[3] Before 1949, torn apart by warlordism, foreign invasions, peasant uprisings and civil wars and drained of its surpluses through imperialist impositions, China displayed the classic symptoms of underdevelopment: economic stagnation, technological backwardness, political corruption and disorder, and social polarisation and impoverishment.

By the time of Mao's death in 1976, it had developed into a considerable power, with a diversified and self-sufficient industrial structure and some advanced technological capabilities.[4]

This transformation rested on the basic system of socialist ownership. In establishing this, the CPC at first moved cautiously to retain the support of indigenous business people and entrepreneurs in the New Democratic period of transition. Economic reconstruction and development in these early years of New Democracy paved the way for agricultural cooperation and the establishment of state ownership in industry, finance and commerce, laying the basis for the transition to socialism. In 1956, China introduced a Soviet-type system of state-owned enterprises (SOEs) and centralised planning which allowed the country's limited investment resources to be mobilised and targeted at the enterprises and industries which were key to establishing a self-reliant economic base. Mao's approach was to differ from Stalin's in adopting a strategy of 'walking on two legs' to drive the dynamic development of both agriculture and industry together, focusing on grain as well as steel, to feed the people as well as create an independent industrialisation.

During the Mao period, the Chinese people began to move out of poverty and ignorance but the achievements were indeed gained at heavy human cost. China's development was severely constrained not only by its own socioeconomic backwardness but also by the enormous pressure from the US-led anti-communist world system. Mao had had to forge a path of 'closed door' self-reliance and limited interaction with the outside world which was very damaging to the country's development. In these circumstances, the aim was to combine 'top-down' commandism with 'bottom up' mobilisation to develop production and for social advance. Mass movements, however, were driven to excess in the Great Leap Forward (1958–60) and the Cultural Revolution (1966–76).

At the same time, though hugely disruptive, these movements had great significance in bringing science and technology to the countryside, transforming both the skills and the consciousness of China's rural people. Such developments clearly provided a springboard for the exceptional economic development and rising living standards of the subsequent reform decades.

While Maoist self-reliance was adopted under severe constraints within the international conditions of 'war and revolution', Deng was able to develop a new approach in the very different conditions following the normalisation of Sino–US relations in 1978, itself indicative of a wider world trend towards 'peace and development'. Increased opportunities for multilateral initiatives, given superpower decline, now allowed China to 'open the door' and make use of export markets and direct foreign investment (FDI) in its development. The aim of self-reliance in these new circumstances as formulated by Deng was to 'keep the initiative in one's one hands' by maintaining control over the country's economic lifelines.

China now began to embark on a process of gradual economic reform. This involved a reorientation in the political direction of the CPC from class-based mobilisation to a focus on 'developing the productive forces' through use of market mechanisms, relying on material incentives rather than political ardour to carry forward the socialist orientation.

Early successes in reforms paved the way in 1987 for a more realistic assessment of China's socialist transformation. China, as a poor, largely agrarian-based developing country, needed, for some time to come, to focus on the development of production and to use the market mechanism to coordinate production of small-scale farmers and workshops. This primary stage of socialism was understood as likely to last for at least 100 years from 1956. As Deng had said 'socialism cannot be built on the basis of poverty' and the 'superiority of the socialist system is based on increasing the productive forces and improving people's material and cultural life'.[5] By 1992, China was declared a 'socialist market economy' in which diverse forms of ownership were to be developed and different forms of distribution allowed so long as these 'contributed to common prosperity' and that public ownership and distribution according to work remained predominant.

Very different from Russia's neoliberal 'shock therapy' in the early 1990s, Deng's economic reforms and open door policy progressed in stages with the aim of strengthening China's industrial base and CNP. The long-term reform programme was set in motion by raising the prices of grain bought by the state, thereby stimulating a rural consumer boom which in turn promoted a spectacular rise in small and medium-sized township and village enterprises (TVEs). This rapid expansion of TVEs created a favourable environment to ease the restructuring of large-scale SOEs. These were given greater autonomy as demand for machinery rose.

As Ross has argued, the approach here was not one of market liberalisation but of planned interventions by the government and managed expansion of the domestic market, using pricing policy to shape patterns of demand so as to create a dynamic balance between the development of agriculture, light and heavy industry.[6] At the same time, a decentralised approach brought local initiative and local understanding of conditions into play to improve the efficiency of planning and the use of local resources.

As Ross maintains, the success of these measures of planning and control would not have been possible without the retention of the country's industrial core under public ownership.[7] This was preserved and enhanced by a controlled opening to trade and investment in which the domestic economy remained highly protected from international competition, whilst FDI was used for technical transfer and training to upgrade the industrial structure.

In the right conditions, exposure to competition can help to improve an enterprise's or an industry's performance. Radical developmentalists such as Khor have therefore argued that in opening up a developing country to foreign trade and investment, what is important is the quality, timing, sequencing and scope of liberalisation as well as the accompanying strength of local enterprises, human resources and technological development and the building up of export capacity and markets.[8]

The open door policy aimed in the first place to promote China's production for external markets by seeking to attract foreign investment into the export sector. The focus was not simply on the large-scale MNCs, but especially on the overseas Chinese investors from Hong Kong, Taiwan and Singapore as well as from elsewhere in East Asia.

Export production allows China to utilise its comparative advantage in labour-intensive manufacturing, an advantage which is unusually high since, with around 22 per cent of the world's population and 9 per cent of the world's cultivable land, China has a high ratio of labour to land. Foreign earnings have then been used to import modern equipment, filling the gaps in China's existing technologies to develop the economy faster.

However, foreign investment was not allowed to flow in freely. The government followed a selective policy limiting FDI to priority sectors in accordance with the state's industrial policies, directing foreign capital inflows into long-term investment projects and into greenfield sites to create new productive capacity.[9] Through joint ventures and the mobility of personnel, the modernising effects of FDI have on the whole been diffused fairly widely, while profits in the fast-growing export sector have largely fed back into the localities though joint venture arrangements, often with the TVEs. In these ways, foreign investment was used to enable China to advance more quickly in technology.

ECONOMIC REFORM FOR INTERDEPENDENCE: DIVERSIFYING THE SOCIALIST ECONOMY

By the latter part of the 1990s, China's economic system was still over-whelmingly made up of SOEs or collectively owned enterprises (COEs). Bankruptcies had been limited and private enterprise only made a small contribution in terms of output. Building on Mao's achievements, Deng's step-by-step approach had proved enormously successful in achieving growth. However, from 1997, China began to embark on a new trajectory of development seeking a much deeper engagement with the international economic system with the decision to speed up WTO accession.

The turning point for the Chinese leadership's thinking in its economic as well as its security approach was the 1995/6 Taiwan Strait crisis. With the United States building advanced military capabilities and its increasingly offensive stance, China's leaders became more and more focused on the technological gap between China and the United States.[10] China's national security was on the line.

Restructuring in the State-Owned Sector

The 1997 15th CPC Congress began to address the need for China to grasp the most advanced technologies, to enhance its ability to innovate and to accelerate hi-tech capability and IT use. Success here would be the key to determining China's future. The development of a knowledge economy was imperative if China was to meet the military and economic challenges it faced, and to catch up with and join the ranks of the advanced nations. This required a two-faceted approach. China would have to build its own group of large corporations mainly by transforming its SOEs into profitable and internationally competitive 'national champions' to provide the core of a strong CNP, and at the same time, in order to do so, it had to become more involved in the global economy to join the trend of technological advance and economic globalisation.

WTO rules would require China to remove the restrictions on MNCs which had been protecting its domestic producers to give much greater free-doms to inflows of foreign capital. But for China the choice was not simply a matter of economics: it was a strategic decision.

In the first place, joining the WTO would help to reduce China's vulner-ability to the pressures of US economic blackmail. For at least one Chinese analyst, threats over access to US markets, which inhibited FDI, were seen as the 'nuclear bomb of economic relations'.[11] WTO membership would help to stabilise economic relations with the United States, so stimulating trade and investment generally. Within the security of the global trade frame-work, China would be able to insert itself into the global production chains linking East Asia to the US and other markets, thus making itself indispensable as a production base for the world economy. This would make it far more difficult for the United States to impose a new Cold War isolation.

Second, WTO membership would also help China in forging closer ties with Taiwan. According to WTO rules, Taiwan's restrictions on direct trade and investment with the mainland would have to be removed.

Third, accession to the WTO would provide China with a chance to join the unprecedented global technological revolution, offering a short cut for the country to accelerate its industrial transformation and upgrade its economic structure. By using new information technologies to propel industrialisation, incorporating IT into the restructuring of SOEs, China would be able to make a leap in development, at the same time using new technologies to increase the state's capacity to control the economy.

Clearly WTO membership is a high-risk strategy. The intense debates on globalisation at the time show that Chinese leaders and analysts were, as they still are, acutely aware of the dangers that economic globalisation poses to its economic security. China's SOEs would have to face the full force of global competition and its economy would be more exposed to the instabilities of world markets. Pressure to abide by international norms and regulations devised by the world's most powerful governments would constrain government policy making. Should the international corporations based in the advanced countries capture the 'commanding heights' of China's economy, central government could become paralysed. If the import and export of goods and capital flows were to be taken out of its hands, the government would lose macroeconomic control, finally surrendering economic sovereignty.

On the other hand, China's leaders saw the WTO as forum within which China could conduct economic diplomacy and bring into play win–win negotiations to promote the New Security Concept (NSC). Above all, and certainly the most important point, joining the WTO would itself be a win–win scenario, a matter of 'pooling sovereignty to enhance sovereignty' with the opportunity for China to become a rule maker in the international economic order rather than just a rule taker. In this way, China would have the chance to exert more influence on the management of economic globalisation in its own interests in order to ward off the risks and redress the imbalances in global development.

China, then, was prepared to take a very daring step to 'embrace globalisation' in order to maintain self-reliance in the long run. WTO accession and greater global integration were indeed seen to hold 'rare opportunities and grim challenges'.[12] The risks would be great, but self-reliance and interdependence, though contradictory, are not mutually exclusive. The key was to balance further opening with self-reliance 'to safeguard the economic security of the country'.[13] China would be able to manage greater global economic involvement on its own terms if it took the opportunities to build up its CNP. But to grasp the opportunities and respond to the challenges called for deeper reforms.

China's SOEs were still largely protected from market forces – generally overstaffed, with 'iron rice bowl' provisions for the health, welfare and education of their workers and their families impeding their competitiveness. To transform them into 'national champions' able to take on the giant MNCs of the advanced capitalist world required drastic measures. At the 15th CPC Congress in 1997 the decision was taken to focus efforts on restructuring and upgrading a limited number of the larger SOEs.

In his keynote speech to the 15th CPC Congress, Jiang Zemin took Deng's 1992 formula of a socialist market economy one step further to argue that state ownership did not have to dominate in every sector in order to maintain broad control of the economy. Instead the state should consolidate its strength in key areas, concentrating its support on selected industries and technologies with an important bearing on national economic and military security and with long-term potential for development. Focusing on those with the greatest assets, generating the most profits and taking a leading role in their sectors, SOEs were to be restructured using IT and the other most advanced technologies, to then release China's own capabilities in independent technological development so that it would have an international presence in these crucial areas.

To do so meant 'letting go the small', that is, the smaller SOEs, which were to be merged, contracted out, transformed into shareholding companies or otherwise privatised.

Jiang further proposed the introduction of a shareholding system to allow SOEs to tap into other sources of capital, raise funds on stock markets, as well as take out foreign loans. Such measures would greatly assist SOE restructuring and mergers, avoiding bankruptcy. The state would retain the controlling share which could be as little as 35 per cent if other ownerships were dispersed.[14]

Such measures required a deeper shift away from planning and a greater use of the market in resource allocation. Direct central planning had its advantages in marshalling limited resources to support key industries but, at China's low levels of development, was very inefficient. Deng's decentralised approach had helped to widely disperse the benefits of industrialisation, but it had led to a lot of overlaps in production. China's industrial structure had become fragmented and prone to over-capacity and over-pricing, with domestic capital often wasted on unprofitable projects.

A wider and more effective scope of market mechanisms would help to improve management and resource allocation to enhance the competitiveness of the state economy. At the same time, WTO-imposed market disciplines would aid the creation of a unified, fair and regulated internal market by helping to remove the bureaucratic barriers erected by local governments which protected their own industries but which obstructed the development of leading nationally based corporations.

Finally, facilitated by shareholding, SOEs were to be opened up to foreign investment to help support their modernisation. What China's leadership recognised was that to enter the knowledge-intensive era required closer links with MNCs in order to gain technological know-how. However, while MNCs could assist in the diffusion of modern techniques and help SOEs to upgrade their production processes, they clearly were not going to give up their advantages easily. The view was that Chinese companies should cooperate with MNCs, in particular with those corporations driving technological breakthroughs, by joining their global production and supply chains, using this role of serving as a production base to forge long-term strategic partnerships as a means to gain access to technology.[15] Foreign partnerships could be used to strengthen the competitiveness of China's own companies, but:

> Only when the interests of transnational corporations are closely linked to that of their joint ventures in China will they take the initiative to provide the newest technology and management which are of great benefit to the development of China's new technology industries.[16]

The 15th CPC Congress in 1997 then marked a new stage in China's reforms, which together with the NSC, constituted a third phase of 'self-reliance in interdependence' – pursuing the national interest in and through global cooperation. The new approach here reflected the CPC's assessment that the international trend of 'peace and development' would continue and that while the US trend towards military aggressiveness was to be taken seriously, growing global interdependence through rapid globalisation was opening up new opportunities for multipolarisation.

To make the most of the opportunities for global economic cooperation, deeper reforms in the ownership structure were seen to be necessary to advance the mixed ownership of the socialist market economy. However, the overall aim of the reforms was to strengthen the state's capacity to control the nation's economic lifelines. The public sector was to remain dominant, with the SOEs as the main body of the economy holding the leading position in the major industries, including infrastructure – energy, steel, and transportation; the lifeline industries including petrochemicals, metallurgical, electrical and chemical industries; the hi-tech sector such as telecoms and IT; as well as finance and banking, space and atomic energy.

The Private Sector

It is hard to estimate the relative sizes of the state-owned, foreign-owned and private sectors in the Chinese economy separately since the different ownerships are in certain respects becoming interwoven. According to official figures for 2005, the private sector comprised 49.7 per cent of GDP, counting not only Chinese-owned enterprises but also foreign-owned, joint venture and other foreign-funded enterprises. Including Hong Kong, Macao and Taiwan-funded enterprises, the figure rises to 65 per cent.[17] Huang, on the other hand, estimates that only 14 per cent of fixed assets are in private hands.[18]

The domestic-owned sector mostly comprises the self-employed, mainly small-scale family-run enterprises. It has been growing very fast indeed, especially in service provision, experiencing a five-fold increase between 1998–2003, not least with the divestment of numbers of smaller SOEs.[19] As a major source of employment of workers laid off from SOEs, the growth of the private sector has been of tremendous assistance in SOE restructuring, easing the pressures of social instability.

A number of limited liability companies have emerged through the reform of small SOEs and from within the TVE sector, although many of the large-scale TVEs remain in collective ownership. Some of these limited liability companies are starting to list in the stock markets.

However, the private sector now emerging in China is not so much an independent economic force of pressure on the government, but rather a creation of both state and market. Many, especially the larger private enterprises, have very close links with government, benefiting from favourable taxation measures, land allocations, grants and loans as well as R&D support and procurement arrangements. Lenovo, for example, has close links with the Chinese Academy of Science and through this a close association with other state bodies.

Foreign Investment

Although again it is very difficult to quantify, the involvement of foreign investment in the Chinese economy has undoubtedly accelerated since the end of the 1990s. Martin Wolf claims that whilst in the early 1990s FDI made up only 4 to 5 per cent of GDP, between 1995 and 2002 its share in industrial output rose from 12 per cent to 29 per cent.[20] FDI has been encouraged especially into manufacturing and export manufacturing, and it is often noted that companies in which foreign investors have a stake – the foreign invested enterprises (FIEs) – make up over 50 per cent of China's exports, exceeding domestic exporters. Linda Lim cautions against exaggerated FDI figures since at least 25 per cent of China's 'foreign' cash inflow is likely to represent investment from domestic companies which routinely funnel money out of the country to tax havens such as Hong Kong or the British Virgin Islands.[21] According to Jiang Xiaojuan, by 2000 FDI still made up only 10 per cent of China's total investment in fixed assets.[22]

Nevertheless, China has opened its industrial sector to foreign investment at a much earlier stage of its development than other developing countries, and China has become a leading recipient of FDI. Foreign investors have been attracted to China not simply because of the cheapness of Chinese labour but because of its productivity given the generally higher educational standards than elsewhere in the developing world, as well as because of its market potential, good infrastructure and stability. Foreign investment has contributed to China's growth, but China's success has also attracted foreign investment. Far from representing a weakening of China's international position, this inflow of FDI reflects its strengthening as the economy's growth gives it leverage to demand significant transfers of technology and training from foreign investors.[23]

The significance of FDI lies not so much in terms of its amount as in its modernising effect in bringing new products, improving managerial practices, as well as improving the competitiveness of exports and opening avenues into international markets. FDI can have negative effects on developing countries, draining economies through profit repatriation or creating a trade imbalance through additional imports, but China has largely been able to use FDI to its advantage, subjecting investment to national development needs and objectives. Foreign enterprises have generally helped to raise the technological levels of their Chinese partners, boosting their R&D, expanding their markets and restoring their profitability.[24] In 2001 FIEs accounted for nearly one-third of total profits of the country.[25]

Lacking in understanding of international markets and the skills to create the necessary technological and logistic chains, some Chinese domestic exporters may find it extremely tough to compete against companies which are far more able to invest in R&D and management know-how. But the FIEs – those state- and collectively-owned as well as private enterprises which work with foreign partners incorporating foreign investment while continuing to hold the majority stake – have greatly benefited from export growth.

The inflow of FDI to China has not been excessive by the standards for the Asia–Pacific region and the proportion of investment by developed countries is unusually low. The explosion in FDI in the 1990s was largely driven by overseas Chinese, and in 2002 some 68 per cent of foreign investment came from developing Asia, while by June 2006 only 8 per cent came from the United States, 8.5 per cent from Japan and 7.75 per cent from the European Union.[26]

It is argued on the other hand that overseas Chinese investors mostly act as subcontractors for companies such as Nike, Reebok, Adidas and Puma, and that through the use of Hong Kong enterprises as intermediaries, the involvement of US and Japanese companies in China takes a disguised form far greater than the trade and investment figures would suggest. What appears as Asian investment in China actually rests on the investment and production decisions of the giant corporations of the advanced capitalist countries.[27]

However, seeking the aid of overseas Chinese to help Chinese enterprises join in with transnational production networks shaped by international capital is of course the deliberate strategy of the Chinese government precisely to ensure the process is not one-way. Overseas Chinese investors have been able to serve as an extremely important bridge in terms of transfers of managerial know-how and technologies as they were heavily involved in the shift in FDI from labour-intensive to capital-intensive sectors in the 1990s. Although their investment has brought only limited advanced technology, their methods have been easier to absorb and they are more prepared to take risks and assist in the restructuring of SOEs into 'national champions'. Their involvement has helped to close the technological gap, so facilitating the transfer of more advanced technologies from abroad, as well as the development of innovative capacities.

Rather than simply playing a compradorising role as suggested above, these investors are influenced by loyalties to China, both local and national, in their desire to contribute to the country's development and to improve conditions in their own hometown districts. As Sen has argued, the overseas Chinese have not merely been instrumental in deepening China's ties with the wider world economy but at the same time have provided a buffer against predatory market forces and associated political pressures. Since they share in some of the Chinese government's political and economic goals or at least lack the backing of other powerful governments, overseas Chinese investors have provided a gateway through which China's government has been able to regulate economic ties with the outside world more effectively.[28]

THE CHALLENGE FROM FOREIGN MONOPOLY CAPITAL

Under its commitments to the WTO, China now has to open even further to foreign competition, lowering quotas and tariffs and eliminating subsidies to give foreign MNCs greater access into its domestic markets. New rules make it easier for foreign companies to expand their businesses more freely, by setting up their own wholly owned enterprises, through takeovers of domestic companies and through acquiring shares as the stock market opens gradually to international investors.

Foreign MNCs are now allowed entry into the service sector – banking and finance, insurance, telecoms, retailing, transportation, legal and professional services as well as railways, electric power, construction and technology-intensive industries. These sectors have survived on the basis of their state monopoly position but will face exposure to competition for the first time.

Since these global corporations are far stronger in their technological innovation and financial capacities, managerial expertise and customer base than China's SOEs, the question is whether or not the latter will be able to survive exposure to the full force of international competition.

Competition in global markets as a whole has become increasingly unequal since the late 1990s. A boom in mergers and acquisitions has seen the emergence of giant corporations with huge R&D expenditures using IT to globalise their systems of production, purchase and sale. As Nolan has reiterated, this global business revolution redefines the scale of what is needed to be competitive in international markets, making it much more difficult for newcomers to gain entry.[29] Developing countries are finding it especially hard to upgrade and diversify their industries since developed countries lock in the benefits of technology, R&D and brand.[30]

With China's five-year adjustment period for WTO accession ending in 2006, the danger was that foreign companies would start an aggressive expansion, acting quickly to take over their joint venture partners.

Through acquisition, MNCs can find a cheap and fast way to create a low-cost manufacturing base. By gaining control of local enterprises with wide sales networks, they can easily grab market share and even establish a monopoly position, if they take over local market leaders. MNCs are able to rely on their advantages to drive out local competition and can then use their monopoly position to raise prices. Alternatively, by using enterprises in different parts of a business as subcontractors, and insinuating themselves as the integrating factor, foreign MNCs could reduce China's production into a part of their own international division of labour.

While China seeks to insert itself further into the world economy on the basis of its advantages in labour-intensive processes in order to gain access to technology and to build its own CNP, the giant corporations have their opposite goal to integrate the China end of their production, marketing and R&D into their global business operation.

Chinese analysts are well aware of the danger that the economy could end up trapped in low-cost production. A wave of mergers and acquisitions could stifle China's efforts to cultivate its own capacity for innovation and create its own brands.[31] If Chinese companies were to go into decline, the economy's industrial capacity would shrink, weakening its technological capacity and accelerating a brain drain. China's own enterprises would become confined to low-technology sectors such as footwear, travel goods, bicycles and electrical appliances and China would end up 'just like a puppet state' under the control of foreign MNCs as a low-cost assembler of imported parts.[32]

As these analysts recognise, China could find itself in the position of many Latin American countries whose high dependence on external markets for growth stems from a failure to develop indigenous industrial systems, their loss of competitive edge together with a weakening of government capacity, especially in financial management, leading to economic stagnation, the polarisation of the population, social conflict and long-term instability.[33]

TAKING ON THE CHALLENGE: COMPETITION, REGULATION, GLOBALISING, INNOVATION

Despite the continued growth in labour-intensive exports, the government has no intention for China to end up simply as a supplier of cheap labour for the world economy, and so has been adopting a wide range of measures to guard against the risks and dangers entailed in WTO accession. Through a variety of strategies the government aims to manage capitalism to the overall advantage of the national economy, ensuring that Chinese companies become internationally competitive and that the economy as a whole is geared up to strengthen independent technological innovation and to develop more sophisticated manufacturing and services.

Creating Competition

Fostering a competitive environment is one way of curbing or shaping MNC behaviour. The creation of 'national champions' is key here. Since 1997 SOEs have been undergoing massive restructuring, and mergers have been encouraged to consolidate sectors such as steel and energy to overcome the problems of fragmentation and overinvestment. The aim is to have around 50 'national champion' companies in the Fortune Global 500 by 2010. As of 2007 there are 24 – all state-owned – such as Sinopec, China Mobile, Baosteel, CNOOC as well as a number of the state-owned banks. Also targeted to become national leaders are a number of rising companies with a more private character such as Haier (white goods), TCL (TVs), Huawei (telecoms) and Lenovo (PCs). China's search engine Baidu is also competing successfully against Google and Yahoo in domestic markets.[34]

Since 2001, Chinese companies have proved to be highly competitive on cost in some areas, gaining ground on global giants.[35] However, where MNCs are so far ahead of Chinese companies in technological terms that competition is not an option, certainly in the short term, China has used the great promise of its market to attract rival bids for contracts. With MNCs rushing in headlong to tap growth in China, it is often possible to encourage two or three to compete to prevent a foreign-controlled monopoly forming or to win concessions on technology transfer. Indeed many foreign businesses in China willingly transfer technology to local partners as a price for market entry.[36]

Strategic Partnerships

The favoured approach is for SOEs to forge strategic partnerships with foreign companies to tap into capital and expertise to modernise. Foreign companies with advanced technologies in energy savings and environmental protection are especially sought after. The state however resists ceding management control to foreign partners, who are not allowed to own majority shares.

Such arrangements help to put limits on the entry of foreign competitors, since once a partnership is agreed, a company will be less likely to set up independently in competition. Partnerships also seem to be the choice of foreign companies even though the WTO agreement makes it easier for them to set up their own subsidiaries, since conditions in China's domestic markets are so competitive.

The restructuring of the banking sector is a case in point. The impact of WTO entry on China's state-owned banks (SOBs) has been a matter of some concern. These banks have had to pump considerable sums into non-viable SOEs and as a result acquired substantial non-performing loans (NPLs). This made the overall system fragile and particularly vulnerable to unequal competition. Banks provide some 80 per cent of funds for investment, with stock markets playing only a supplementary role, so banking reform is particularly critical for the economy's overall financial stability. SOB staff are often poorly trained, and with foreign banks gaining full access to China's markets in 2007, SOBs are at risk of losing business to them. If foreign banks were to succeed in creaming off the best customers this could trigger a bank run on SOBs if they were thought to be insolvent. Such a crisis occurred in Argentina in 1999 when control of the banking sector was lost to foreign banks which only gave credit to MNCs leaving local businesses badly squeezed. Foreign banks also provide a channel for the inflow of speculative capital or 'hot money', which has become a serious problem in China since 2002.[37]

To help China's SOBs to recapitalise and become more efficient and commercially oriented they have been linking up with foreign investors as well as listing shares. Foreign banks, lacking knowledge of Chinese markets, have made partnership arrangements their first choice and China's four big SOBs have now received foreign investment. The injections of capital have helped to restore the banks to financial health, so reducing the problem of NPLs. This in turn has assisted Chinese banks in gaining listings on overseas stock markets to access additional capital inputs from international markets. The arrangements have been tightly regulated, guaranteeing the state's majority control and limiting foreign ownership to minority stakes of 25 per cent. Although foreign investors have tried, as minority shareholders, to get agreements to exercise management control, the CPC retains powers to appoint managers.[38] It remains to be seen however, whether foreign banks will be able to increase their influence from within by acquiring more shares through the stock market.

Overall the reforms aim to help foreign banks enter into China's markets in an orderly way harmonised with the country's long-term development strategies.

Going Global

In 2001, Hu Jintao, the then vice-president, called for Chinese enterprises to 'go global', a momentum that accelerated after 2003. Key SOEs have begun to set up joint ventures in extractive industries, for example in iron ore, copper and oil, in Australia as well as in Latin America, Africa and South-East Asia, as part of their strategies for technological upgrading to meet the challenge of the WTO. The SOE's role is generally as a buyer of output under long-term contract.[39]

China's consumer brands have also been encouraged to 'go global' in the face of stiff competition in domestic markets in order to secure a market position through exporting. Huawei has spearheaded these efforts with success in telecoms markets in a number of developing countries as well as in Russia.[40] The move to 'go global' is mainly driven by the need to acquire technologies and design skills to maintain competitiveness. Some companies, having gained technological capability through licensing and joint ventures, have then upgraded further by buying assets and patents to build global brands. Lenovo's US$1.75 billion purchase of IBM's PC unit in 2004 which allows the use of the brand, makes it the third-largest PC supplier. The Shanghai Automotive Industry Corporation (SAIC) was eventually successful in obtaining intellectual property rights for the Rover brand.

Nor are the ambitions of Chinese companies limited to markets in developing countries. Haier has offices in 100 countries, though still so far operating in niche markets. TCL bought France's Thomson TV business with the aim of becoming the Chinese Sony.[41] SAIC is aiming to be among the world's top six car companies by 2020 having bought South Korea's Ssangyong Motors.[42] Chinese automobile companies are opening assembly plants in Asia and Latin America and Chery, Geely and SAIC all aim to export in Europe, the Middle East, Latin America and United States. Not all these ventures are success stories: TCL's links with its French partners fell apart after only a couple of years. Nevertheless, China's automobile and telecoms sectors, which were considered to be particularly vulnerable to international competition after WTO entry, are evidently fighting back.

Anti-Monopoly Measures

Mergers and acquisitions of Chinese companies have been on the increase, with US companies topping the list of takeovers followed by European Union and Japan.[43] To reduce risk of foreign companies using acquisitions to gain control in strategic sectors and establish monopolies, the ground rules on foreign investment are being tightened up. Restrictive anti-monopoly legislation has been introduced to 'guard the pass', requiring foreign takeovers and investment in sensitive sectors, where an issue of industrial or national security is at stake, to pass national security reviews.[44]

Encouraging Long-Term Investment

To limit stock market volatility, access to China's stock markets is being tightly controlled. China has refined its Qualified Foreign Institutional Investors Act to make it more effective in deterring speculators by establishing quotas for international investment funds with access to domestic equity markets.[45] Foreign investors are to be allowed to buy shares on stock markets but restrictions favour long-term investors.

Research and Development

Chinese companies have yet to prove they can compete on more than just low-cost manufacturing. The main battle between China's 'national champions' and the MNCs is not so much over market share as over technology. In computers and consumer electronics, for example, while foreign brands may only account for a minority share in these markets, the core technologies are monopolised by a handful of foreign companies.[46]

Although R&D spending has trebled in the last seven years and China now has overtaken Japan to become the second-biggest spender on R&D, much of the research carried out in China is still at a low level, involving international firms and organisations which are responsible for filing two-thirds of the patents.[47]

To support industrial upgrading, China's FDI policies have turned to encouraging hi-tech investors to help drive local technology and stimulate new ideas. Science and industrial parks have been mushrooming not just in the coastal provinces but also in the cities of central China – Wuhan, Chongqing, Chengdu – and many of the top Fortune 500 firms rushed to set up labs. For the MNCs, outsourcing R&D is part of a strategy to integrate their Chinese production, R&D and marketing with the global market in order to realise integrated operations worldwide. For China, however, these centres constitute a 'brain drain': the MNCs hire the major proportion of Chinese graduates and compete for China's best talent. At the same time, they tend to keep their core technologies at home so as not to give away their secrets, restricting technology transfer to maintain their dominant market position. The bulk of China's hi-tech companies meanwhile just do assembly work for foreign companies, with little or no technological content, producing low-margin electronic products such as DVDs with the 'smart bits' imported.

The major drawback of Chinese industries is their lack of core technology. The 11th Five Year Plan (2006–10) has placed hi-tech industries at the top of the agenda with the focus of economic restructuring and transformation on increasing innovative capability through support for science and technology, as well as strengthening the diffusion of knowledge and investing more in education. The aim is to create internationally competitive new growth segments especially in hi-tech sectors such as robotics, biotechnology, computer software, biology and nanotechnology, and to forge new innovative capacity in space, laser and other areas that have implications for the country's industrial competitiveness and national security.

China has a greater skills capacity than is traditional for developing economies, and in fact produces two and a half times more graduates each year than the United States. Although only one-eighth as many graduates are engaged in R&D,[48] this is still a high number by world standards, and while China's research is often at a low level and impeded by the shortage of scientists, educational levels are rising to standards comparable with the West far more quickly than predicted. Plans for a massive expansion of higher education with the development of 100 world-class universities are underway. People are highly motivated and young Chinese appear to have an aptitude for new technology.

China is also able to draw on a diaspora of knowledge workers. A quarter of foreign PhD students in the United States are Chinese and a growing number of them are returning to China.[49] With returnees from Silicon Valley joining China's technology-driven development effort, the basic computer software industry is slowly breaking the monopoly of the MNCs.

Some MNCs are now beginning to move genuine research to China to do breakthrough work because of the high numbers of skilled scientists they can recruit.[50]

But SOEs have now also begun to file thousands of patents. Joint research projects and joint patenting may be the way forward as Chinese companies, universities and research institutes set up R&D projects together with the MNCs, especially in pharmaceuticals, software and communications technologies. Huawei, for example, is setting up research partnerships with Siemens and Motorola. In this way, China can combat the 'brain drain' and become part of the development of cutting-edge technologies.

China is leapfrogging ahead in certain areas. Its successful launch of a manned spacecraft in 2004 took the world by surprise, demonstrating its technology in that area as near the world's best. China has now produced its own satellite navigation system and its hi-tech sector has had success in digital cameras, cell phones, computer and TV chips, as well as in developing the first successful anti-SARS vaccine.[51] China also now comes second to the United States in the number of papers published in top nanotechnology journals.[52]

China is also developing its own core competences to promote its national champions by setting domestic technical standards. In 2005, the government issued an international standard for audio-video coding to support its own version of a DVD aimed to break into a field whose core technologies are highly monopolised by a handful of foreign MNCs.[53] This attempt has faced difficulties. However, the government is now advancing plans to establish standards across a range of technologies from 3G mobile telephony and optical discs to nanotechnology and bioengineering.[54] If China's own companies can get their technologies accepted as standard then the size of the Chinese market will force international giants to support it.

CONCLUSION

China's reforms have achieved remarkable success: a near double-digit growth rate year by year with generally low inflation and dramatic improvements in living standards and poverty reduction as well as in the creation of numbers of 'national champion' enterprises. This success is owed mainly to its independent course of development based on a foundation of socialist ownership, with growth essentially driven by the very large domestic savings and with poverty reduction helping to fuel domestic markets.[55]

China's self-reliance has advanced step-by-step, each stage a new move forward given changing opportunities and challenges, tackling the limitations of the preceding stage. So Maoist self-reliance, underpinned by central planning and mass mobilisation, built a foundation of a socialist industrialisation, which took off once Deng was able to break through 'closed doorism' as China's Cold War isolation ended, to make new advances through opening up and reform. The SOEs were gradually brought under the discipline of market competition, and small-scale experiments in shareholding, stock markets and the private sector in the early 1990s paved the way for further far-reaching changes after 1997 as Chinese leaders, concerned over the growing technological gap between China and the United States, aimed to bring China into the knowledge economy. WTO accession meant adapting Deng's formulation of the self-reliant principle – 'keeping the initiative in one's own hands' – with deeper reforms to allow China to take advantage of the new opportunities of globalisation while at the same time guarding against the dangers by providing a framework within which to cultivate innovative capacity.

The recent reforms to enhance the role of the market and competition have meant further changes in the ownership system with the level of government intervention in economic activities reduced significantly. But as Guo Sujian points out, the reforms are not about replacing public ownership with private ownership as in a capitalist system; on the contrary, they have been introduced and extended to strengthen the public ownership system and the capacity of the state to control the economy.[56] Resource allocation under a market economy is now recognised as being more efficient, but as former premier Zhu Rongji stated, 'public ownership of property can better maintain social justice and increase common prosperity than systems which encourage private ownership'.[57]

Instead of a 'creeping privatisation' China's reform path has been led by a conscious state strategy to nurture a group of large enterprises to challenge the world's leading MNCs. Liberalisation has been selective, with foreign investment and competition introduced to assist the modernisation of SOEs as an alternative to privatisation, with ownership transfer for the most part limited to the smaller SOEs.[58] Chinese stock markets have been developed to alleviate the pressure on SOBs which provide the bulk of investment funds so as to promote greater stability for economic growth. The stock markets are mostly used by SOEs and at the same time, through a certain limited sale of shares in the large SOEs to overseas investors and the listing of these companies in world stock markets, financial markets are being used to raise capital to strengthen SOEs, not to hand them over to private shareholders.

The exact reach of state ownership is much disputed. According to the *Economist,* SOEs still account for more than half of all industrial assets, although reduced by 10 per cent since 1998.[59] As Guy de Jonquieres of the *Financial Times* confirms, the prevalence of SOEs in 'strategic' industries leaves little doubt that the state continues to dominate the economy's. commanding heights and to ensure that it serves the social objectives not least of stable employment.[60] Since they continue to play such a key role in economic growth driving China's industrialisation, improving the competitiveness of the SOEs through reform and restructuring helps to strengthen the ability of the state to control the national economy as a whole and to bring into play the advantages of socialism. Now most of the enterprises have been restructured and are generally in profit, the government can use dividends on state shares to help fund further reorganisations as well as R&D, hi-tech industries and welfare provision.[61]

Economic reform has strengthened the state sector, with the 169 largest centrally controlled enterprises growing by nearly 28 per cent in 2005.[62] It is true that private and foreign enterprises have generally grown faster, a fact often used by China's critics as evidence of the superiority of capitalism over a public ownership-based system. However, the private sector and foreign investment have increased from a very low base and their comparatively faster growth is partly to be explained by their concentration in consumer goods and exports while state ownership predominates in the inevitably slower growing capital intensive heavy industry which is only just completing its restructuring.

The approach of 'using capitalism to construct socialism' was previously followed, in different circumstances, during China's period of New Democracy between 1949 and 1956, when the domestic business elite was encouraged to take part in economic development. Almost since its earliest days in the 1920s, the CPC has recognised that in certain periods 'patriotic capitalists' retained an element of revolutionary opposition to domination by foreign capital. These domestic-based businesspeople and industrialists, since they had to compete against the foreign monopolies, were more interested in developing the domestic economy, and so quite distinct from the compradore bourgeoisie or intermediaries and bureaucrat bourgeoisie whose interests were tied up with those of foreign companies and foreign loans respectively.

Now, as compared with the earlier period, public ownership and the Chinese state are in a vastly stronger position to harness the dynamics of both internal and international capitalism to assist in the socialist transition from a less developed to a more advanced economic stage.

The precedent in 'using capitalism to build socialism' was set by Lenin under the New Economic Policy (NEP) in the USSR in the 1920s, when he advocated the hiring or borrowing technologies from the West in order for the USSR to catch up. However, whilst using tried and tested technologies minimises risk for Chinese companies, as the demand for technology increases along with industrialisation, China risks paying huge costs in having to licence technology from abroad. If it simply relies on 'hiring or borrowing' technologies, China will always lag behind and never join the ranks of the advanced countries. China's approach has therefore moved beyond Lenin's recommendation to seek ways of combining foreign investment with domestic industrial technological progress through partnership arrangements in order to enter the knowledge economy swiftly.

Conditions in China favour partnerships, and although MNCs have technology and know-how on their side, the cultural, linguistic and operational barriers they face in China are formidable. Chinese companies then have the advantages of wide networks, local knowledge and the government on their side.

Nevertheless, the whole approach of attracting FDI by using 'markets for technology' has come under fire as China has yielded markets only to gain outmoded technologies with the MNCs maintaining overall technological control. Over-dependence on FDI is criticised as driving a low-cost labour-intensive and energy-consuming growth mode which produces an extremely unbalanced economic structure.[63] Debates continue. In which industries and sectors should SOEs remain dominant or even in a monopoly position? Which are crucial to the national economy and national security? Which core technologies should be developed indigenously and which can be bought elsewhere? To what extent can China continue on the path of borrowing technology and how fast should it speed up its shift to the knowledge intensive end of the division of labour? Meanwhile private entrepreneurship is now being encouraged further by the government to contribute to innovation and the development of indigenous technological capacity, and private enterprises are likely to continue to surge ahead in the future.[64]

In 2007, a landmark Property Law, aimed not least at protecting farmers from illegal land transfers without compensation, was adopted after extensive public debate. Whilst the law granted private property the same legal status as state property, at the same time it confirmed that public ownership remained at the heart of the country's economic system, and also contained provisions to make those who cause losses of state-owned assets through mismanagement or abuse of power legally liable.[65]

Private enterprise is particularly being encouraged in the non-strategic sectors of the economy but the question nevertheless arises as to whether China is nurturing a new national bourgeoisie, or even a new compradore class, since the larger private entrepreneurs have a dual aspect, both collaborating with and competing against foreign investors. The key point nevertheless is that the terms or rules of the market, which enable them to do so on an equal basis, are set by the state. Retaining close government links, the role of China's private entrepreneurs in the economy is essentially underlined by nationalism. On this basis, as with the overseas Chinese operating in a regional context, their interests are encompassed within the Third World globalist agenda identified by Harris, which seeks a full integration of developing countries into the global economy on an equal basis.[66]

'Using capitalism to construct socialism' remains problematic. Nonetheless, the government continues to play the leading role in economic development and social stability. The heavy industrial sector which drives the economy remains almost entirely in state hands. The state not only regulates the market but continues to exercise critical levers of control. Through tight management of capital allocation and stock market listings, it maintains its key position in making investment decisions to guide the country's path of development. With control over sites for a new plant and loans, the state is in a powerful position to direct private interests and is able to keep both foreign and domestic businesses in line. In this it acts as a formidable gatekeeper: even after years of trying to gain entry for News Corporation, Murdoch had to admit his efforts had 'hit a brick wall' in 2005.[67] Meanwhile, the rate of foreign takeovers is subsiding.[68] China's economic reforms have meant not so much a withdrawal of the state from its role in the economy, but rather a redefining of its role as a regulator of the market as well as increasingly in nurturing scientific and technological innovation.

China has followed its own development path, diverging from the Soviet model in taking a much more open approach to the market, while differing fundamentally from the neoliberal prescriptions of 'free markets' and privatisation. Its growth pattern shares something in common with the export-oriented industrialisation strategies of the other East Asian developmental states, which have also used their comparative advantage to upgrade industrial structure and productivity. However, China's active and controlled insertion into the progress of globalisation is very different from an economic strategy of prioritising exports. It has aimed at gaining bargaining power not only in relation to MNCs but also with other governments which now have too much to lose from China's instability. In particular it has sought to revolutionise US–China relations.

At the same time, as admittance to the WTO has released its scope for economic diplomacy, China is in a far stronger position than the other East Asian states to use its new development trajectory of 'self-reliance with interdependence' – pooling sovereignty to enhance sovereignty – to influence and shape the international order.

China's emphasis on innovation refers not only to science but also to social transformation and it is through new approaches to social reform as well as through the development of hi-tech capability that China aims to keep the initiative in shaping its own development. As Wen Jiabao said at Harvard University on 10 December 2003:

> China today is a country in reform and opening-up and a rising power dedicated to peace. It is neither proper nor possible for us to rely on foreign countries for development … [W]hile opening still wider to the outside world, we must more fully and more consciously depend on our own structural innovation, on constantly expanding the domestic market, on converting the huge savings of the citizens into investment and on improving the quality of the population and scientific and technological progress to solve the problems of resources and the environment. Herein lies the essence of China's road of peaceful rise and development.[69]

8 DEVELOPMENT WITH CHINESE CHARACTERISTICS

China's high-speed growth over the last nearly three decades has not been without serious social and economic costs. Remarkable reductions in poverty are taking place alongside widening gaps in income, growing regional disparities and rural–urban inequality. Economic reform has seen the rise of new socio-economic groups of rich farmers, rural and urban entrepreneurs, white-collar professionals, technicians, managers and the self-employed, which have all benefited disproportionately as the economy has grown. In the cities, laid-off state-owned enterprise (SOE) workers and a large 'floating population' of rural migrants coexist with the comfortably off middle class as well as a nouveau riche, which, though comparatively tiny, is highly visible. Meanwhile, for the majority of farmers, improvements in livelihood have so far failed to keep pace with the country's overall double-digit growth. A decline in socialised services has led to increasing inequity in access to health care and education in rural and urban areas and this, together with widespread corruption and environmental degradation, has become a major social and political issue in China.

For China's Leftist critics, these failings are the inevitable consequences of a capitalist restoration as China's working people are transformed into a cheap, dependent, insecure, exploitable labour force. As collectivist values have become eroded in the pursuit of personal enrichment, it is argued, the Communist Party of China (CPC) and the state have become alienated from worker–peasant support, even suppressing labour organisations while tilting increasingly to favour the interests of the urban elites.[1]

This chapter sets out not only to examine the wider social and environmental record of the reform period but also to consider the current Chinese leadership's efforts to address the problems of the country's unbalanced growth pattern.

The emergence of a more plural society made up of diverse interests inevitably creates more potential for conflict. The country is now seen to be entering a particularly painful stage of development with a per capita income of between US$1,000 and US$3,000 signalling a danger zone for modernisation in which the different interest groups will find it hard to come to terms with each other.[2] With World Trade Organization (WTO) accession threatening to exacerbate unequal development, the government, seeking to avoid 'Latin Americanisation', has begun to pay far more serious attention to the social and environmental costs of China's growth path. After all, when Deng Xiaoping advocated that some people should be allowed to 'get rich' first, this was in order to achieve common prosperity in the longer term.[3]

China's growth path of the 1980s and 1990s, reliant on investment and exports, is now under question as the leadership seeks to adopt a new more equitable, balanced and sustainable development strategy to achieve a more 'harmonious' society. It is in this context that issues of human rights and democracy are now being placed more firmly on the agenda of reform. China's immature political and legal system is seen to have become an obstacle as the Party and government seek to shift the basis of their legitimacy from fast-growth performance to delivering a better quality of growth.[4] Taking a rights-based 'people first' approach and increasing grass roots empowerment, the aim now is, as this chapter will show, to balance economic growth with a social policy of fairer redistribution.

THE COSTS OF RAPID GROWTH

The social achievements of the Mao period in many ways provide an example for the developing world. In 1950 average life expectancy was 40, only slightly higher than India's at 32. However, by the time of Mao's death, the figure stood at 62 as compared with 47 in India, a 15-year gap which reflected enormous strides in improving rural health care and reducing income inequality.[5]

Rapid growth in the reform decades has succeeded in lifting millions of people out of poverty. Between 1978 and 2002, incomes in China have increased more than eightfold and poverty, at the $1-per-day standard, has fallen by three-quarters, from 490 million to 88 million, a decline in poverty incidence from 29 per cent to just 6.9 per cent of the population.[6]

Having reached a per capita GDP of over US$1,000 by 2003, China is now ranked as a lower-middle income country. Remarkable progress has been made in the wider sense of human development. Overall levels of health in China are now higher than average in developing countries and roughly the same as in medium-income countries. Primary school enrolment is 11 per cent higher than the average level for developing countries in 2002 and at the same level as medium-income countries. Adult and youth literacy rates are also above average levels in developing countries and equal to those in medium-income countries.[7]

This success has rested in the first place on Mao's 'barefoot' rural doctors schemes and the anti-illiteracy drives, while during the reform years themselves the system of collective ownership of land allowed townships and villages to distribute land plots on a local equal per capita basis for use by farmers as a subsistence guarantee. Rural industrialisation has also significantly boosted rural incomes.

However, China's development pattern under reform, taking GDP as the priority, has centred on the modernisation of heavy industry to drive growth, supported by the Open Door policy. This has produced an unbalanced economic structure, which is now clearly unsustainable. Resources have largely been concentrated on the coastal areas, big cities and the SOEs, with capital being pumped into sectors such as iron and steel which are low in efficiency, high in energy usage and highly damaging for the environment. The very high levels of investment required has meant that the portion of national income given to improving living standards has been kept low, in fact far below that of many other developing countries. These investment rates have risen even higher since the late 1990s to support the upgrading of the SOEs.

Social Inequality and Urban Bias

Rapid industrialisation and urbanisation has brought considerable levels of social inequality. Although China's 'stellar growth rates have filtered down to make the bottom 20 per cent better off than in most countries', according to a recent report from the Asian Development Bank, it now has Asia's highest Gini coefficient.[8] According to World Bank figures for 2005, China remains home to 18 per cent of the world's poor, and while the middle class has flourished, conditions in some of the poorer inland areas have in certain ways deteriorated.

Between 1997 and 2000, at least one-quarter of the state sector workers, who in total made up 40 per cent of the urban workforce, were laid off as overstaffed and inefficient SOEs underwent restructuring.[9] Many other SOE workers faced cutbacks in their 'iron rice bowl' entitlements, reducing health and welfare provision. Women workers have been disproportionately affected by redundancy and early retirement, finding it harder to get another job. Although the rate of job loss has now slowed, unemployment has become a new and persistent feature in China's cities.

However, it is in the rural areas, where some 750 million[10] of China's 1.3 billion population live, that the major problems lie as rural development has failed to keep pace with China's rapid modernisation. The agricultural sector has served as the foundation of the economy since the early days of the People's Republic of China (PRC), with the government maintaining controls over grain production to ensure stable and cheap supplies of food for the cities to sustain the high investment regime. While peasant subsistence needs have been secured, rural migration has been tightly controlled through a household residence registration (*hukou*) system. This has ensured that as market reforms have deepened, China has largely kept at bay the dangers of an emerging destitute landless class feeding into an underclass of urban poor with the growth of urban slums on a large scale, a pattern which has blighted the development experience of other poor countries.

However, this rural–urban segregation has also meant that the rural areas have become the weakest parts of the country's economic and social development, given the concentration of population of the land. Farming remains small scale, using mostly traditional methods with low productivity, and rural surplus labour is China's biggest problem. The growth of township and village enterprises (TVEs) in the 1980s and 1990s eased the situation, creating jobs for an estimated 40 per cent of rural workers (200 million). However these enterprises tend to operate beyond regulation: pay is low, safety and working conditions are poor, sometimes quite appalling, and pollution levels are a big problem.

In recent years, particularly as competitive pressures have slowed growth in the TVE sector, rural–urban segregation has generated a pronounced urban bias in development, clearly evident in disparities in education, health and welfare provision. Rural residents who make up around 60 per cent of the population have access to less than 30 per cent of the nation's total health resources, and almost 100 million have virtually no access to medical services. The problem arises because of China's decentralised administrative system in which, while having vastly different resource levels, each community is 'left to find its own way'. The system was adopted to take advantage of local initiative and local understanding of conditions of production as well as to minimise the costs of bureaucracy. However, given the poor economic state of many rural communities, especially in China's western provinces, local governments have themselves fallen into debt and have been unable to maintain the cooperative medical insurance system which in Mao's time covered 90 per cent of the people's communes. Now around 50 per cent of village clinics are run on a private basis, with only about 20 per cent of the rural population remaining covered by insurance.[11]

A similar pattern of urban bias is reflected in schooling. The government now estimates that children under 15 in rural China receive on average three years less education than their urban counterparts.[12]

Rural Migrants

With urban cash incomes averaging more than three times rural ones, migrants from the countryside have flooded into the cities as the government has gradually lifted barriers to migration to ease the rural surplus labour problem. Over the last ten years, China's cities and towns have absorbed about 150 million of the rural population, more than twice the size of the entire population of Britain. These rural migrants tend to form a marginal, unstable 'floating population'. Lacking official residency status, they enjoy fewer rights and social security entitlements than urban residents, and their children are often denied access to urban schools. As virtually second-class citizens, they are more vulnerable to exploitation, often working under dismal conditions below the minimum wage and without restrictions on overtime.

Environmental Problems

Overcrowding in the cities is creating huge pressures on water, energy, housing and waste disposal. Now China's cities are considered amongst the worst in the world in terms of air and water pollution.

China's rapid industrialisation is worsening problems of environmental degradation day by day. Coal provides around 70 per cent of China's energy and the numbers of coal-fired power stations are increasing weekly. China became the world's largest emitter of greenhouse gases in 2007 although on a per capita basis its emissions are seven times less than those of the United States.[13]

With per capita land and water resources way below the world average, China forms one of world's most environmentally stressed regions, prone to both flood and drought, and facing serious problems of desertification and deforestation. In addition, pollution means that at least a quarter of the population does not have access to clean water, while arable land is shrinking, cutting into farm production levels.

Social Protest

In recent years, social protest has become much more prevalent. The end of the 1990s for example saw a wave of discontent among laid-off workers over severance packages and pensions concerns.

The CPC has sought in the short term to limit the impact of SOE reform to avoid alienating the working class as a whole. Both central and city governments have done much to keep unemployment in check in the urban areas, exercising constraints on redundancies and bankruptcies so that, by and large, SOE restructuring has proceeded only as the non-state sector has developed sufficient job-creating potential to absorb redundant workers. City authorities have introduced unemployment benefit schemes, albeit rather basic, along with enterprise centres, distributing basic livelihood expenses, and re-employment centres, while some SOEs continue to support their laid-off workers for two or three years.

Rural areas have also experienced heightened tensions between villagers, village leaders and township officials as a result of increasing local taxes and the crisis in rural public provision.

Since 2001, the numbers of 'mass incidents' have escalated yet further, with official reports from the Ministry of Public Security indicating a 28 per cent rise from 58,000 in 2003 to 74,000 in 2004, jumping to 87,000 in 2005.[14] Evidently, since joining the WTO, many of China's social problems have been exacerbated. Although the World Bank has praised China's continuing success in poverty reduction work between 2001 and 2004,[15] in 2003 the number of farmers living in poverty surged by 800,000,[16] even as the economy as a whole continued to steam ahead.

An estimated 20 million farmers have been forced to leave their land as a direct result of China's entry into the WTO, unable to withstand the competition of imports from subsidised US farmers.[17] Increasingly, with farmers a declining source of tax, local governments have turned instead to the sale of land for urban or commercial development for revenue. However, urbanisation has not kept pace with the transfer of land, leaving more than 30 million farmers without land or jobs.[18]

For China's Leftist critics, the rise in social protest indicates a growing worker resistance to a repressive regime. However, while there have been some large-scale demonstrations, on the whole these tend to be the exception. 'Mass incidents' are vaguely defined, and appear to include anything from organised petitions, strikes, sit-ins and demonstrations to impromptu scuffles. By far the majority of incidents are localised and short-lived. They are not explicitly political but rather raise economic grievances, for example, over excessive local taxes, property rights abuses, seizures of farmland and forced relocations, non-payment of wages and social security benefits, as well as environmental concerns. As such, they express quite widespread popular dissatisfaction with official behaviour and corruption at local levels. Rather than being directed at the political system itself, as critics suggest, the protests represent a rising consciousness over issues of social justice. In this they indicate the fault-lines of China's fast growth pattern: the weakness of the agricultural sector, the problems of local government capacity especially in the rural areas, and an over-rapid pace of urbanisation which is leaving workers and farmers without a safety net.

TOWARDS BALANCED DEVELOPMENT

While China's urbanisation has remained at a relatively low level, the vast rural labour surplus makes large-scale urbanisation and rural-to-urban migration inevitable. The Chinese government envisages that some 300 to 500 million more people will be transferred out of subsistence agriculture by 2030, equivalent to the entire population of Western Europe.

The key question is how this shift of the rural labour force to non-farm occupations is to be accomplished. On the one hand, this transformation represents a huge opportunity as a great growth driver for at least the next 20 years. But there is also potential for huge disaster – landlessness and joblessness on a massive scale, further overcrowding and environmental damage, and the exacerbation of rural–urban and income inequalities, with migration draining the countryside.

In promoting a gradual reform of the *hukou* system, the government has sought a dispersed pattern of urbanisation through the expansion of not only big and small cities, but also towns, around the development of local enterprise and rural service sectors.[19]

However, in the face of increasing competition from international agricultural products, experts forecast that by 2010 the number of landless farmers may reach more than 100 million.[20] Since the SOEs also continue to shed labour, job creation is an extremely urgent task. According to Wen Jiabao, the government needs to create jobs at a rate of 9 million per year.[21] Yet the current development pattern with its emphasis on heavy industry together with exports is actually producing 'jobless growth', increasing capital intensity on the one hand, while reliance on 'fake foreign investment' using low-waged labour for exports adds more to growth than it adds to disposable income and the generation of new jobs.[22]

In order to realise the key objective to 'build a moderately well-off society in an all-round way' by 2020 put forward by Jiang Zemin at the 16th CPC Congress in 2002, China's leadership has been looking for a new way of industrialising.[23] The aim is to shift the growth mode away from its focus on capital accumulation and exports towards a more consumption-driven path. So far, China's economic growth has been driven largely by intersectoral transfers of labour from low-productivity agriculture to higher-productivity manufacturing. Now it is looking for new ways of generating growth through innovation to promote technological progress in agriculture and services as well as manufacturing, especially through the use of IT.[24]

The new growth mode is to feature high scientific and technological content, good economic returns, low resource consumption and little environmental pollution.[25] Increased productivity will help to increase fiscal revenues to support government social provision. It involves less concentration on energy-intensive, environmentally polluting heavy industries. Finally, it opens the door to employment creation through expanding the service sector, and developing self-employment, small and medium-sized enterprises and the private sector.[26]

The goal of delivering a better quality of growth lies at the centre of the 11th Five Year Plan launched in 2006. The plan aims to start to rein in excessive investment and moderate growth to a target of 7.5 per cent per year, and sets out a vision for a more socially equitable and sustainable development pattern in terms of five linked inter-relationships between inland and coast, rural and urban, society and the economy, the environment and society, and domestic consumption and export. In each, to bring the situation back into balance, the aim is to favour the first consideration over the second.[27]

Increasing Consumption

While continuing to make good use of overseas markets, China's intention is to gradually raise the proportion of consumption in GDP in the medium term and increase average per capita GDP from US$1,000 to US$3,000 by 2020.

Especially since the 1990s, growth in China's internal market has relied largely on stimulating the domestic demand of urban elites. Now the government is looking to raise the living standards of those with the lowest income, while gradually increasing the proportion of the middle class with an average income of US$5,000, from 100 million to 300 million by 2020, and effectively regulating the extremely rich, in order to narrow income gaps and living standards in the longer run.[28]

High-income earners are likely to remain a key force in the consumer market but the real development in the domestic market will come in other ways: from the country's upward adjustment from a low-wage and low-cost production economy, the increased purchasing power of the farmers and rural workers, the gradual shift of population to urban areas, and from opening up the inland provinces through infrastructural investment.

A major reason that personal spending is low in China is that families have to put money aside for housing, education and medical costs. To release this spending power, the government is focusing on improving income security by setting minimum salary levels, increasing employment opportunities, gradually increasing public investment in health and education, as well as building up a social security safety net.[29]

Society and Economy

Since the development of a mixed economy and the reform of the SOE 'iron rice bowl' have seen a decrease in the ability of the state to provide social welfare directly through the workplace, it has become necessary to devise a completely new system of welfare protection and provision. At the same time, the discriminatory segregation of rural and urban areas needs to be broken down in order to address the problem of urban bias and achieve a better balance between social progress and economic development. Such a move towards a unified rural and urban labour market will allow more freedom for rural labourers who want to pursue urban employment, but for the stable development of a national labour market a national social security and welfare system is essential. This is something the country finds difficult at the moment to afford.

At its 16th Congress, the CPC made the choice, alongside a gradual reform of the *hukou* system, to proceed towards a social security system, including pensions, which would cover the whole population by 2020 but with relatively low benefits. At the same time, the aim is to compensate for low provision with job creation,[30] while focusing on the establishment of social safety nets for excluded vulnerable groups.

A start has been made to expand social security coverage to include migrant workers, TVE employees and the rural areas. Plans have also been announced to set up a minimum living allowance for rural residents which, together with the urban subsistence allowance initiated in 1997, would cover the whole population.[31] A safety insurance scheme for rural migrants was also launched in 2006, and plans for a new old-age insurance scheme which rural migrants could join were announced in 2007.[32]

According to researcher Anita Chan, adjustments to the *hukou* system are also having some effect in making migrants far less vulnerable to manipulation and bullying by employers and local authorities.[33] At the same time, measures to improve skills training for women and migrants as well as their access to resources are also high on the government's agenda. Schemes for people in substandard housing have seen the building of 20 million homes over the last five years.[34]

Plans for a Socialist Countryside

At the NPC in 2006, Wen Jiabao set out a proposal for building 'a new socialist countryside', putting agriculture and rural initiatives more prominently on the modernisation agenda, seeking to reverse the trend of urban bias with a policy of 'getting industry to assist agriculture and cities to support the countryside'.[35]

As China begins to shift its economic base towards industry, it has to develop agriculture in order to provide a market by raising farmers' demand for industrial technologies and consumer goods. The aim now is to promote a sustainable, resource-efficient and environmentally friendly modern farming system. Since this will mean reducing the agricultural population further, it is to be balanced by a programme of technical innovation in TVEs to increase job opportunities within the village or township vicinity, promoting industrialisation and urbanisation in the rural areas.

Vocational training centres are being set up across China to raise rural people's skill levels and earning capacity, increasing their access to technology. Such improvements are bringing the Internet revolution to the Chinese countryside, with computerised wholesale markets helping farmers to integrate into a national agricultural market and compete against foreign imports.[36] Special training schemes to ensure the inclusion of women in rural development are also being extended. Improvements in roads, electricity and power supplies, clean water and irrigation aim to create a modern, unpolluted countryside while opening up the domestic market.

As a first step to raising farmers' purchasing power, in 2006 the government scrapped the agricultural tax which had been in existence for 2,600 years. Then in 2007, Wen Jiabao announced plans to increase spending on agricultural subsidies, while maintaining a minimum purchase price policy for key grain varieties in the major grain-producing areas.[37] Improvements in rural banking and finance have also begun to make it easier for farmers to obtain loans to develop their business.

The problems in the rural health care and education systems have been placed centre stage in the government's 'people first' agenda. In 2006, a rural cooperative medicare system was started in low-income areas, with farmers, central and local government all making equal contributions. According to government estimates, the new scheme already covers 83 per cent of the rural population, and the aim is for complete coverage of the whole population by 2010.[38] Although the system is rather modest, it has begun to make steps towards relieving the situation, with central government funding doubling at the end of 2007.

To improve the situation in rural education, the government is abolishing fees for all 150 million rural students in primary and secondary education, while increasing support for teacher training.[39]

The 'Go West' Strategy

The government is seeking to address regional disparities through massive investment and infrastructure programmes in the least developed areas, opening up the west and north-east of the country. The western regions in particular are critical to the supply of energy, since they contain much of the country's minerals and coal as well as water resources. Developments in the 1990s included the controversial Three Gorges Dam project as well as the opening of oil and gas fields in Xinjiang. The 'Go West' strategy itself was formally launched in 2000 as a main focus of the 10th Five Year Plan to prepare for the shift of manufacturing activity away from the coastal regions. Some US$200 billion has been pumped into deprived inland regions for road and rail networks, river navigation in the Yangzi, dams and power lines. There are plans for 15,000 miles of motorway by 2010, and over 60,000 miles of rail lines by 2020, including an intercontinental railway link to Europe, across Central Asia.

The most high-profile project has been the rail link from Qinghai to Tibet which opens the Tibetan economy to trade and tourism. Tibet's economic growth at 13.4 per cent is now one of the highest in China.[40] Many ordinary Tibetans have benefited from development in recent years: lifespans have increased, public health has improved and opportunities to explore the outside world have opened up for urban Tibetans. Rural Tibetans have seen widespread benefits from improvements in irrigation and their incomes have risen sharply since 2002.[41] The 'Go West' programme aims to promote local specialised industries, such as herbal medicine, and improve the ecological environment to prevent deforestation and desertification. Huge sums of money have been poured into the renovation of the Potala Palace and the protection of its treasures. There are efforts to improve educational standards and skills levels so that the benefits of the boom are spread widely. The Tibetan language is increasingly used in schools and universities, and a Tibetan middle class has benefited from the growth.[42] However, high-speed growth can be disorientating, and ethnic tensions have been exacerbated as it is widely thought that incoming Han Chinese are benefiting disproportionately from the boom.

Clearly more needs to be done, and with greater sensitivity to Tibetan needs and religious culture. There is still discontent on which international campaigners have been able to play, with demonstrations leading to riots in March 2008, bringing a heavy Chinese military and police presence into Lhasa. While the Chinese government needs to avoid excessive use of force and more generally modify its top-down approach, this is not so easy to do given the Dalai Lama's equivocal stance – denying that he seeks independence yet failing to explicitly recognise Tibet as a part of China's territory – which itself generates uncertainty and tension. While his concept of a 'Greater Tibet' covers almost a quarter of China's territory, his complaints of 'cultural genocide' are not without an element of antipathy towards development.

Looking further to the future, much of the 'Go West' boom has been fuelled by state subsidies, and how self-sustaining this development will become once government support comes to an end remains in question. Western China still suffers from a weak legal system, local government inefficiency, poor infrastructure and labour quality. Nevertheless, tourism is clearly thriving and there are signs that businesses are shifting inland as wages in coastal provinces and big cities rise.[43] The often critical *Guardian* reporter Jonathan Watts, reporting on a tour in 2006 of the western provinces of Yunnan, Sichuan and Shaanxi, was clearly inspired by the 'huge energy, immense optimism and an encouraging open mindedness' he found. 'In terms of raising living standards,' he wrote, 'China has come much further, much faster than many outsiders think.'[44] Meanwhile, the high investment in infrastructure is likely to see pay-offs in future years.

Environmental Policy

The 11th Five Year Plan enshrines a green agenda, addressing the need to conserve energy resources and cut environmental pollution by calling for a

20 per cent reduction in energy consumption per unit of GDP, a 20 per cent increase in forest coverage and a 10 per cent reduction in the discharge of major pollutants by 2010. This is to be achieved by moderating economic growth; increasing the proportion of the hi-tech and service sectors in the economy, while cutting steel and aluminium; stepping up research in, and employing, advanced energy-saving technologies widely; and encouraging energy-saving, water-saving and environmentally conscious behaviour among the people.[45]

The Chinese government takes the problem of climate change seriously since this could be highly damaging for its agriculture and long-term grain security. While prioritising poverty eradication, the 'growth first' agenda has been modified to one which seeks to reconcile the need for development with the need for environmental protection. A national action plan on climate change was released in 2007, a move welcomed by Greenpeace China's climate change campaign manager as a first for a developing country, which 'shows China has done its homework about what needs to be done'.[46]

On the energy front, China has no easy options. It has the third largest coal reserves in the world. However, while the United States is planning to increase its coal capacity, China aims to reduce the rate of increase in new coal plants and increase the overall share of renewables, hydropower and nuclear power in its energy mix. These choices are also clearly not without cost. In building the Three Gorges Dam, for example, more than 1 million people had to be relocated.

The government's plan to invest almost US$200 billion in renewable energy by 2020 would make it the biggest investor worldwide in this area. Its aim to ensure that 15 per cent of the country's energy comes from renewables by 2015 compares with European goals for 20 per cent energy renewables consumption by 2020.[47] A number of projects in wind, biofuel and hydro power generation have already been approved, and the implementation of plans to build five British-designed eco-cities, which will be almost entirely zero-energy communities, is also a world first. Plans to reduce vehicle emissions are far more stringent than those in the United States, including limits on car use in the overcrowded cities.[48] Nevertheless, while China is managing to reduce the energy intensity of its fast growth, the pace remains below target. According to Xie Zhenhua, vice-chairman of China's National Development and Reform Commission, the situation regarding environmental targets overall remains 'extremely bleak'.[49]

At the international level, while China together with India and other developing countries do not accept that they are equally as obliged to cut emissions as the developed countries, to break the deadlock on a post-Kyoto agreement in 2012, the Chinese government has proposed a two-track approach of 'common but differentiated' responsibilities and has said that 'China will be a follower if the US leads'.[50]

THE CHANGING POLITICAL LANDSCAPE

The extension of market relations through reform has meant that the Party and state can no longer rely so much on direct measures to shape the economy and society. The control of prices and investment, of jobs through the work unit (*danwei*) and housing with the *hukou* residence system were the key mechanisms of social control in the planned economy. Now the government has to develop new and more responsive institutional structures and mechanisms in order to deliver its economic and social goals: to regulate the market, alter the patterns of economic behaviour that sustain high investment and manage an increasingly diverse society.

The CPC Constitution adopted at its 16th Congress called on the Party to gradually put all work of the state on a legal footing to 'rule the country according to law and build a socialist country under the rule of law'.[51] In fact throughout the reform period, the state has been steadily building up a new regulatory framework of laws, institutions and networks in order to exert control over the market economy through standard setting, supervision, monitoring and enforcement. Between 1978 and 1998, the National People's Congress passed more than 200 laws while local people's congresses drew up 7,500 local regulations.[52]

This shift from direct controls to a regulatory environment shaped by the rule of law to back the progressive policies adopted by the central government on a wide range of issues has frequently received praise from international bodies such as the United Nations as well as leading international NGOs. However, problems lie in the implementation of policies and rules at local levels.

Central government is limited in the extent to which it can impose its will at local levels since China's government system is decentralised, geared towards fostering local self-governance. The system lacks effective oversight and for example, as local governments compete to develop their regions by attracting foreign direct investment (FDI), they may be slack in their enforcement of labour laws and pay lip service to health and safety regulations. Local judges often owe their first loyalty to the local governments that employ them, so that the local law courts may be compromised, while whistleblowers are often persecuted by the people they are trying to expose.

The question of regulation in the coal-mining industry provides a revealing case study.[53] The industry involves tens of thousands of notoriously unsafe small-scale mines operating across China. Coalmine safety has now become a very high priority for the government, and a raft of

new regulations and measures to improve conditions have been introduced. New teams of safety inspectors, operating independently of local
governments, have been trained to ensure that the regulations are implemented more effectively. However, the fact is that these measures are
often insufficient in overcoming powerful local resistance to pit
closures.[54] Conditions in these small mining operations may be
hazardous but often they provide virtually the only source of income for
poor rural communities, providing much-needed employment opportunities while township and village governments, otherwise strapped for
cash, depend on them for their revenues. So while thousands of mines
have been closed down on central government orders in recent years,
many reopen illegally.

The danger is that problems in the implementation of the rule of law will
have a detrimental effect on its credibility. As it aims to foster self-government
at local levels, central government needs to create a strong framework within
which to do so. While seeking to recentralise authority from the top down
through the rule of law and a regulatory environment to rein in irrational
investment and corruption at lower levels, it is at the same time exploring new
methods of government supervision from the bottom up. In this dual
approach, demands for greater accountability and transparency in government
practice, especially in the area of tax expenditure, exercised from below, are
seen as an essential element in shaping a more 'harmonious society' with a
balanced development.

To this end, the new CPC Constitution also calls for more effective
measures to 'protect the people's right to run the affairs of state and of society', improving democratic decision making, enhancing people's supervision of government work, encouraging the 'free airing of views' and
strengthening mass organisations.[55] The 'people first' approach of the
current leadership team of Hu Jintao and Wen Jiabao aims to coordinate a
more balanced social and economic development with political reforms to
promote a rights-based system. As the latter sees it, the two major tasks of
China's socialist system are to develop the productive forces and to 'gradually realise fairness and social justice so as to encourage the creativity of the
entire nation'.[56]

Political Reforms

A broad programme of political reform is now underway, with the strengthening of individual rights, the building-up of the legal infrastructure, an
increasing the role for local elections and expanded opportunities for popular participation at grass roots level in order to make government at the local
levels more accountable.[57]

Significant legal and policy changes have been introduced to advance individual rights. In 2004, the National People's Congress (NPC) amended the country's constitution to include the protection of both property rights and human rights in order to uphold the interests of the individual against corruption and abuses of power, to outlaw discrimination, and to provide the basis for the new system of social protection.[58]

The NPC, once derided by critics as a rubber-stamp organisation, is now much more a forum for debate. Indeed there have been long debates in the NPC over key legislation such as the Bankruptcy Law, Anti-Monopoly Law, the Labour Law as well as modification of Three Gorges Dam plan. Tens of thousands of people took part in public debate on the draft Law on Property Rights which was publicised in the media, and thousands of suggestions were collected. A law barring sexual harassment in the workplace was also put to public debate.[59] At local levels, the people's congresses are also becoming more assertive, publishing draft bills and holding hearings on important local issues to solicit public opinion.

The government's efforts to recruit large numbers of lawyers and judges demonstrate its commitment to increasing the autonomy of the individual. New specialised agencies backed by law have been created to enforce standards and regulations. Judicial courts at city level are now to be funded centrally and judges' performance brought under review by local people's congresses.[60] The growth of lawsuits and trials reflects an increasing confidence in the courts.

State interference in personal and economic lives has been much reduced as basic freedoms of expression and association have been steadily expanded. Public demonstrations have been allowed to take place in recent years in China's major cities. In 2007, for example, major protests took place in Xiamen over the location of a chemical plant and in Shanghai over the Maglev rail extension.

Experimentation in arts and intellectual matters is encouraged, and the media, no longer simply an instrument of propaganda, play a greater watchdog role in supervising government practice with, for example, more exposure of accidents and disasters. The media play a key role in raising ordinary people's awareness of their rights, popularising new laws and regulations through television programmes as well as investigating and reporting actual cases.

Competition across the sector is encouraged: there are huge numbers of publishers, newspapers and newspaper readers. The Internet has 137 million Chinese users and there are thousands of websites, chat rooms, bulletin boards and blogs full of discussion and critical debate.[61]

The government is also making itself more accessible to the media. According to Xia Li Lollar, e-government plays a massive role in improving government transparency and building bridges between officials and citizens. The public can track government information online, although reports are still biased towards the good news, reporting very little of the bad. It is also possible for members of the public to report corrupt officials anonymously and instantaneously.[62]

There are still limitations placed on the freedom of the press and publishing, with periodic banning of books and restrictions on the Internet. Controls on foreign journalists are more relaxed but foreign ownership of the media is barred. Government caution is hardly surprising given Murdoch's claim that satellite TV was 'an unambiguous threat to totalitarian regimes everywhere'[63] as well as Madeleine Albright's repeated calls on the US government to make the best use of the Internet to spread 'freedom and democracy'. Google, on the other hand, has suggested that the controls are as much driven by protectionism as by 'ideological policing'.[64]

Electoral systems are improving as practices of multiple candidates and secret ballots have been introduced at both grass roots and national-level elections. However, the representative processes remain constrained, as only those candidates who accept the guiding role of the CPC, as set out in the Constitution, are allowed to stand. On the other hand, the small democratic parties which cooperated in the United Front with the CPC to set up the PRC in 1949 and subsequently followed Party leadership are also active at all levels, and have been able to exercise more influence.

A visit by leaders of the KMT and other political parties from Taiwan in 2005, the first since it lost the civil war, augurs well for democratisation in China, in the first instance opening the way for a less dogmatic portrayal of China's history of resistance to the Japanese invasion.

Empowering the Grass Roots

In exploring innovative practices for participation at local levels, the Party is also seeking to strengthen mechanisms that give voice to the demands and complaints of the ordinary people, in order that these might be channelled in institutionalised directions to exercise supervision over both government and practices in enterprises.

China's mass organisations such as the trade unions and women's organisations are generally regarded by critics as powerless transmission belts, too closely linked to an authoritarian Party and state to serve the interests of their constituents. However, these collective organisations, along with the system of workers' congresses in enterprises, and the city residents' and villager committees, are now being reinvigorated through, for example, improved electoral systems.

The Trade Unions

China's official trade union organisation, the All-China Federation of Trade Unions (ACFTU), plays a role on the one hand in supporting government policies on economic development by seeking to secure harmonious relations in the workplace, and on the other hand in protecting workers' rights. From a Western point of view this dual role is an impossible one which can only compromise the unions' ability to fight management on behalf of workers. However, as a recent Communist Party of Britain pamphlet points out, this is consistent with Lenin's approach during the New Economic Policy (NEP) period, when he called on trade unions to act as mediators and endeavour to avert disputes. It was also the practice in Britain in the Second World War when the Party itself supported the postponement of industrial class struggle, calling for maximum production to defeat fascism.[65]

Anita Chan, by no means an uncritical researcher into the conditions of Chinese workers, notes how the ACFTU's close links with the Party and government have had certain highly significant advantages. With its president amongst the highest ranks in the Party hierarchy, the ACFTU has considerable political influence, playing a major role in drafting labour law legislation and in drawing up legal definitions concerning working time, the minimum wage, social security contributions, prohibition of child labour and special regulations for women and young workers.[66] One example of the positive benefits here was its success in reducing the maximum working hours as well as securing the inclusion of workers' congresses in enterprise law.

Chinese workers have the legal right to join trade unions; unions by law have the right to defend their wages and conditions against offences which violate labour legislation, and unlike in Britain, union officials have the right to enter the premises of non-union enterprises in order to recruit. Strikes in China are not uncommon and are not specifically outlawed, but the state aims to minimise workplace conflict within a legal framework of labour relations emphasising the rights of workers in order to allow labour and capital to meet on a more balanced footing. The findings of Anita Chan with regard to SOE and collectively owned enterprise (COE) employees, and of Zhang Yunqui in his study of conditions in foreign-invested enterprises (FIEs) in Shandong province,[67] suggest that labour legislation has proved a successful channel for workers to settle their disputes with management and protect their interests. Zhang argues that the ability of the ACFTU to intervene in the workplace to establish unions and train leaders, rather than bringing workers under the control of the state, helped in strengthening the capacity of inexperienced 'green' labour to handle powerful and often hostile foreign employers. He found the labour law to be widely publicised through legal education campaigns and the media – one locality even ran a quiz on the law in which 30,000 workers participated – and the workers won the majority of lawsuits.[68]

As reforms in the urban economy have deepened, the ACFTU has developed new skills in collective bargaining, legal affairs training and arbitration as well as running labour service and law centres. But with WTO accession, both government and the ACFTU have become increasingly concerned over the informalisation of employment and the growth of part-time and casual workers. Recently China's labour laws have been improved primarily to prevent abuse of rural migrants, providing for stronger contracts and redundancy payments as well as setting a minimum wage.

The problems of migrant workers, as well as issues of health and safety, and age and gender discrimination, have all been highlighted in the media, and the draft Labour Contract laws received intense interest from the public, who sent in around 200,000 emails and letters over 70 per cent of which were from ordinary working people. EU and US employers also raised dozens of objections, complaining that the new laws made it too hard to dismiss workers.[69] Although the final legislation took into consideration some of the employers' views, it still gives labour a certain advantage to balance market conditions which disadvantage workers.[70]

The new law also covers temping agencies and permits workers in small enterprises to form neighbourhood or community trade unions.[71] A group of 50,000 rural migrants formed the country's first Labour Union Federation in 2007.[72]

The new powers will help to control private sector expansion, as private suppliers, under pressure from multinational corporations (MNCs) to produce goods ever faster and ever cheaper, often violate labour laws. However, it is the FIEs themselves that have fallen under the media spotlight as underpayment of part-time workers by McDonald's and KFC hit the headlines recently. With only about 26 per cent of FIEs unionised, the ACFTU has gone on a new recruitment drive.[73] The rabidly anti-union Wal-Mart was compelled by law to recognise a trade union for the first time anywhere in the world in one of its outlets in Fujian province in 2006.

The government, then, is shifting its thinking away from policies pursuing labour cost advantage at the sacrifice of reasonable pay and working conditions, even at the risk that some foreign companies might withdraw from the country.[74] Indeed, labour costs overall are predicted to rise by 40 per cent in 2008.[75] As greater emphasis is put on improving the quality of human resources, infrastructure and R&D capacities to attract foreign investment, trade union activities are now to be bound more tightly with workers' interests to help balance development.[76]

Workplace Democracy

The government has also followed through the CPC's 16th Congress commitment to improve democratic management in enterprises. The system of workers' congresses has been revived. These are to be composed of 60 per cent shop floor workers, 20 per cent technicians and 20 per cent senior managers.[77] The practice of worker-shareholding is common in the restructured SOEs and COEs, and worker representatives may be elected onto the boards of directors or shareholder committees. Company law requires that Chinese companies also establish a board of supervisors, usually chaired by an employee representative from the ACFTU, with the role of supervising the company's finances as well as its board of directors and senior management to ensure the company's stability.[78]

Village Elections and Village Self-Governance

Since 1988, the rural population have been covered by elected village committees which operate below the lowest levels of state power – the township and county people's congresses. Since village committees decide on land and related matters, and villagers are dependent on them for their livelihood, committee affairs carry weight with the farmers.

Village elections are seen as an important means of tackling problems of corruption, nepotism and inefficiency, gradually strengthening villager self-governance as the provision and administration of rural services has shifted to the local level. Elections have become more competitive and not only Party members stand. Problems exist in some places of election rigging and vote buying where rival clans compete, and generally the Party secretary continues to wield considerable power. Women comprise only 16 per cent of village committee members. Nevertheless, researchers such as Zweig and Chung found that in the area they researched in the late 1990s, village elections had strengthened rural democracy.[79] For them, village self-governance has been one of the major innovations of the reform era.

Farmers' demands for land and subsistence rights, and for more accountability and transparency of government at village level, have mounted since the late 1990s. With increasing local taxes, the rise in land sales and the privatisation of many deeply indebted TVEs, villagers are demanding the publication of minutes of meetings and financial accounts.

With rapid urbanisation, the sale of farmland near cities for factories or housing has become a particular point of friction. The rules on compensation to farmers aim to cover for loss of income for 30 years. However, the farmers have not always received the benefits due, or at least not benefited to the full.[80] Deals are often done between township governments, village leaders and businesses behind closed doors without gaining the consent of farmers to sell land.[81] The problem is that local governments are often themselves deeply in debt, unable to pay for local services, and are heavily dependent on land rental and sales to raise money. While their own performance is measured by GDP growth, local governments have every incentive to sell land to businesses, in return for which they can receive lucrative deals covering investment, jobs and tax revenues.

The farmers on the other hand are being asked to give up what amounts to their 'iron rice bowl', that is, the security, if minimal, of their subsistence plots. Many end up with jobs and there are no complaints. However, problems arise where farmers only get a lump sum and are left to find their own jobs, or when local governments fail to use the fees for low-rent apartments but spend all their gains on prestigious projects. Such situations prompt protests, sometimes violent, in the countryside.

As Yu Jianrong notes, the peaceful protests of the farmers against local government are actually based on the authority of the central government which has passed laws prohibiting illegal fees and land seizures. Judging local government behaviour by central policies, the farmers are exercising their rights within the law and, in demanding democracy in the management of financial affairs, are taking collective action as supervisors of local government.[82]

The government is making efforts to safeguard farmers' rights in land transfers and to improve their access to the courts. At the same time, within the plan for a socialist countryside emphasis is placed on training and job opportunities for farmers who lose land to ease the urbanisation process. There are now plans for market-based compensation if land requisitioned is used commercially, and new regulations require local governments to build more affordable housing.[83]

New measures for assessing local officials other than simply by economic growth and job creation are also being introduced on an experimental basis, with promotion prospects also made dependent on performance in protecting the environment, raising education and health standards, energy efficiency as well as levels of participation in village elections.[84] At the same time, the conditions under which ordinary villagers may call for the removal of unsatisfactory leaders from office are being defined more clearly.

However, it is the problem of local government indebtedness that most needs to be addressed. The shift in policy towards 'industry supporting agriculture' should see increases in central government transfers to local levels. Proposals are also being reviewed to increase farmer representation in local people's congresses which control fiscal budgets, in order to ensure that their rights and interests are taken into consideration when it comes to fiscal distribution.[85] By limiting the tenure of leading officials to a maximum of ten years in any one locality and position, the government intends to tackle problems of bureaucratism, over-concentration of power, and official assumptions of privilege.[86]

In urban areas, social organisation is also being transformed as, where available, the services of the SOEs are opened up to the community and as new community-based services are established. There had been 17,000 community clinics set up across China's cities by the end of 2005,[87] and there are new experiments in community congresses with expanded responsibilities for the improved delivery for example of health care and environmental protection.[88]

NGOs

As the relaxation of direct Party controls over society has opened up spaces for more autonomous social action, NGOs have sprung up all over China. These are taking up a wide range of issues covering environmental protection; social welfare, poverty alleviation and health care; problems of rural migrants, domestic violence and legal advice. Recently an AIDS clinic was set up funded by government health institutions but run by a gay volunteer organisation with networks throughout the country using gay chat rooms.[89]

Environmental issues provide the biggest area of NGO growth. There are over 2,000 working with government support to raise environmental awareness. These have created openings for scientists, journalists, officials and the public concerned about sustainability, to participate in environmental policy making.

China's environmental legislation is even stricter than European law, but the state environmental protection agency, SEPA, is thought to lack clout in standing up to vested interests, and the hope is that public opinion will give it extra strength.[90] A recent campaign to close polluting factories is yielding results after names of the worst polluters, including around 70 MNCs from Japan, the United States and Europe, which unlike domestic companies are not short on capability to deal with dirty discharges, were published on the Internet and they were ordered to stop production.[91]

While NGOs are still at an initial stage of development, often dependent on funds from the government, their numbers and reach are increasing, and their advocacy role is beginning to develop.

CHINA'S APPROACH TO DEMOCRATISATION

The emergence of a new strata of entrepreneurs and managerial and technical staff employed in FIEs, linked in to the global market and communication network, presents a particular challenge for the CPC as it devolves power downwards while at the same time seeking to engage more deeply with the global economy.

The CPC recognises that in these circumstances it would be a fatal error to take its current 'ruling party' status for granted. The working class, which forms the social foundation on which the Party socialist orientation depends, has become more diversified as many laid-off workers have become self-employed or private entrepreneurs as well as freelance professionals, so it is less easy to define a single voice. How the Party continues to develop its mass base and strengthen its role in the wider society, 'handling the contradictions' between the different interest groups to maintain collectivism and national solidarity, is critical if the CPC is to ensure its continuing relevance in the changing domestic and international conditions and to safeguard the long-term interests of its socialist cause.

Tackling Corruption

Tackling corruption is seen to be a 'life and death' issue for the CPC. China is not amongst the most corrupt countries in the world, and while its SOE-restructuring and privatisation processes have undoubtedly been marred by asset stripping and the undervaluation of state properties, this is on nothing like the large scale of looting that took place in Russia in the early 1990s. The majority of China's new elites have attained affluence through their own hard work and abilities.

Nevertheless, the problem is widespread and serious, and could threaten the credibility of the Party and state legitimacy at least in the long term. A great deal of effort is being made to crack down on asset stripping and capital flight. According to Transparency International, China has shown the biggest improvement in anti-corruption in the world for the period since 1995.[92] Investigations have reached to the highest levels and some top leaders have been sacked, and if necessary put on trial, even in some extreme cases executed.

Corruption is both a legacy of feudalism, in practices of excessive bureaucratism and extravagance, and the result of exposure to global capitalism. Inviting foreign investment has meant opening the system up to bribery. Indeed some foreign companies keep friends of high officials on their payroll or pay for officials to take luxury 'training' trips abroad.[93]

The problem also arises as a result of the decentralised government system, which has given more discretionary power to the local levels, allowing local governments to retain a larger share of the income, leading some officials to misuse their position in the state for their own private benefit.

However, corruption owes more to incompetence, failure to understand government policies, and local conflicts of interest with national policies, than to criminality. Social pressure against corruption is high, and success in the long war against it ultimately lies not only in strengthening the role of Party investigators but also in harnessing these pressures to strengthen supervision over government decision making from below, as well as in professionalising financial and accounting practices, especially at local levels.

Party Leadership and Membership

The CPC has built up a collective leadership style which draws on diverse experiences: while some high-ranking leaders have been educated in the West, the top leaders, Hu and Wen, both spent their early careers in China's poorest provinces. To improve its own leadership and accountability, the CPC is now making it compulsory to solicit ordinary members' recommendations and opinions before selecting cadres, with methods including doorstep surveys, appraisals of probationary work performance and secret ballots of all Party committee members.[94] Contested elections have been introduced within the Party itself at local and workplace levels as a means of breaking down local factions and cabals.[95]

A breakdown of Party membership shows a heavy male bias, with only 13.6 million women members out of a total 70.8 million membership. While only 20.6 million are educated to junior college level and above, 16.3 million are aged below 35.[96]

The decision allowing private entrepreneurs to become eligible to be admitted into the Party after the 16th CPC Congress has been highly controversial. For China's Leftist critics, this represented the ultimate convergence of Party and private business interests, and the CPC's final abandonment of the working classes. In fact, making ideology and outlook rather than social status the fundamental requirement of Party membership it is nothing new to the practice of communist parties elsewhere in the world.[97]

At any rate, the CPC is far from making private business its main recruiting ground, but has sought to strengthen its involvement in the SOEs and COEs as well as initiating a drive to set up Party committees in the private business sector, comprising both managers and workers. Meanwhile, it is also building up village-level Party organisations by establishing villager Party support groups. These new forms of organisation are precisely the means to restrain any unhealthy relationships developing between the Party officials and private business interests.

Chinese Conceptions of Democracy

The leading role of the CPC in the Chinese political system is anathema to liberals, who see the system of multi-party competitive elections as best adapted to complex societies made up of different groups with conflicting interests. However, the fact is that fledging democracies in developing countries often struggle to form stable governments and so fail to make much progress in achieving the tasks of development. Many operate only partial democracy, and are in a mess, as political parties and voting processes get tangled up by religious, tribal and ethnic divides, or are easily hijacked by elites – the middle classes, Western-educated technocrats and professionals, and landed interests – so creating political systems riddled with corruption, elitism, and even the criminalisation of politics, as in parts of India.

Western views of democracy also lack resonance among the Chinese people. An early attempt to establish a Western-style parliamentary system in 1912 ended very soon after in warlord rampage. Later, in the broad urban popular movement which helped to bring the CPC to power in 1949, the call for democracy was directed against the corruption of the 'four big families' who, seeking to monopolise political and economic power for themselves, placed themselves at the bidding of the United States. This popular view of democracy as a tool against corruption and for better government and higher living standards remains key to people's understanding of democracy in China. It is this, rather than any calls for a Western-style political system, that inspired the vast majority of students in the months leading up to the Tiananmen Square tragedy of 4 June 1989, and that continues to press forward the orientation of political reform.

For China's leaders, Western-style democracy is neither feasible nor desirable: China instead should take its own road to strengthening people's democracy. The democratic basis of the Chinese state lies in its ability to determine China's path of development free from external interference. As the 2005 government *White Paper on Democracy* states, with public ownership in the dominant position as the economic foundation of the socialist system, China's democracy is prevented from being manipulated by capital.[98] This is what is meant by the commonly used phrase 'the people are the masters'.

The emphasis here, in common with socialists worldwide, is more concerned with the substantive nature of democracy, the content of political life, than with its form. Democracy and human rights, while inherently universal, are recognised as defined within particular political, economic and cultural circumstances. Therefore from 1949, the main focus of government was on the realisation of subsistence as the primary human right. But now that these material foundations for democracy have been laid, the people-first approach of Hu and Wen marks a shift in political orientation to a broader focus on economic rights to advance people's independence and self-determination, extending their individual rights and choices by strengthening their position within a market system.[99]

The growth of rights-based movements in China is quite unlike democracy movements seen elsewhere in the world, which have largely been led by the middle classes seeking to assert their civil rights and liberties in opposition to authoritarian rule. In China, a wide variety of groups, mainly ordinary workers and farmers, are asserting their rights in relation to employment, income distribution, social security, health care and education, at the same time demanding increased supervision of government work. This broad social awakening is being actively fostered by the Party and state as part of the ongoing project to involve people in the construction of their socialist future.

Shaping the Boundaries of Class Relations

So far during the reform decades, the interests of different communities and sections of society have been handled by government through a process of bargaining and consultation directly with the mass organisations. Now, in accordance with China's own democratic traditions of 'letting a hundred flowers bloom and a hundred schools of thought contend',[100] the government is extending the practice of 'letting the people speak' in order to manage social diversity through more open debate.

In some ways, this is returning to the 'great debates' of the Cultural Revolution about what kind of society China's should be and what kind of social relations should take shape. This time, though, the means of tackling corrupt authorities, abusive managers and class privilege from below are to operate within a clear legal and institutional framework.

So far however, China's leaders have been proceeding with political reform very cautiously, endeavouring to 'develop diverse forms of political participation in an orderly way'[101] to prevent destabilisation. Political liberalisation is still contained within a strong framework of the state as its direct involvement in society is gradually reduced. The Party and state stand ready to intervene to contain the emergence of contradictions not compatible with their broader and long-term goals.

The credibility of the CPC's effort to strengthen political participation and create a government under the rule of law is put into question in particular when it fails to act against local government clampdowns on rights campaigners, lawyers, journalists, writers and NGO activists. Even lawful protests have been suppressed at local levels.

In any society it generally takes the most tenacious and committed social activists to make headway in challenging blinkered outlooks, prejudice and vested interests, which block progress on minority rights and concerns. In China, however, where the use of law as an instrument to settle grievances is still very new, activists may risk stepping into grey areas where legislation is yet to be clarified, particularly in relation to the operations of foreign NGOs and foreign funding.

In these early stages of establishing the rule of law and institutionalising the channels of the people's voice, the risk is that small protests may grow into mass incidents, so authorities have stepped in to prevent situations from escalating. But China is not the only developing country to repress protests. In one incident in India in 2007, police shot eight activists demonstrating for promised land reforms in Andhra Pradesh.[102] However, in China, when some protestors died in a clash with police in a village incident also in that year, those responsible for the killings were put on trial and prosecuted.[103]

Yongnian Zheng highlights the central government's dilemma as it seeks popular support to counter local government resistance to central policies, yet when people are mobilised, it starts to worry about social order and stability. Clearly this dual role of both agent provocateur and defender of public order is one that requires a delicate balance,[104] something not always achieved.

As the CPC sees it, class struggle will continue to exist in China 'within a certain scope for a long time' and 'may possibly grow acute under certain conditions'.[105] While the potential for internal conflict increases with the widening social divisions, externally, 'hostile forces are still pursuing their strategic attempts to westernise and divide our country'.[106] Kenny Coyle, for example, reports how two bodies associated with the US-based National Endowment for Democracy have been channelling substantial funds to anti-Beijing parties in Hong Kong.[107] Nevertheless, the international environment is generally seen to be advantageous for China's reform, and the CPC seeks to build the 'broadest possible united front' among the Chinese people.

Internal conditions also favour a wide unity, with the possibility of handling potentially antagonistic class contradictions in non-antagonistic ways. Unlike India for example, where caste consciousness still marks social and political relations very deeply, in China barriers of privilege are far less tenacious. Although elitism and patriarchal thought are far from eradicated, feudal and upper-class values and attitudes were subjected to severe challenge, not least during the Cultural Revolution. China's educated elites accept more readily not only appeals to patriotism, national unity and social solidarity in the face of difficult international circumstances, but also the democratic principle of 'serving the people'.

At the same time, since the Chinese state continues to exercise the critical levers of economic control, it is able to play a decisive role in mediating class relations. As So points out, the All China Federation of Industry and Commerce and the Private Business Association require official endorsement from the state, and their leaders, budgets and activities have to get state blessing. In return for acceptance, they get privileged access to state information, state funding and other forms of state support.[108]

The state then is able to define the political conditions for class formation and shape the contours of class relations, and so may channel potentially antagonistic class differences in conflict-free directions through the existing legal-institutional framework.[109]

CONCLUSION

In accordance with WTO requirements, China is setting up a viable legal system but using this to strengthen the socialist orientation of its market economy, not only to provide legal guarantees to property rights but also to set legal limits to investor behaviour and strengthen the rights of working people and marginalised groups.

Seeking to avoid the 'Latin American problem', the Chinese government is focusing on raising the living standards of the poor, combating unemployment, addressing the conditions of under-development of the rural areas and improving the conditions of migrant workers. Its approach is to reform the *hukou* system gradually, using pro-poor, rights-based measures to ensure adequate protection of peasant subsistence rights as a safety net; to relieve the farmers' tax burden; to develop a basic safety net of social protection and welfare; and to improve education and training in order to guide rural-to-urban migration in a positive direction as a force for development rather than a drain on the countryside.[110]

To achieve its social goals, China has to rein in its high investment rates, while streamlining the industrial sector, and allow public pressure to help shape growth and consumption patterns. Political reforms are now gradually releasing a bottom-up impetus for democratisation against bureaucratism, corruption and state capitalism within a strengthening legal-institutional framework. There is a steady expansion in the scope of self-governance, and the widespread cultivation of rights awareness enhances the ability of the mass organisations to serve as 'voices of the people' demanding more accountable government. This bottom-up participatory process is seen as key to changing the local practices and expenditure patterns that drive excessive growth, and to integrating local governments into the centrally defined regulations and policy measures, so as to achieve a more balanced development and the equitable distribution of its benefits.

That the government is nevertheless struggling to overcome the problem of high investment rates is evidenced in the continuing blistering rate of economic growth at 11 per cent per annum over the last two years. But to turn the entrenched growth process around to a more balanced mode is like trying to turn a battleship – it can only be done inch by inch. However, concluding his study of the coal industry, Tim Wright rejects the view that in this area at least, China faces an overwhelming crisis of governance, although he warns against over-optimism in the success of regulation.[111]

Part of the problem of fast growth lies in local government incentives which, in looking to local GDP performance, have encouraged local officials to seek high growth by all available means in order to advance their careers. Now, as has been seen, new performance objectives for local governments are being put in place. In addition, an SOE dividend payments scheme should also help in limiting over-investment and in rebalancing the economy.

But the problem also lies in the demands of development: moderating growth, creating jobs, maintaining stable prices, upgrading industrial structure, and controlling the trade surplus and the explosive growth of foreign exchange are contradictory tasks. The priorities of the Party and government are job creation and improving people's livelihoods. But how are these priorities to be met alongside the goals of reducing dependence on labour-intensive exports and promoting hi-tech industries which are inevitably labour-replacing? Technological upgrading will help to strengthen the fiscal base of local governments and wean them from dependence on FDI and on dangerous and polluting local enterprises. Yet how is a hi-tech knowledge-intensive sector to be developed without a widening income gap? How is a balance between ecological as well as social responsibility on the one hand, and employment and financial efficiency on the other, to be achieved? These all remain difficult questions yet to be answered.

The real challenge lies in developing and implementing a regulatory framework which honours the contradictory interests involved in the development process. This is a question of the achieving the right top-down bottom-up balance, that is, balancing between private short-term interests and national long-term interests, as well as between the different social groups, in ways that are accepted as fair. By opening up public debate and encouraging more political participation, the aim, as Li Peilin puts it, is to bring about a reasonable order of social stratification with the aid of the legal system, moulding values of social justice compatible with fair competition among different interest groups through dialogue, communication and understanding.[112] How far the Party and state allow the political system to shift towards greater institutional autonomy and a relationship of more equal partnership amongst government sectors, corporations, civil society, NGOs and working people's economic organisations is perhaps the ultimate question for the future in shaping a more balanced development pattern.[113]

PART 3

AN INTERNATIONAL TRIAL OF STRENGTH

9 TOWARDS A NEW INTERNATIONAL POLITICAL ORDER

The new central theme of the 16th CPC Congress in 2002 was China's peaceful development.[1] Taking forward the long-established principles of non-confrontation and self-reliance, the new emphasis signalled China's intention to become more active on the world stage in pursuit of the global agenda for 'peace and development'. Now with its growing strength, China was ready to move beyond Deng's caution 'to lie low and bide one's time', and instead, setting aside the 'victim mentality' so deeply embedded in its century of 'shame and humiliation', to put itself forward as a major power on the world stage.

Did this now mean that China was no longer 'dissatisfied' with the international order? Or was this deepening embrace of the multilateral order just bowing further to the inevitability of US world dominance following the expansion of its military power since 9/11?

Some commentators argue that in shifting the emphasis towards 'peaceful development', China's new leaders have quietly abandoned the New Security Concept (NSC) strategy of 'multipolarisation' with its connotations of balancing and containing US aggression, in favour of 'multilateralism', a term thought to have a less anti-US spin.[2] Other critics have taken China's offer of assistance to the United States in the 'war on terror' as yet another effort to curry favour in order to gain further acceptance.

On the other hand, China's active regionalism clearly indicates a shift in diplomatic stance from one mainly of accommodation with the existing multilateral order to one of advancing strategic initiatives. The US challenge to the existing UN order has played no small part in China's decision to do so. In order to secure a peaceful environment for its own development, it has become necessary for China to play a more active role in shaping it. At the same time, while opportunities to influence the global agenda have been growing, China, after years of sustained growth, can now bring more influence to bear in multilateral negotiation rather than simply playing a reactive role.

Meanwhile, in the face of worldwide opposition to the invasion of Iraq, the United States has been forced to adjust its unilateral policy and seek cooperation with other powers within the UN framework. In 2005, when the then US deputy secretary of state, Robert Zoellick, called on China to act as a 'responsible stakeholder in the global system' this seemed to open a new phase of dialogue in Sino-US relations.

Now both China and the United States have declared their interest in a negotiated international order. However, they come to this from very different perspectives and with very different agendas. Exploring the new context of multilateralism, this chapter sets out to contrast their political differences on issues of key international importance.

From the US perspective as set out in Bush's National Security Strategies (NSSs), corrupt dictatorships that abuse their own defenceless citizens and harbour terrorists pose the greatest risk to world stability. In the US mission to 'end tyranny', China is often made out to be playing an obstructionist role. At the same time, the Pentagon constantly hypes up the threat from China's military modernisation. China's stance, on the other hand, reveals how, through negotiations, its government is playing a major role in restraining the US hegemonic project by presenting alternative solutions to world problems.

THE NEW MULTILATERAL INTERNATIONAL ORDER

China's decision to step forward as a more activist world power should be understood first in the context of its accession to the World Trade Organization (WTO). This meant, as China saw it, that although its economy would now be more reliant on other countries' economic policies, so diminishing its national sovereignty, it would actually have more sovereignty, as 'our actions are of more universal significance'.[3] As has been seen, WTO membership gave new momentum to China's economic diplomacy and activity in promoting South–South economic cooperation as a basis for North–South dialogue.

Second, while condemning the terrorism of 9/11, China was able to gain strategic advantage from the situation. Given that China had its own concerns over domestic terrorism, its leaders used the issue of the 'war on terror' as leverage to shift Bush from his view of China as a 'strategic competitor' and to restore partnership relations on the basis of shared interests in tackling global terrorism. However, far from being coopted into the 'war on terror', China had considerable reservations regarding the attack on Afghanistan which it never explicitly endorsed, and was openly opposed to the US-led invasion of Iraq, which it did not regard as part of the 'war on terror'. The Chinese government constantly criticised the 'war on terror' for its over-dependence on coercive means, stating that any force used should be based on evidence, should be proportionate and must not target civilians; that the authority of the United Nations should not be bypassed; and that terrorism should not be treated as synonymous with any particular nation, culture or religion.

Nevertheless, despite the fact that the United States was using the 'war on terror' for its own strategic purposes, strengthening its military position in China's surrounding areas, at the same time, improved relations with the United States meant that when the US–North Korea crisis broke in 2002, China was well positioned to initiate the six-party talks. In doing so, it in effect stepped right into the path of the US unipolar drive.

Then, seizing the moment in 2003 to ride the multipolar tide of world opposition to the Iraq invasion, China stepped up its diplomacy worldwide. Between 2003 and 2005, President Hu Jintao toured Europe, Asia, Latin American and Africa with a view to promoting negotiations on strategic cooperative partnerships, moving China into position as a major global player. If the language of multipolarity was toned down to emphasise multi-lateralism, China was actively moving forward to promote multipolarity in practice. As Wang Jisi saw it, 'so long as the United States' image remains tainted, China will have greater leverage in multilateral settings'.[4]

Meanwhile Bush, shifting back into a multilateral mode, was preparing to attack the UN norms of non-intervention from within. The 2006 NSS was a more ideological document than its predecessor in 2002, highlighting the question of 'values' to strengthen and institutionalise a market-based 'Community of Democracies' with the aim of promoting 'responsible sover-eignty'. Nevertheless, with the goal of absolute military advantage and pre-emptive strike still upheld, the neocon vision remained firmly at the heart of US foreign policy.

Following on from the 2002 NSS, the 2006 NSS addressed the issue of how to organise 'coalitions of the willing' to 'augment' the permanent insti-tutions of the United Nations, WTO and North Atlantic Treaty Organization (NATO). Amongst the 'tools to protect freedoms', it lists the application of sanctions to target those who rule oppressive regimes, encouraging other nations not to support these regimes, the use of foreign assistance to support democracy and human rights, and working with the United Nations to help reinvigorate its commitment to promoting democracy and human rights. In this way, the United States seeks to determine the rules defining global citizenship in its own image, thereby constructing a political order in which its own ideology reigns supreme.

Whether it has been Iran's right to develop nuclear power, the handling of the crisis in Darfur, Israel's attack on Lebanon in 2006 as a 'legitimate form of self-defence', the principle of national sovereignty, which protects nations from external interventions and interference, is under constant pressure as the United States endeavours to draw a line through the international community, demarcating the 'responsible democracies' from tyrannies and repressive regimes.

With regard to China, the 2006 NSS sets out the US expectation that it acts as a 'responsible global player', sharing the burden of maintaining international stability and security, working with the United States and other major powers both within and beyond the UN Security Council (UNSC). The United States sees its task, according to Condoleezza Rice, as trying to 'push and prod and persuade China to a more positive course',[5] and is pressing China hard on a series of international issues, at the same time strengthening its own military hedge not least to ensure that China makes the 'right choices' about the 'fundamental character of its state'.

China for its part has chosen to join the multilateral system, using the arena as a platform from which to challenge the United States and its 'China threat' arguments rather than seeking to form an anti-US coalition. In declaring its commitment to peaceful development, China has made clear its intention, as it steps up to its major power role, not to challenge or disrupt the US-led international political and economic system. Rather, by participating in regional and global affairs, it seeks to play its part as a rising power in improving the unjust international order.[6]

CHINA AND THE UNITED NATIONS

The United Nations has long been regarded by China as an instrument in which developing countries could make their opinions known, thereby acting, if only as yet to a limited extent, as a brake on the ambitions of hegemonic powers. For China, the main role of the United Nations is to promote a more balanced world order. It envisages the United Nations emerging as the central organisation of the new international order – the political and economic coordinator of a diverse but peaceful and interdependent multipolar world based on sovereign equality. A 'responsible global power' should then commit to safeguarding the authority of the United Nations and to furthering UN principles in tackling key global issues.

China's critics in the West, on the other hand, regard its role in the UN Security Council as rather less than principled, as pragmatic at best, self-serving at worst. It is often claimed, for example, that China abstained from the crucial UN vote in 1991 authorising the use of force to evict Iraq from Kuwait, in order to gain the reward from the United States of further moves towards normalising relations post-Tiananmen Square.[7] From China's viewpoint, although it was certainly not in favour of the use of force despite the fact that Iraq had transgressed the UN non-intervention rules, had it used its veto, this would not have prevented the US action.

However, as its strength and influence have begun to grow, China has become more active on the UN front. Particularly since the 1999 war on Yugoslavia, China has been more determined than ever to defend the relevance and authority of the United Nations against the challenge from the US-inspired concepts of 'limited sovereignty' and 'humanitarian intervention'.

China was president of the UNSC at the time of the critical UN resolution 1441 on Iraq and did a great amount of mediation work in order to find a peaceful solution. China believed that the methods of peaceful resolution of the Iraq issue had not been exhausted and took great care in the wording of the UN resolution.[8] The United States realised that as a result it could not secure sufficient votes of support. Although the combined force of France, Russia and China could not stop the US attack, China's work, by ensuring that the UN resolution did not directly authorise war, averted a fundamental change to the UN principle of non-intervention. Without this, the doctrine of pre-emptive strike would have been allowed to substitute for this fundamental guarantee of world peace, other powers would have followed the US 'go it alone' example and the United Nations would have broken down completely.

When China subsequently accepted the UN resolution in October 2003 legitimising the US-led occupation of Iraq, this was not so much a case of 'buckling under'. Rather China's view was that bringing the United States back into the United Nations and thereby restoring its role, no matter how weak, was to be encouraged at all costs as preferable to US unilateral militarism since it allowed room for diplomacy and the peaceful resolution of conflict. But as China's UN representative, Wang Guangya, made clear: '[It] does not mean that the resolution is good ... [or] that China ... want[s] to yield to the pressure of the US.'[9] Without US engagement with the United Nations, the organisation would not work effectively, but at the same time, the United Nations needed to appeal to 'the interests of the developing countries' and be made 'relevant to their concerns'.[10]

Since 2003, in further negotiations whether over Iraq, Iran, North Korea and Sudan, China has sought to uphold the fundamental norms of the United Nations and maintain the sovereignty and territorial integrity of its members.

It is often argued that China hesitates to endorse international intervention lest the precedent be used to legitimate possible intervention in North Korea, the Taiwan Strait or Tibet. However, the question is rather a matter of upholding the principles of the United Nations against what is hardly a measured case-by-case assessment but more a pattern of intervention in the interests of a hegemonic United States.

UN Reform

Since the failure of the United Nations to ratify their attack on Iraq, the United States and Britain have displayed an almost obsessive determination to drive their agenda against 'abusive states' through the United Nations. They continually call for a more activist UNSC to exercise its powers more forcefully, especially through the wider use of sanctions, and to extend the scope of its actions in order to 'widen the circle of market-led democracies'. The stakes are constantly being raised over controversial and highly sensitive issues, with continual referrals to the UNSC.

The invasion of Iraq has left the legacy of a deep lack of trust within the United Nations. The UNSC in particular, given its key role in matters of international security, including decisions on sanctions and peacekeeping, has become the site of intense dispute. The United States and Britain, and Russia and China backed by members from the G77, are ranged against each other across a series of issues from reform of the UNSC to climate change in a struggle to defend the non-intervention principle and to democratise the United Nations itself. For its role in these issues, China has frequently been singled out and presented in the Western media as obstructionist.

The 60th anniversary of the founding of the United Nations in 2005 provided the occasion to consider the organisation's reform to meet the challenges of the twenty-first century. For China, as indeed for the G77, the problem is that developing countries, which comprise two-thirds of the UN membership, are seriously under-represented in the UNSC and that as a result, as it is dominated by developed countries, UN operations have a tendency to over-emphasise individual rights as well as civil and political rights to the neglect of the rights of developing countries to survival and development. Throughout the 1990s, the United States and its allies, clearly preparing the ground for 'humanitarian intervention', sought to politicise the human rights agenda and prevent the United Nations from fulfilling its main goal of achieving a more balanced world order to meet the needs of developing countries.[11]

China's stand, on the other hand, has been for a depoliticised agenda in which economic, social and cultural rights on the one hand and the civil and political rights on the other are given equal importance, supporting UN work with member states to bolster their human rights promotion regardless of political system.[12]

The ultimate goal of the 60th UN Summit reform agenda, as far as China was concerned, was to revitalise the organisation and strengthen its ability to achieve balanced world development by enhancing democracy and the rule of law in international relations, and thereby lay down a solid political basis as well as create a favourable atmosphere for safeguarding world peace and promoting common development.[13]

In the first place, this meant that the United Nations 'must hear more voices from the developing countries' in order to make the world body more representative and authoritative, and capable of restraining unilateralism.[14] This claim to stand for the democratisation of the international order may seem hypocritical since China supports the power of veto in the UNSC.[15] On the other hand, the veto serves as a guarantee against the manipulation of smaller powers by any of the major powers.

China sees two ways in which the role of developing countries in the United Nations should be strengthened. First, it favours regional representation to the UNSC to achieve overall balance and has been particularly supportive of an Africa seat. Second, China favours building closer links between the UNSC and the General Assembly to allow more countries, especially small and medium-sized countries, to have more input into the decision making of the UNSC.[16]

At the same time China calls for the remit of the General Assembly to be extended to encompass all areas key to the international order, for example through closer links between the WTO and the UN Conference on Trade and Development (UNCTAD),[17] by 'opening a line of communication' to the Bretton Woods institutions to cater to developing countries,[18] and restructuring the G8 as a supplementary organisation of the United Nations.[19] From China's strategic perspective, then, UN reform stands at the centre of a 'fair globalisation'.

In the event, the debate at the summit became narrowly focused on the question of UNSC expansion. A group application for permanent membership by Japan, Germany, India and Brazil, however, omitted Africa, and arguably would have further strengthened the US position in the Security Council, since both Japan and Germany are US allies and India a prospective US partner.

With regard to Japan's application, which was supported by many developed countries on the grounds that it already provides a considerable proportion of the UN budget, China argued that 'global responsibility' should not be defined in terms of how rich a country is, but by its commitment to the UN's Peace and Development goals. Japan's failure to face up to its wartime atrocities raises questions here.

With Mexico opposing Brazil's application, Pakistan opposing India's and both China and South Korea opposing Japan's, the UNSC reform debate threatened to split the organisation. China's position was that regional groupings should hold their own closed-door meetings to determine their candidates.[20]

The proposal for a UN Democracy Fund also bore the markings of a new US-inspired effort to draw a dividing line between 'democracies' and 'non-democracies'.

UN reform was clearly seen by the United States as an opportunity to press for changes in the rules on non-intervention.[21] The issue of the 'responsibility to protect' was potentially the most threatening to the organisation. This calls for international intervention when a state is unwilling or unable to stop massive human rights violations. The concept has long been rejected by developing countries which feared that the West could use it as a pretext to interfere with their internal affairs. However, if the primary responsibility to protect people from crimes against humanity lies in the hands of their sovereign state, the question is: where a state fails or is failing, as increasing numbers have been doing since the end of the Cold War, what would be the responsible thing to do?

The US position as stated in its 2006 NSS completely disregards the matter of sovereignty by insisting that the world must act against mass killings and mass atrocities even if 'local parties are not prepared for peace'. The Chinese view on the other hand, as stated in its *Position Paper on UN Reform*, while maintaining that basically it is the state that shoulders the prime responsibility to protect its own population, also recognised that nevertheless internal conflicts may be caused by complex factors, such that:

> When a massive humanitarian crisis occurs, it is the legitimate concern of the international community to ease and defuse the crisis. Any response to such a crisis should strictly conform to the UN Charter and the opinions of the country and the regional organization concerned should be respected.[22]

Such responses should be decided by the UNSC case by case.

The compromise reached at the 2005 UN Summit, on the one hand reconfirmed respect for national sovereignty and individual states' primary 'responsibility to protect', while on the other hand also admitted that the international community, through the United Nations, should be prepared to take collective action should national authorities manifestly fail to do so. The stipulations were that such action should only be taken on a case-by-case basis, in cooperation with relevant regional organisations, and only where diplomatic, humanitarian and peaceful means conducted in accordance with the UN Charter prove inadequate. These indicated considerable restraint compared with the US position.

The Darfur Question

Since the UN Summit, China's 'value-free' foreign policy and its dealings with Sudan, Myanmar and 'other troublesome states' have come under heavy criticism from the West. Indeed the US 2006 NSS criticised China specifically for 'supporting resource-rich countries without regard to the misrule at home or misbehaviour abroad of those regimes'.

Things came to a head in 2006 around the problems in Sudan, where it is said that 200,000 people have lost their lives since war erupted again in 2003. Bush raised the temperature on the issue by describing the Darfur situation as one of 'genocide' at the United Nations in September 2006, and demanding that the United Nations get tougher, calling for thousands more peacekeepers to be sent. Although much of the opposition to the US approach has come from other African countries, with Russia and South Africa as well as China opposing sanctions, the issue has become an opportunity for China-bashing as the United States focused on the involvement of the Chinese government and its state-owned China National Petroleum Corporation in the extraction of Sudan's oil. In fact, the top recipient of Sudan oil in 2006 was not China but Japan.[23] Nevertheless, a campaign, mounted with the support of over 100 US Members of Congress to force China into pressuring Sudan further, targeted the 2008 Beijing Olympics – dubbed by the campaigners as the 'Genocide Olympics'.[24]

China has maintained that the Darfur crisis must be resolved through dialogue not punitive sanctions to avoid destabilising the area.[25] The point is that a UN mission cannot succeed if it alienates the Sudanese government. As China's UN representative Wang Guangya sees it:

> In some countries there is a problem where the protection of their own people is neglected. The UN can come in a quiet way, providing help, providing advice. But the role to play is not to impose it when the government is functioning. Of course there are cases where you can say that the country is a failed country. But where there is a government, I think the best way to do it is by giving good advice, wherever you can ... to let the government pick up on its main responsibility.[26]

For some analysts close to the situation, the problems are in fact being exacerbated by the West's preoccupation with an international force.[27] As one former UN envoy to the Sudan said recently:

> I have been struck by the constant lack of knowledge about this situation in the capitals of western countries as shown by visiting ministers and diplomats, together with arrogance, and that is in particular the American arrogance ... nobody is dealing with the political issues. New York is not focusing on them, the SC is not focusing on them; everyone is obsessed by how to get in the peace-keeping mission. That is useful but you cannot intervene militarily. Any force has to sustain peace; if you don't have peace, a peace force doesn't make any sense and it can become part of the problem.[28]

Clearly, the situation in Darfur causes deep concern. But it does not admit of an oversimplified 'abusive state, helpless citizens' analysis. Not only are there ethnic and religious dimensions to the problems but, as some commentators point out, the situation in Darfur is the first climate change conflict. Jeffrey Sachs argues that the first problem to be addressed is 'water and food to survive – not sanctions and peacekeepers. They need a development approach.'[29] This is precisely what Chinese investment potentially offers, as its government looks for a long-term solution to the situation. The Chinese government has also delivered concrete help to Darfur, building 20 small power plants with the aid of over 300 Chinese engineers as well as giving US$500,000 to the United Nations for Darfur projects with additional similar aid to the African Union.[30] Critics of China's arms sales to Sudan, which have been exaggerated, might take note that its arms sales to developing countries as a whole make up a mere 3 or 4 per cent of the total, with nearly 46 per cent coming from the United States and 13 percent from Britain.[31]

China is credited with eventually persuading the Sudanese government to accept an increased joint UN and African Union force of 20,000 peacekeepers. However, the Sudanese government has become reluctant to accept this force as difficulties arose over a political settlement when the French government failed to encourage one influential Sudanese rebel leader, based in France, to attend peace talks in 2007.[32]

Democratising the International Order?

The United States stakes its international leadership of 'a growing community of democracies' on its mission to 'end tyranny'. But according to a recent study, democracies comprise little over half of all world states. The number of 'autocracies' has indeed declined since the end of the Cold War, but there has been instead a sharp increase in the numbers of failing and failed states. This shows how very fragile democratic political systems often are, and how ill suited they may be to the challenges of nation building and development. According to this study: 'It is not clear how much democracy actually fosters peace and facilitates peace-building and how much democracy is the culmination of economic performance and peace-building efforts'.[33]

To a large extent, the problems of failing states in the developing world lie in their shattered plans for economic construction under the impositions of the neoliberal order. Yet, while the West insists on improving standards of domestic governance especially in Africa, shifting the responsibility for development failure on to Africans themselves, it ignores the problems of the instabilities and lack of governance of the global economic order which destroyed the hopes for development.

Meanwhile the constant insistence of the developed countries led by the United States on the need to impose human rights monitors, peacekeeping forces and sanctions on regimes in Africa, does not measure well against their parsimony over aid.[34] The work of the United Nations meanwhile is very much limited by a large amount of back dues, the United States being the largest debtor, paying only the minimum to entitle it to vote.[35] Actually, China provides more UN peacekeepers than any other UNSC member, and they have a reputation for good quality.

The continual efforts by the United States to refer issues to the UNSC, not only to sanction Iran and North Korea but also to censure Myanmar, yet at the same time stalling on a resolution condemning Israel for the bombing of Lebanon in July 2006, ratchets up the tensions in the United Nations. China and Russia, frequently coordinating with India and South Africa, have challenged these attempts to establish the 'tyranny of a minority'[36] marginalising the views of the General Assembly on matters of worldwide concern.

Pursuing a divisive agenda to support 'humanitarian intervention', the United States has also attempted to 'democratise' international proceedings by introducing majority voting.[37] China is not in favour of forcing through votes on a proposal when consensus is lacking, remaining committed to the UN principle of consensus as a basis for building trust and support on a broad basis.[38]

Where the United States attempts to 'ring fence' contentious issues within the UNSC, separated from their regional context, China instead favours an approach which coordinates regional and UN efforts. If the Gulf States, the states of the Middle East, Africa, North-East Asia and so on, were all to play a key role in conflict resolution within their neighbourhoods, making their own regional security arrangements within the wider UN framework, this would build a firm foundation for a multipolar world with the United Nations as its coordinator.

The UN system remains in a very fragile state. Nevertheless, though not always leading from the front, China has done much to keep the United Nations going by insisting on the resolution of disputes by peaceful means, working quietly and determinedly to limit the extent to which its authority is diminished or bypassed, and to maintain unity and the solidarity of its membership. As the ambassador for Singapore noted:

> They [the Chinese] play a very skilful game at the UN …. They make their opinions felt without much talking. They never come in first and make a statement. They always listen first and then make a statement which captures the main thrust of what the developing world wants.[39]

MAINTAINING DEFENCE: PROMOTING NUCLEAR DISARMAMENT

The most crucial areas of international negotiation are those concerning global nuclear disarmament and the non-proliferation of weapons of mass destruction (WMD). Pursuing a confrontational 'sword plus shield' approach to achieve nuclear primacy, the United States, as Gerson has highlighted, asserts that the responsibility for non-proliferation lies not with the United Nations but with the Pentagon.[40] Following its withdrawal from the Anti-Ballistic Missile (ABM) Treaty in 2002, US policy seems set to undermine the rest of the international non-proliferation treaty system, substituting instead its own 'full-spectrum dominance'.

To secure its own nuclear primacy, the United States is in the first place, as detailed in the 2006 NSS, aggressively pursuing a Fissile Material Cut-Off Treaty (FMCT) to 'close the loophole' in the Non-Proliferation Treaty (NPT) which allows non-nuclear states access to nuclear materials.[41] In addition, while refusing to negotiate a treaty to prevent an arms race in outer space (PAROS), it unveiled a National Space Policy in October 2006, asserting the right to deny access to anyone deemed 'hostile to US interests'.

At the same time, also in line with the 2006 NSS, the United States has introduced its own instrument of non-proliferation, namely, the Proliferation Security Initiative (PSI), which contravenes the UN Convention on the Law of the Sea. Devised by key neocon John Bolton, the PSI is used to take actions against Iran and North Korea by stopping and searching shipments for WMD. In effect, the initiative maintains a 'coalition of the willing' in support of pre-emptive strike, and serves as a model for new voluntary-based partnerships oriented towards action and results rather than rule making, to meet new global challenges.[42]

However, what without question is threatening to change the whole world situation on nuclear disarmament and non-proliferation is the proposed US nuclear deal with India. The double standards exercised by the United States in seeking to constrain Iran and North Korea, yet giving tacit consent to India's nuclear status in favour of its own nuclear and missile technology exports, are driving non-proliferation negotiations into an impasse, creating divisions within the New Agenda Coalition and the non-aligned movement, the main advocates of global disarmament. The US stance seems set not merely to perpetuate the division between the nuclear 'haves' and 'have nots' but to demarcate 'responsible' from 'irresponsible' nuclear weapons states.

Meanwhile, the United States has declared China as having the 'greatest potential' to compete militarily with its own capabilities, and the Pentagon constantly whips up fears of China's military expansionism. For China, the US deployment of missile defences together with its development of space weapons, and the US arms sales to Taiwan, are the two security issues it cares most about.

China as a Nuclear Weapons State

China pursues a strategy of minimum nuclear deterrence, maintaining a small force of nuclear warheads, enough only to be able to retaliate in a nuclear attack. According to a 2006 report issued by the Federation of American Scientists and the Natural Resources Defense Council, its total nuclear stockpile numbers about 200 warheads, with about 20 silo-based intercontinental ballistic missiles (ICBMs) capable of reaching targets in the United States, while the United States has nearly 10,000 strategic and tactical warheads and more than 830 missiles, mostly with multiple warheads, that can reach China.[43]

China developed nuclear weapons after being subjected to US threats over Korea and the Taiwan Strait in the 1950s and early 1960s. When the USSR withdrew all of its scientists in 1960, China was left with little option but to develop its own bomb.

From the outset, China has been the only recognised nuclear weapons state with an explicit policy of 'no first use' under any circumstances and with unconditional commitment not to use or threaten to use nuclear weapons against non-nuclear states or nuclear weapons-free zones (NWFZs). India's claims of a 'China threat' to justify its own nuclear weapons have been dismissed by South Asian anti-nuclear campaigners Praful Bidwai and Achin Vanaik as 'utterly abstract, never exercised or articulated'.[44]

China has joined all the international treaties related to non-proliferation, including the major conventions on biological and chemical weapons.[45] It has also declared its readiness to ratify the Comprehensive Test Ban Treaty (CTBT) and since signing the treaty has not carried out any tests.[46] Meanwhile, the Bush administration has made it categorically clear that the United States does not support the CTBT. China is also the only recognised nuclear weapons state to declare its support for a Nuclear Weapons Convention.

The Chinese position remains that states with the largest nuclear arsenals bear special responsibilities for disarmament and should take the first steps.[47] But this has not been taken as an excuse for inaction. The Chinese government is particularly concerned to create the right conditions and atmosphere for global disarmament, pursuing mutual non-targeting agreements with other nuclear weapons states, successfully in the case of Russia. However, a similar approach to the US government was turned down.[48]

As has been seen previously, China supports NWFZs, and in addition values the role of NGOs in urging nuclear weapons states to dismantle nuclear weapons.[49]

China holds that a mechanism for non-proliferation should be fair and reasonable: its basic principles should be non-discrimination and undiminished security for all countries, and it should be universal, with all countries participating on the basis of democratic decision making.[50] China has then refused to join in with the US extra-legal PSI scheme, arguing instead for strengthening non-proliferation by negotiation, not force. It agrees the need to close the loophole which allows countries to carry out nuclear development under the guise of peaceful utilisation of nuclear energy, but argues also for the necessity of removing the pressure on non-nuclear states to gain nuclear weapons, by writing into the NPT the requirement that nuclear powers declare policies of no first use and no threat of use against non-nuclear states.[51] It also calls for the UNSC to reiterate the authority of the NPT and to set up a nuclear technology production and management body as the sole legal market for nuclear technology and nuclear materials.[52]

Space Weaponisation

China's main concern over missile defence is the possible inclusion of Taiwan in such a system, and the disabling effects of US interceptors and space weapons on its own defence systems. Even a limited missile defence system would neutralise China's few ICBMs. The fear is that the military superiority a missile defence (MD) system offers may allow the United States freedom to intervene in China's affairs and encroach on its sovereignty, including undermining China's reunification with Taiwan.

China has made clear its view that US plans could lead to a new costly and destabilising arms race since it may be forced to build more warheads to maintain its nuclear deterrent. However, as its first and best option, China has been pursuing an arms control agreement.

The US planned development of space weapons has made their banning an urgent issue for China. In 2002, together with Russia, it put forward a proposal to the UN Conference on Disarmament for a treaty on PAROS, including a ban on MD. Initially, the Chinese government insisted that PAROS be linked to a Fissile Materials Cut-Off Treaty (FMCT), since if the Outer Space Treaty failed and US missile defence goes ahead, China would need more fissile materials to expand its nuclear warheads.[53] The United States, supported almost alone by Britain, has staunchly opposed any negotiation on the outer space issue while pressing ahead for the immediate negotiation of an FMCT. In order to release the resulting deadlock at the UN Conference on Disarmament, China agreed in 2003 to delink the treaties as a gesture of compromise.[54] However, this goodwill effort is yet to be matched.[55]

While declaring its commitment to the peaceful use of space, China has made some significant advances in space technologies, not least with its successful launch of astronauts into space in 2003, a development which took the United States by surprise. The Chinese government has made its interest in international cooperation in this area very clear, and the European and Russian space agencies have been willing to build closer ties. The United States however, has frozen all space cooperation with China, often banning its space scientists from visiting the United States.[56] The United States insists that such cooperation should be linked to membership of the

Missile Technology Control Regime (MTCR), yet at the same time will not allow China to join, making constant allegations regarding the export of material from China to states hostile to the United States. But China has made efforts to comply with international standards of export controls and has been admitted as a member of the Nuclear Suppliers Group, while again the European Union is reported as willing to endorse China's application to join the MTCR.[57]

In early 2007, China successfully tested an anti-satellite device by shooting down one of its own old satellites. This was widely condemned around the world as hardly a peaceful use of space. The action was not, however, illegal since there is no PAROS, and this was the point that China was making. China was responding to the October 2006 US National Space Policy and the timing of the test, just before an upcoming UN Conference on Disarmament, suggests that the motivation behind it was to nudge the Bush administration towards a space weapons ban.

The Question of China's Military Budget and Military Development

In recent years the Pentagon has been issuing annual reports which seriously exaggerate China's military expenditure. These Cold War portrayals of China as an aggressive power seeking regional hegemony, a threat to the United States and to its Asian neighbours, are intended to cast doubt over China's claim to peaceful development and help to whip up 'China threat' fears.

The July 2005 Pentagon report to the US Congress claimed that Beijing's defence spending could be two or three times the official budget of US$30 billion, making it the third-highest in the world.[58] On the other hand, the 2006 SIPRI report estimates China's military spend to be in the region of US$41 billion.[59] As a percentage of GDP, China's 2004 spend was given as 2.4 per cent, below that of Britain's at 2.8 per cent and Russia at 3.9 per cent, as well as that of the United States at 4 per cent, and commensurate with its neighbour South Korea. SIPRI, furthermore, gives the US 2005 budget as US$478 billion, making it responsible for 48 per cent of the world total, while China accounts for just 4 to 5 per cent. On this basis, US military spending is more than twelve times as high as China's and more than 50 times as high in per capita terms.

The Pentagon claims that China excludes the costs of new nuclear weapons and R&D from its calculations. But equally the United States keeps the costs of its own space weapons programmes hidden in a classified 'black budget', so making it hard to determine what progress the United States has been making.[60] The report also draws attention to increases in China's arms purchases from Russia, but the fact is that Russia tends to sell more sophisticated weapons to India than to China.[61]

It is, though, quite true that China's military spending has been increasing by double-digit figures in most years since the early 1990s, and in 2007 the government announced another 18 per cent boost. Nevertheless, an alarmist interpretation of China's increased spending is not justified.[62] Less than 20 years ago, China's military was essentially geared simply towards fighting a people's war. When military modernisation was placed on the agenda, this was pursued throughout the 1980s as a rather low priority, high priority being given to economic growth. However, particularly since the 1991 Gulf War, this approach has been adjusted to one in which more equal weight is given to national defence building and economic development.

The increases in military expenditure in recent years have mostly gone to fund salaries, equipment and fuel costs, as Goldstein argues, to 'lift the PLA from what has been a position of near impotence against all but the smallest of regional adversaries'.[63] Military power remains the weakest link in China's comprehensive national power (CNP), and according to its *National Defense White Paper* in 2004, the increasing technological gap with the United States remains a major security issue.

The main focus of China's military enhancement has been to establish superiority in conventional forces in case of possible conflict over Taiwan. But most recently, China has prepared to deploy more mobile ICBMs although, despite Pentagon predictions, it has not developed a multiple warhead system. However, according to the 2006 report of the Federation of American Scientists and the Natural Resources Defense Council, China's efforts to update its forces have been moving slowly and are to a considerable extent a reaction to US nuclear deployments and military policies.[64]

Meanwhile, the Pentagon's exaggerated reports on China's military expenditure have been used to provide fuel for the pro-nuclear lobby in India and help to boost US weapons sales to Taiwan against mounting opposition from the Taiwanese people themselves, who prefer welfare over warfare.[65]

China now has hundreds of short-range conventional missiles pointing from Fujian province across the Strait. According to its new 2005 anti-secession law, China continues to reserve the right to invade if Taiwan were to attempt to gain full independent statehood. This is taken by China's critics to give the lie to its avowal of peaceful development. But the Taiwan issue is a special case where China considers its national interests at stake, and not an indication of an expansionist agenda of which its neighbours should beware, as the Pentagon reports. In fact, the anti-secession law marks a softening of China's position to focus on preventing independence rather than seeking unification within a certain time scale. At the same time, by clarifying the 'rule of law' in the situation, China has increased its transparency.[66]

What drives the arms race across the Taiwan Strait is the US insistence that 'peace comes from the balance of power'. In 2001, the United States offered a US$30 billion arms package including Patriot missiles, and in 2007 the United States put forward plans to sell 450 air and ground missiles to Taiwan.[67] China on the other hand has sought to trade off a decrease in Chinese missile deployment in Fujian for reductions in US arms sales to Taiwan.[68]

On Non-Proliferation: The Iran Issue

The Bush administration has claimed Iran's alleged nuclear weapons development to be the single most important issue at stake in US–China relations.[69] Depending on how it responds, China may be made out to appear as an 'irresponsible' nuclear weapons state.

However, as China sees it, success in preventing the proliferation of WMD would be aided by a general improvement in international relations with the fair and rational settlement of security issues. While the United States has engaged in high-tension tactics in its dispute with Iran, hauling the issue before the UNSC and insisting on sanctions, the Chinese government has supported efforts to prevent the dispute from being brought to a head.

Although clearly recognising that the problem arises from Bush's foreign policy in the Middle East, the Chinese government, in line with its cooperative security win–win approach, has taken an even-handed position. On the one hand, the United States should address Iran's security concerns and guarantee non-aggression, at the same time, Iran, even though it is not in breach of the NPT, should also show willing by suspending its uranium enrichment operations in acknowledgement of the security concerns of the United States and other states.

China attaches importance to the fact that the EU3, Britain, France and Germany, have different views from those of the United States, given their own economic interests in the Middle East and their preference for diplomacy. Yu Jun argues there is a problem in that Iran broke its promise to the EU3 to suspend its nuclear activities, thereby undermining trust, but that if this situation were diffused then the differences between the European Union and United States would resurface.[70] China then has looked to Iran for greater flexibility and called on its compliance with International Atomic Energy Authority (IAEA) resolutions.

As it is, with Iran maintaining a hardline stance and the United States adopting a more hostile policy, the danger is that the situation will deteriorate to the brink of war.[71] While joining efforts to deflect harsher measures, China has supported minimal UN sanctions, as it did over the North Korean nuclear issue, in line with its own policy of not providing assistance to any nuclear facility that is not placed under IAEA safeguard.[72] Meanwhile, appealing to the positive lessons to be drawn from the six-party talks on Korean denuclearisation, China strongly supports Iran's quest for inclusion in the current framework of multi-party negotiations, at the same time encouraging US–Iran face-to-face talks.[73]

Nuclear Capability: Peaceful Intent

While the United States pursues global hegemony in the name of non-proliferation at the expense of the existing international arms control regime, China is standing by the gains made in the treaty system since the 1980s and is seeking to strengthen them. Its declared intention of peaceful development then means far more than simply the absence of threat.

Apart from its efforts in arms control negotiations, China has demonstrated its peaceful intentions in many ways, not least in its willingness to settle border disputes with its neighbours on generally favourable terms to them. China has no military alliances and no troops occupying, or military bases in, foreign territory.[74] It has adopted an extremely restrained attitude towards the development of nuclear weapons. However, given the United States' continued pursuit of missile defence, the Chinese government announced in its 2006 *White Paper on National Defense* the intention to build a 'lean and effective' nuclear force. Although it is not in a position to conduct an arms race with the United States and does not intend to do so, China 'will not sit idly by and watch its strategic interests being jeopardised'.[75] While reaffirming its peaceful intentions, China aims to develop as a military power capable of defending its development in line with its policy of minimum deterrent and no more: it is not seeking an armament level beyond what it sees as its legitimate defence needs.

CONCLUSION

The concept of peaceful development is essentially China's response to the US turn towards unilateralism and pre-emptive strike, aiming to highlight its own new activist diplomacy for peace, linked with the opportunities through win–win exchange for development.

While the second Bush administration has sought to place more emphasis on multilateralism to create greater consensus for US hegemonism not only with the European Union but also within the United States itself, its commitment to absolute security is undiminished. The United States is now working within the multilateral system to change to the existing international rules and principles and remove any constraint that these might have on its own decision making.

This multilateralism is more of a disguised form of unilateralism, a multilateralism for a unipolar world, with the United States acting not so much in isolation but bending if not seeking to break UN principles and international law. In contrast, genuine multilateralism involves a search for dialogue and for negotiation between multiple partners in a multipolar world.

The United States and China now meet in the international arena with two very different ideas about global responsibility. For Bush, global responsibility is defined in ideological terms: democracies are the most effective in 'extending peace and prosperity', that is, the most willing to share the burdens of US-defined goals for a successful global order. The test for China as far as the United States is concerned is its willingness to take a greater share in these burdens.

China has indeed accommodated the United States in a number of respects, not least in introducing restrictions on exports of missile technology as a significant concession to US non-proliferation pressure.[76] Yet its concern above all has been to maintain the United Nations and defend its principles. Although not always at the forefront of the international stage, in its opposition to the invasion of Iraq, its refusal to join the PSI, its stance on global nuclear disarmament, its emphasis on conflict resolution and building trust together with its key role in the six-nation diplomatic dialogue dealing with nuclear weapons on the Korean peninsula, China is demonstrating that its peaceful development means it intends to play a greater role in securing the conditions of international peace against the destabilisation of the US hegemonic drive.

China's peaceful development is not a strategy for pacifism but a preference for the resolution of disputes in a diverse world by peaceful means. It is the United States that has become the 'revolutionary' force of change in the international order, and China is now the defender of the UN 'status quo' and the legacy of resistance against aggression.

10 TOWARDS A NEW INTERNATIONAL ECONOMIC ORDER

Bush's political and military strategy to forge a 'community of market-based democracies' is matched by a set of economic policies which drive a neoliberal dollar-centred globalisation. As set out in the 2006 National Security Strategy (NSS), these are the promotion of free trade agreements (FTAs) to open markets, the reform of the international financial system to refocus the International Monetary Fund (IMF) on its core mission of maintaining international financial stability, the promotion of flexible exchange rates and open markets for financial services, and the protection of intellectual property rights (IPR).

These policies, as Bello and Malig note, mark out a strategy of economic hegemonism, less a recipe for 'economic freedom as a moral imperative' and rather more an aggressive attempt to reverse the US economic decline and its huge and ever-growing trade and fiscal deficits.[1] While pursuing protectionism in its own trade and investment matters, the United States has sought to negotiate FTAs to press trade and financial liberalisation on others beyond the current World Trade Organization (WTO) framework. It endeavours to manipulate multilateral agencies, in particular, the World Bank and IMF, to push the interests of US capital. With the US economy's increasing reliance on profits from IPR, it has sought to extend the scope and length of patents, to make up for the decline in manufacturing competitiveness and exports. Above all, by manipulating the dollar's value, it seeks to regain competitiveness for the US economy and to pass on the costs of economic crisis to rivals through flexible exchange rate regimes.[2]

The Chinese economy has borne the brunt of US protectionist threats since, after acceding to the WTO, its trade surplus has widened, creating new tensions in Sino–US economic relations. The 2006 NSS singles out China in particular to do much more in moving to a market-based, flexible exchange rate regime if it is to be considered 'a responsible major global player'. The renminbi (RMB) has come under considerable pressure from the United States to revalue, while US investment bankers pursue an agenda of greater financial liberalisation, looking to China's fast-growing economy as a potential goldmine for their financial services.

Identifying China as a major cause of global imbalances and instabilities, in aggressive pursuit of its self-interest at the rest of the world's expense, the 2006 NSS in effect seeks to scapegoat China for the United States' own economic failure. As this chapter sets out to show, China's development is indeed starting to challenge the dominance of finance and monopoly capital, to undermine the US dollar-based hegemony through its own independent management of its exchange rate, and to weaken the grip of the developed countries over the developing world in its efforts to promote South–South cooperation. But while the US drive for global economic hegemony is deeply destabilising, China's efforts to establish a more firmly based international economic system display novel approaches to trade, investment and international currency arrangements, making concrete moves towards a fair globalisation.

THE QUESTION OF THE SINO–US TRADE IMBALANCE

Protectionist interests in the United States constantly whip up fears of China as an economic threat. China is endlessly accused of being a 'currency manipulator' and an 'unfair trader', deliberately cheapening its labour through state intervention in markets. The charge that cheap Chinese labour is stealing US jobs is one that is exaggerated by the media and used by both political parties to generate support among US workers. Anti-China rhetoric in the US Congress is fuelling a spate of demands to slap tariffs on its imports and to haul its government before the WTO on charges of dumping, improper subsidies, piracy and copyright violations.

The particular focus of agitation is China's large surplus in trade with the United States, which according to Bush reached US$233 billion in 2006, although Chinese figures put this at more like US$170 billion.[3] The surplus has grown since China joined the WTO, not least as a result of increasing foreign investment in its export sectors. It is seen to be feeding the accumulation of China's huge foreign exchange reserves, which contrast sharply with the United States' own unprecedented deficits. By the first half of 2007, China's forex reserves had topped US$1,330 billion, equal to approximately 50 per cent of its GDP.[4]

However, China is seen not just as competing but cheating in trade, with an undervalued currency subsidising its exports which can then flood US markets while the outsourcing of jobs speeds up. According to some US claims, the RMB has been running at 40 per cent below its true rate.[5] What inflames the situation further is that China uses a substantial portion of its reserves to buy US Treasury bonds.[6] US Sinophobes claim that China is preventing dollar devaluation to artificially hold up US demand for its exports,[7] and fear that, as these purchases hold down Treasury bond yields, China can influence US interest rates, so eroding US sovereignty over its own monetary policy.

Calls by the United States for China to revalue its currency have been growing since 2002. However, the case regarding the bilateral trade imbalance is overstated. China is not the only US trading partner to accumulate large trade surpluses: other countries in East Asia, the Middle East and Europe also do so. China's share has hovered at about a fifth of the total US merchandise deficit since 1995.[8] Even by US figures, China's exports to the United States, at least up to 2004, had not reached 5 per cent of total US imports, far less than Europe's exports to the United States.[9] It seems unfair to say the least for the United States to pick on China.

The figures for the US trade deficit with China are exaggerated by counting the whole value of exports, but much of the growth in the latter's exports is in low-cost assembly products which have high import content with little added value. The United States meanwhile runs a large surplus of trade with China in services. Furthermore China's total surplus in its overall trade is much smaller than its surplus with the United States.[10] With its demand for imported raw materials and manufactured inputs rising, China's economy is particularly vulnerable to increases in oil and other primary commodity prices. Its surplus could easily disappear if these prices were to continue to rise.

The trade imbalance is hardly helped by the fact that the United States maintains a 7,000-page list of commodities and hi-tech products whose export to China is restricted because of the supposed risk that these might be diverted to military use. Germany, which sees China as an important destination for its manufactured exports, on the other hand enjoys a balance in its China trade.

US trade deficits could also be offset by capital inflows from China, but here again the US government has put up barriers. In 2005 anti-China rhetoric fuelled a sustained campaign forcing the Chinese state-controlled oil company, CNOOC, to drop its US$18.5 billion bid for the US company Unocal. The bid was considered a threat to US national security, but this argument hardly held water given that Unocal provided a mere 1 per cent of the US total consumption of oil and gas.[11] Then again in 2006, following the Lenovo takeover of IBM's PC division, the US State department decided to limit use of Lenovo PCs on security grounds.[12]

Such barriers have enhanced China's accumulation of foreign exchange reserves, which have increased against a background of soaring currency reserves around the world. China's reserves, now the largest in the world, only surpassed Japan's in 2006. However, Japan escapes criticism even as the yen has declined against the dollar, while India, Indonesia and Korea all have considerable reserves which they also use to buy US assets and Treasury bonds.

Countries generally hold reserves as a guard against debt crisis or inflation caused by speculation. These tend to be held in dollars because, as the international currency, it can easily be liquidised in an emergency. The particular build-up of forex by Asian countries is in part a reaction to the financial crisis of 1997, reflecting fears of speculation and a lack of faith in the IMF. In China's case, the maintenance of substantial reserves would seem to be a particularly wise precaution, given the warnings by Western economists of the risks of WTO-induced macro-economic shock after 2001 to its banking system.[13]

The US government claims that since China's industries are subsidised through 'soft' loans from the state-owned banks, it is not playing by market rules. The US refusal to recognise China as a 'market economy' fuels protectionist demands for WTO rulings to be brought against it. Yet China has made itself one of the most open markets in the world. It is more liberalised than both Russia, which was accepted by the United States and the European Union as a market economy in 2002, and India, whose claim is also supported by the United States. When it criticises the Chinese government for creating political obstacles to free trade and investment, the United States itself is practising double standards: through its own subsidised agriculture, for example, the United States is among the world's worst offenders in dumping cheap exports on others while protecting its own markets. According to a report from Oxfam (Hong Kong), China lost an estimated 720,000 jobs in 2005 as a result of the increase in imports of subsidised cotton from the United States.[14]

Contrary to protectionist beliefs, the United States has benefited enormously from China trade. According to the recent admission of the US trade representative herself, US exports to China increased by 190 per cent after 2001 when China removed numerous tariff and non-tariff barriers.[15] China now is close to overtaking Japan as the third largest export market for US goods. Inexpensive and generally good-quality Chinese imports to the United States have saved US$600 billion for consumers, who have more to spend on services and housing, creating jobs in the retail sector and beyond.

China's export growth at any rate is attributable more to rising productivity than dumping by excess-capacity industries at cutthroat prices.[16] The loss of jobs in industrialised countries cannot so easily be attributed to Chinese cheap labour. According to Will Hutton, citing the US Bureau of Labor's survey of mass layoffs, of the 884,000 jobs lost in the United States in 2005 only 12,030 went overseas, with two-thirds of these going to China and Mexico.[17] The United States easily remains the top manufacturing nation, producing almost a quarter of global output, yet is convinced that it is the loser to China in globalisation.

The fact that China is not the only country to run a trade surplus with the United States strongly suggests that the asymmetry in trade relations is a symptom of a far wider problem of global imbalance. China's trade surplus with the United States actually has little to do with the exchange rate: what underlies it is the internationalisation of production and the conditions of monopoly capital.

The Sino–US trade imbalance has arisen as the Chinese economy has inserted itself into the global and regional division of labour, and is a phenomenon that is partly owned and orchestrated by Western business, as foreign investors have moved in to use China as a production base. In other words, US deficits with China are, in considerable part, triggered by US investment. Big corporations such as Ford and General Motors source key parts from China, while Wal-Mart imports around US$20 billion of goods from China a year.[18] As Bo Xilai, then China's commerce minister, pointed out, once the profits generated by such companies are taken into account together with their sales revenues in China, bilateral economic relations are relatively balanced.[19]

Particularly since China's WTO accession in 2001, enterprises from Japan, South Korea, Taiwan and South-East Asia have been relocating the production of their labour-intensive US exports – clothing, toys, footwear – to China, and as China's trade surplus has risen, the US deficit with the rest of Asia has fallen. The US trade deficit with China is in effect largely a disguised deficit with the region as a whole.[20]

Although China runs a trade surplus with the United States and the European Union,[21] its actual position within the global economy as a developing country is perhaps better demonstrated by the fact that about 70 per cent of its exports to the United States, Japan and the European Union are low-profit, low value-added labour-intensive goods, while 80 per cent of its imports are capital intensive.[22] The question of the Sino–US trade imbalance therefore needs to be set in the wider context of an international division of labour structured by the global capitalist economy and its uneven development, rooted in the historical legacy of colonialism and reinforced since by the monopoly practices of multinational corporation (MNCs).

The problem of the US deficit is less about unfair Chinese competition and more about the fact that the United States consumes more than it saves. The import of cheap goods that are produced overseas is the result of the export of capital. Capital export, which from the Leninist perspective provides the basis of imperialism as an economic system, is driven by the need to offset falling rates of profit created by the capitalist tendency of over-investment and over-production. The United States seeks to open the rest of the world ever wider to investment so that its corporations can reap vast profits overseas to compensate for falling profits in the domestic economy. Cheap imports help to hold down wage pressures at home and ease recessionary downturns. At the same time, domestic demand is expanded to support the economy's addiction to capital export and the US deficit in trade is the result.

The deficit in turn is sustained by the inflow of funds from US trading partners who seek to hold the dollar as a reserve currency. Dollar primacy, as Gowan notes,[23] has allowed the United States to manipulate its exchange rate and enhance the competitive edge of its corporations, passing on the burden of economic adjustment to others.

In 1985, the United States used protectionist pressures to force the Japanese government to revalue its currency under the Plaza Accord. The value of the yen jumped by 51 per cent against the dollar over just two years.[24] This triggered a massive inflow of overseas capital, jacking up house prices and the stock market. The bursting of the bubble wrecked Japan's financial stability and it fell into a prolonged period of stagnation throughout the 1990s.

The United States is now placing China under similar pressure to substantially revalue its currency as a means of reducing the trade imbalance, benefiting the competitiveness of its own corporations while also cutting the cost of its debt. However, since the problem is rooted in the structural inequalities of global monopoly capitalist relations, resolving the situation will take some time: a change in China's exchange rate would make little difference.[25]

THE UNITED STATES AND CHINA: MUTUAL HOSTAGES?

The Sino–US economic relationship has its advantages for both sides. Apart from the benefits to its consumers and businesses as well as in job creation, for example in the retail and service sectors, the United States receives, through the Chinese purchase of its Treasury bonds, the additional reward of cheap loans to finance its current account and so can keep its interest rates low. This encourages consumption which benefits China's exports, and although the purchase of low-yield US bonds is hardly a lucrative proposition, for China, jobs are more important than maximising returns. Meanwhile, although the US motive for developing economic and trade ties with China is to help itself, as has already been argued these ties have also helped China, spurring its economic prosperity and technological advancement.[26]

However, this relationship of interdependence might equally be described as one of mutual hostage.[27] China's growth has been heavily dependent on US markets to absorb its exports. At the same time, the United States is equally dependent on China, along with other Asian governments, to finance its deficits. If China were to stop buying US debt, interest rates would rise, causing problems for the US economy. Indeed, in the event of a trade war, a political dispute over Taiwan, or a banking or financial crisis in

China, if its government decided to sell off its substantial dollar holdings rapidly, this could set off a chain reaction among other holders to dump their dollars, send US interest rates soaring, and in turn cause the economy to crash.

On the other hand, Sinophobes have a tendency to hugely exaggerate China's hold over the US economy. Warning against such views, analysts such as Breslin point out that a crash in the United States would have an equally devastating impact on China's economic growth.[28] Not only would the value of its dollar reserves collapse but the loss of US markets would feed through into factory closures, causing massive unemployment and recession. If Japan and South Korea as US allies were also to be involved in a conflict, the United States could close more than one-third of China's trade outlets and cut off the vital supply lines bringing in components to be assembled into finished products.[29]

As Breslin sees it, China then has no desire to halt US growth which helps to drive its own domestic development. Stiglitz on the other hand argues that the 'mutual hostage' nature of this US–China relationship is weighted in China's favour since, rather than export its goods to the United States 'in return for paper of diminishing value to fund tax cuts for the rich', China could use its reserves to increase its own consumption by lending them to its own people or use them to finance its own investment.[30]

But regardless of who has the upper hand, the economies of China and the United States are so interconnected that open conflict would clearly be catastrophic for both. The important point to recognise is that the United States is now in a far weaker position than it was at the time of the Plaza Accord in 1985 and cannot easily pass on the costs of economic adjustment to others. US growth is heavily based on debt and deficit such that a sharp rise in interest rates could cause the economy to collapse. While the sheer size of its deficits makes the US economy far more dependent on the inflow of funds to keep it afloat, it can no longer take these inflows for granted. China on several occasions over the last two or three years has made it clear that it will not keep underwriting US debt levels.

However, for China to diversify its reserve holdings is not so easily done given their size. A reduction in holdings of US bonds in favour of European assets would not only weaken the US dollar but also cause an unwelcome appreciation of the euro.[31] Nevertheless, China's warnings over its dollar holdings are designed to have some impact on US behaviour to encourage debt reductions and interest rate rises.[32]

In other words, even if the asymmetry of the relationship is weighted against it, China, by deliberately making itself indispensable in Asian production networks, has entered further into the loop of global imbalances, to gain bargaining power. If not through the threat of a sudden offloading of US assets which would spell disaster for itself, China can nevertheless exert some pressure on the United States through a managed reduction of its dollar holdings and the redirection of its capital flows.

MANAGING THE RENMINBI

Faced with US threats of trade wars, the Chinese government has taken an approach of 'making some concessions, changing some behaviour but resisting what in Chinese eyes are excessive demands', in order to defuse tensions, keep relations with the United States stable and avoid any deterioration in the international economic environment which would hinder its own development.[33]

In July 2005, the Chinese government made the first move to undo the deadlock by agreeing to a loosening of the exchange rate mechanism to allow the RMB to fluctuate within a narrow band. Over the next two years, the RMB gradually moved upwards in relation to the dollar by roughly 7 per cent.

While a stronger RMB would see benefits accruing to China's middle classes, who would enjoy imports of luxury goods, a large upward movement of the currency could be very damaging for the weaker sections of Chinese society that have benefited least from the country's rapid growth. The labour-intensive exporting sectors, where margins are low, could see wage reductions and layoffs, and small farmers too could be damaged, facing increasing exposure to the even cheaper subsidised agricultural exports from the United States.

So, as leading economist Fan Gang puts it, while China recognises that it 'has to step up its responsibility to address global currency imbalances', at the same time, the government has resisted a steeper rise since it 'also has to consider the plight of its rural poor'.[34]

A sharp RMB hike would at any rate produce a 'lose–lose' scenario. Since most of China's exports to the United States are goods used regularly by the majority of ordinary US citizens, a rapid currency appreciation would affect their daily lives, especially hitting the less well-off who otherwise benefit from cheap essentials such as clothing and shoes from China. Jobs would be lost in the retail sector. US companies would also lose returns on their investment in China as exports fell and inflation in the United States would rise, forcing interest rates upwards, which could lead to a painful contraction of the economy.

As an alternative to further currency appreciation, the Chinese government has looked for other 'win–win' measures to reduce its US trade surplus. Visits by high-level Chinese officials and leaders to the United States have become occasions for billion-dollar spending sprees, which help to boost US industries and jobs, as do measures to cut tariffs and lower taxes on a certain number of imports from the United States. In particular, the

Chinese government has proposed to gradually reduce rebates to exporters of polluting and energy-inefficient products.[35]

The 'managed float' of the RMB has allowed the government to adjust China's export profile towards higher value-added products while monitoring the effects of revaluation on wages and employment, and since July 2005 exports have continued to grow fast as a result of increases in productivity. Nevertheless, the adjustments made to avoid trade frictions have been at no small cost to Chinese workers, and it might reasonably be expected that the United States should make some corresponding move to persuade its citizens to save more by raising interest rates and ending tax giveaways to the rich.

CHINA VERSUS THE US INVESTMENT BANKERS

From the end of 2005, the US government began to pursue a 'softer line' for China to reduce exports by increasing domestic consumption. This approach, while still one-sidedly holding China responsible for the trade problem, nevertheless corresponds with the new direction of the government itself in seeking a new growth mode, increasing the proportion of consumption relative to investment in GDP, while using capital more efficiently to improve the quality of growth. However, deep divergences remain between the US and Chinese governments on how China's domestic consumption should be increased.

The US treasury secretary, Hank Paulson, representing the interests of the US investment bankers, has been pushing for China to open its financial markets in banking, insurance and brokerage more widely. The perspective here focuses on China's high rates of savings which, it is argued, occur because capital markets are not liberalised enough for these funds to be used to finance consumption and efficient investment.[36] Instead, China's policies of low interest rates and capital controls are causing overheating as the over-supply of capital leads to problems of over-investment and over-production. This builds up inflationary pressures and puts the banking sector in danger by aggravating the problem of non-performing loans while also feeding into asset price and property bubbles. Thus, US analysts warn, China risks repeating Japan's experience of 'bubble', bust and stagnation.

Meanwhile, these analysts continue, as low domestic consumption depresses demand for imports, Chinese companies are forced to look abroad for markets while at the same time the Chinese government, with excess funds to lend, releases liquidity onto global markets by buying US bonds in order to finance US purchases of Chinese exports. Instead of intervening especially in capital markets, generating excess liquidity which then feeds into the problems of the US trade deficit and global imbalance, what the Chinese government should be doing, these US advisors maintain, is improving financial services. The Chinese banking sector, in particular, in which Western banks have taken shares, should be increasing the issuance of credit cards as a means to push up consumption as well as increasing lending to private entrepreneurs.[37]

Chinese analysts on the other hand, while not denying that excessive savings, low consumption and inadequate banking and financial services are problems for their economy, also point to the excessive consumption, low savings and over-dependence on finance of the United States.

From a critical perspective, the main cause of excess liquidity in global markets is in fact the over-issuance of dollars as the United States, consuming more than it produces, seeks to cover its trade deficit by printing dollars. This it does with impunity – that is, without the corresponding contraction in its own economy – since the dollar, as the main international currency, is always in demand. As Nordhaug explains, the oversupply of dollars or 'hot money' generally ends up in the reserves of its trading partners, who are left to mop up the excess liquidity through a process of 'sterilisation', whereby governments buy dollars coming into their country with local currency and then drain the local funds out of the system by selling central bank bills. This causes reserves to soar along with the local money supply, multiplying credit creation.[38] It is the US policy of printing dollars then that generates conditions of over-investment in the global economy.

'Hot money' is a very volatile form of finance and is highly sensitive to changes in the global economy. As Mei Xinyu points out, emerging markets in developing countries are made particularly susceptible to boom and bust cycles since Western investors regard investment in these economies as 'marginal', supplementing low domestic profits, and park their idle funds temporarily, only to reverse the flows with catastrophic consequences when global economic conditions change.[39] On the other hand, as Gowan has argued, the US economy, and especially its financial services sector, has been able to benefit from these instabilities and crises.

For China to follow US advice to reduce savings and liberalise the financial sector at a faster rate would expose its economy to the mercy of 'boom and bust' speculative flows, destroying its banking system and delivering its economic future to US financiers. Instead China, while encouraging the inflow of foreign investment, has 'maintained a guard at its financial door' to restrict its outflow, accumulating foreign exchange as a result.

Since 2001, as Ba Shusong notes, the United States has been pursuing a slack fiscal policy and low interest rates to minimise the negative economic impact first of the burst of the hi-tech bubble and then of 9/11. Instead of taking responsibility for its dominant reserve currency status, the United States has simply printed dollars, acting like a 'spoiled child' expecting developing countries like China to assume the consequences of the economic imbalances.[40] Not only do the US trading partners end up accumulating staggering reserves in a continually declining 'junk currency', which they have to keep buying in order to reduce losses, they also risk stock and property market bubbles as, with the attractiveness of the dollar weakening, 'hot money' is on the move.[41] Indeed, as Justin Yifu Lin argues, speculative flows into China have been encouraged by the US hype about RMB revaluation, contributing significantly to the trade surplus, since, despite China's capital controls, some businesses have been able to sneak 'hot money' in by exaggerating their export value while under-reporting import value in order to increase their foreign currency reserves so as to profit from an RMB appreciation.[42]

However, although China is faced in many ways with a situation similar to that experienced by Japan in the 1980s and 1990s, it is managing the situation very differently. By resisting US pressures and maintaining a stance of gradual and moderate currency appreciation, China is keeping the exchange rate subservient to the aims of economic growth and job creation. With 300 million rural labourers still needing to be transferred to non-farming sectors, the dangers of undermining labour-intensive export industries through RMB revaluation are seen as greater than managing the problems of 'sterilisation' – foreign exchange inflows, credit creation, and stock market and property bubbles. In other words, in a trade-off between financial and social stability, the choice has definitely been with the latter.

This measured and controlled approach to currency appreciation limits the excessive movements of 'hot money'. While floating the RMB against an undisclosed basket of currencies to avoid exchange rate instabilities and keep speculators off balance, the government is also limiting currency convertibility to financial purposes not related to trade or direct investment to make it difficult for hedge funds to manoeuvre in its financial market.[43]

Some limited outflow of capital is being allowed to ease the build-up of reserves, and curbs on foreign investment made by Chinese investors are being relaxed to encourage the 'go global' strategy. However, unlike Japan which in effect exported its problems of over-investment and instability by recycling its trade surplus with the United States into investment in the rest of the Asian region, thereby fuelling the financial crisis, China is absorbing most of the US-generated excess liquidity itself.

Indeed, China's leaders have affirmed the positive benefits in accumulating large reserves which have helped to improve its overall national strength.[44] Not only do these increase the economy's ability to fend off risk, but surplus foreign exchange has been used successfully to recapitalise the big state-owned banks, helping to resolve the bad loans problem, attract foreign partners and support stock exchange listings. The government has also started to use its surplus reserves to create stabilisation funds or reserves of oil and other key primary commodities, to buy hi-tech equipment to improve its environmental protection, modernise its state-owned enterprises

(SOEs) and upgrade its processing trade, and expand imports to help reduce the trade surplus.[45]

At the same time, and again unlike Japan at its time of crisis, China has begun to reform its financial systems. In fact, China has every intention of developing its own financial services to become a leading financial centre within the East Asian region. As it reforms its financial mechanisms, regulatory institutions in banking and finance are being given wide-ranging powers to keep a close vigil on how the sector functions. Sen argues then that:

> The success [China has] achieved so far in taming financial flows and gearing them in the direction of the real economy indicates the exemplary ability of the state to keep control of speculative advances in the era of financial globalization.[46]

Chinese analysts, while seeing Japan's economic problems as stemming from its willingness to accede to US pressure on its exchange rate, also recognise that Japan made its own errors in macroeconomic management, which compounded the situation.[47] China aims to address its own problems of high savings and over-dependence of economic growth on exports by expanding domestic demand gradually.

In this its approach is radically different from that of Paulson. As Chinese analysts explain, the real reason that Chinese people save rather than consume is not because of the poor performance of the financial sector – the problem is the yawning income gap and the absence of a social security net.[48] The US agenda for rapid financial liberalisation would not resolve this but would rather fuel the problem of inequality since US financial institutions are only interested in 'skimming off the cream', focusing on the more lucrative business sector as well as gaining access into China's credit card market to increase middle-class consumption and boost demand for US imports.[49]

On the contrary, China's approach to reducing savings and developing the domestic market puts government spending first to improve the conditions of the farmers and ordinary workers, unleashing their spending power by reducing poverty, increasing social security funds, recapitalising the Agricultural Bank of China which lends to farmers, funding infrastructural investment to further open China's poorer western provinces as well as investing in health and education.[50]

Paulson's recommendations of financial market liberalisation carry enormous risks, and China's agenda is to move at a rather slower pace. Nevertheless, from the Chinese viewpoint, his dialogue approach is preferable to threats of trade wars. The opening of a 'Strategic Economic Dialogue' towards the end of 2006 has been seen as an opportunity to defuse tensions and develop a long-term and strategic focus in Sino–US economic relations, making room to address a wider range of common interests such as energy and the environment while not allowing the United States to dictate the agenda.[51] Indeed, in the light of the subprime crisis, China's approach to financial reform is even more cautious.

However, the continuing fall of the dollar means China is losing billions of dollars on its reserves, at least on paper, and looking for ways to diversify their use, the government decided in 2007 to create a sovereign wealth fund, the China Investment Corporation, to seek better returns through investment overseas.[52] Sterilisation is becoming more difficult to manage and with food prices rising, curbing inflation has become a higher government priority. Since early 2008, in accordance with its own needs, the government has allowed the RMB to rise more rapidly, reaching about 15 per cent against the dollar since mid-2005.[53] At the same time, food subsidies have increased for the poor to alleviate any negative fallout. As Zhou Xiaochuan, then governor of the People's Bank of China, made clear, domestic factors remain more important for the management of the economy than the dollar.[54]

REFORMING THE GLOBAL ECONOMIC ARCHITECTURE

With the United States and China at odds over the causes of global financial instability – the deliberate misalignment of exchange rates or US profligacy – and the global economy verging on crisis, pressures to reform the global financial and economic architecture away from dollar dependency have been rising, with widening debate over the role and structure of the G7 and the IMF as well as over the WTO's Doha development round.

The IMF and G7

The Bush administration has been lobbying the G7 and IMF for support to back the message that China's artificially weak currency is damaging to the global economy. But although in 2004, US treasury secretary John Snow was threatening to hold China's 'feet to the fire' over its RMB policy,[55] the United States has struggled in its efforts to persuade other countries that the RMB is massively out of line and to secure sufficient multilateral pressure on China. The concern is rather that a rapid revaluation of the RMB would be widely destabilising.[56] The United Nations has been the most outspoken against blaming China for what is in fact a global problem.[57]

The IMF and G7 both look increasingly irrelevant to the task of solving the world's economic problems as they were set up to do.[58] Asian economies have virtually delinked from the IMF, making their own arrangements to insure against financial instability, while Latin American countries have also sought to cut ties with the IMF by paying back loans ahead of schedule.

Both the IMF and G7 have a serious problem of legitimacy since developing countries have very little say in their decisions. Belgium, for example, has more voting power in the IMF than China or India.

The G7 made a breakthrough of sorts in 2004 when it extended its dialogue to include the big developing countries, widening its agenda to cover energy security and the future of Africa. However, their denomination as 'outreach' countries clearly indicates their marginality to what are regarded as the main agendas. The character of the organisation as a Western-dominated and discriminatory great-power club appears to have changed little.

The IMF has also reached agreement to increase the voting power for East Asian countries, including China, though only by a small amount. This is little more than tinkering with the system since the US power to veto decisions remains untouched. China, welcoming the move, stated that 'more needs to be done to increase the representation of developing countries especially Africa'.[59]

The underlying difficulty concerns what the role of the IMF should be. In line with its 2006 NSS strategy, the United States has called for the organisation to play a more rigorous role in monitoring exchange rate policies, undoubtedly aiming at putting China in the hot seat over the RMB. But there has been much criticism that an aggressive pursuit of a policy of global flexible market-determined exchange rates would lead to 'exchange rate wars'. Others favour negotiated exchange rate coordination through an international agreement to include China, on which interventions by central banks in currency markets to achieve balance could be based.[60]

The Chinese government itself calls for increased supervision by the IMF of member states issuing 'major reserve currencies that play a pivotal role in the global systemic stability'.[61] From the Chinese perspective, as Fan Gang puts it:

> it seems that no matter how large the US fiscal deficits, no matter how loose the monetary policies and how much the excessive liquidity provided are, the US is not likely to run into financial crisis that other countries have faced. With the dollar as the global reserve currency, the US is able to spread its financial risks. They do not see the deficits as their problem.[62]

Since the United States is no longer a stable anchor in the global financial system, nor is it likely to become one, he suggests it is time to look for an alternative that is independent of the interests of any particular country.[63]

Clearly, then, the IMF and G7 are both in a dilemma: while they are becoming increasingly ineffective without the full participation of China, China will not join simply on their terms.

The WTO and FTAs

The shift of power underway in the global economy from the developed to the developing world has been most evident with the emergence at the WTO meeting at Cancun in 2003 of the G20 group of larger developing countries. Headed by Brazil, India and South Africa, the G20's cohesion upset the trade agenda of the United States and European Union by calling for a 'win–win' deal in which the developing South would only open its frontiers further to trade and financial flows from the North and agree to IPR protection, in return for the North opening its frontiers further to trade flows from the South, not least in textiles and agricultural products.

As a new member with its hands full in implementing its own accession commitments, China has been playing a relatively low-key role in the WTO, though coordinating closely with the G20 coalition in line with its 2001 Doha declaration that the 'developmental dimension' should be fully implemented into the multilateral trading system.[64] Given its growing trading power, China clearly looms large in the considerations. According to Martin Jacques, the difficulties in the Doha round very much reflect the rise of protectionist sentiment against China in the United States.[65]

In the same way that the United States used the North American Free Trade Agreement (NAFTA) to pressure the European Union in negotiations over the WTO Uruguay round in the early 1990s, so, in line with its 2006 NSS strategy, the United States is vigorously pursuing a WTO-plus agenda through a series of regional and bilateral FTAs, in what is clearly an attempt to counter the G20 and divide the developing world.

East Asia in particular has become a field of contending FTAs which have proliferated with the weakening of Asia-Pacific Economic Cooperation (APEC) after the Asian financial crisis. While Japan and South Korea are starting to pursue their own bilateral deals within the region, it is China, through the ASEAN+1 and ASEAN+3 processes, that has become particularly influential in shaping a new regional governance pattern for trade and investment geared towards development first. In contrast, new US bilateral and multilateral FTAs press ahead with unequal terms, including measures kicked out of the WTO negotiations by the G20 at Cancun, to give US institutions greater access into domestic markets for financial services. In the case of Singapore and Chile, the United States additionally insisted they renounce the use of capital controls. The treaty with Australia lengthens the time period for which patents are valid, to extend the monopoly privileges of US companies.[66] These FTAs are not simply an aggressive bid for new markets but aim to undermine the trend towards a China-centred East Asian Community. Linking economic integration and growth with strategic goals through the inclusion of terms covering cooperation on security,[67] the FTAs form an integral part of US efforts to embrace the region in its China encirclement strategy.

However US proposals for a WTO-plus multilateral Free Trade Area of the Asia-Pacific to counter ASEAN+3 have yet to succeed.[68]

WESTERN DOMINANCE UNDER CHALLENGE

While the ability of the United States to manipulate global multilateral economic institutions is evidently weakening, the dominance of developed countries and their corporations over the developing world is also under challenge. Patterns of trade and finance are starting to change as countries of the developing South emerge as more active global economic players, using new forms of cooperation to enhance their position.

According to a 2005 World Bank report, more than one-third of foreign direct investment (FDI) going to developing countries came from their peers. In addition South–South trade, as opposed to trade between industrialised and developing countries, accounted for 26 per cent of developing countries' total trade.[69] In this, China is a central player.

Since its accession to the WTO, China's lower tariffs and rising imports have helped boost trade with other developing countries, many of which are experiencing significant trade balances in their favour for the first time in decades. So far China's overall role in world trade is having a certain equalising effect since, while running a trade surplus with many developed countries, it is in deficit with many developing countries, as it sucks in imports of both primary commodities and processed goods. Thanks to increased demand from China, the value of exports by all developing countries rose by 25 per cent, bringing their share in world trade to 31 per cent in 2004, the highest since 1950.[70]

Since 2004, China has also taken major steps in its commitment to cooperation through large-scale investment in the developing world. From Latin America to Africa, countries are increasingly looking to China as a source of investment and a future business partner, as China seeks synergies in South–South cooperation.

In Latin America, the United States' own backyard, investment from China is expanding at a dizzying rate: in 2004, the year of President Hu Jintao's visits across the continent, over one-third of FDI into the region came from China.[71] This helps Latin American countries to reduce their dependence on US capital. For Chavez, China is a world power without 'imperialist airs', and the 2006 Sino–Venezuela trade agreement, a 'Great Wall' against US hegemonism.[72]

By funding infrastructure projects in other developing countries China is helping to boost trade so that they can lift themselves out of poverty. In addition, China has reduced or cancelled debts owed by 44 developing countries and has provided assistance to more than 110 countries for 2,000 projects.[73]

However, for many developing countries, the problem in developing their trade with China is that its low-cost production presents them with a considerable challenge. In the case of Africa in particular, the continent's weak industrial base makes it particularly vulnerable to a flood of cheap Chinese imports, and critics claim economic relations with China are replaying the old story of Africa's trade with Europe, namely that 'we sell them raw materials and they sell us manufactured goods', which could lead to an unfavourable trade imbalance.[74]

China has become Africa's third largest trade partner after the United States and France. However, its deals with African states are far from one-sided. Sub-Saharan African countries have been major beneficiaries of China's removal of tariffs on goods from least developed countries. The sourcing of cheaper products from Asia in general as well as from China, has also helped to turn African trade deficits into surpluses. Meanwhile, imports of cheap manufactured goods from China are much appreciated by African consumers, filling a 'development gap', despite complaints of quality, since it means they can now buy many goods they could not previously afford.[75]

The relationship with China gives African nations an opportunity to 'diversify risk' and hedge against unpredictable Western aid.[76] With regard to investment, the Chinese government and Chinese SOEs are more willing to face risks, extending loans and funds in difficult African markets which Western investors shun. In oil exploration and production, long-term packages with no strings attached are offered, which no Western countries are prepared to do.[77] The Central African Republic, devastated by years of civil war, ignored by the IMF and World Bank, for example, signed a cooperative agreement with China in 2006.[78] As a diplomat from Chad is quoted as saying, 'From now on, if the World Bank imposes too many conditions, N'Djamena will tell it that it has a ready alternative – Beijing.'[79]

Although China's investments have so far been concentrated heavily in the minerals and energy sectors, its interests are not restricted to raw materials extraction alone. Sino–African economic cooperation is shifting from trade to investment, technology and project contracting in areas long neglected by Western investors and aid agencies: agriculture, manufacturing, power generation and public projects closely related to people's lives as well as infrastructure.[80]

Over 30 African countries have benefited from China's debt cancellations to the tune of US$1.3 billion, and to encourage Chinese businesses to engage in joint ventures, the government has pledged to support investment in Africa with preferential loans. Investment credit is to be doubled to US$3 billion by 2009.[81] Chinese companies offer technical assistance and build highways and bridges, sports stadiums, schools and hospitals to ensure projects deliver clear benefits to locals, for example in helping to restore Angola's war-ravaged infrastructure. A proposed deal with Ghana includes discussion on the provision of finance for a dam.[82]

Certainly, Chinese investment has its negative sides. There have been reports of conflicts between African workers and Chinese employers that need to be addressed by African governments. China's poor level of environmental protection is also a cause for concern. Nevertheless, the jobs created offer a way out of poverty, holding prospects for the future, and African leaders have broadly welcomed China's expertise and financial assistance as a 'cooperation that results in our development'.[83]

As Yao Graham argues:

> Currently the Chinese embrace is nowhere near as stifling as the frameworks offered by the World Bank, IMF and their political masters in the industrialised world. For us in Africa the challenge is to ensure that as China's global power increases, its role in Africa does not become more and more like that we have experienced with the west.[84]

In other words, for Africa, China is a chance and a challenge rather than a threat.

Sino–African developments are based on the long-running strong collaborative strand in their relations established within the anti-imperialist framework of the Bandung conference. Today African, as well as Latin American, leaders view their growing economic relations with China as a useful counterweight to the United States and Europe. China's large-scale investment and trade deals are starting to break the stranglehold of international capital over the developing world.

Breaking the MNCs' Monopoly

With predictions that in a decade or two Chinese multinationals will be as 'pervasive and dominant as the United States, European and Japanese ones are today',[85] the global monopoly of Western-based MNCs is coming under challenge. A change in the pattern of monopoly capitalism has become evident in the oil industry in particular, where the influence of the world's traditional oil giants is on the wane as not only China's state-owned oil companies but those from Russia, Iran, Saudi Arabia, Venezuela and Brazil, which together control almost one-third of the world's oil and gas production and reserves, are emerging as the industry's new rule makers.[86]

South–South cooperation in cross-border collaborations between firms is particularly significant in breaking the grip of giant corporations of the developed countries. A 2006 Sino–Indian agreement on joint bidding for overseas energy assets drew worldwide attention as posing a significant challenge to the likes of BP and Shell. The initial collaboration in the purchase of a Colombian oil producer was seen as demonstrating that China and India were serious about cooperating, and as a sign of bigger joint deals to follow which could have a noticeable impact on the global energy market.[87]

These developments however are weakened by a lack of necessary know-how in refining and extraction technologies. The difference in knowledge levels is a fundamental cause of the global wealth gap. In order to close the gap, developing countries need to diversify into higher value-added activities in which they are not efficient. Instead, developed countries are making it more and more difficult for them to 'borrow' ideas and obtain technology in order to 'catch up', by unjustifiably extending the scope and heightening the degree of protection for IPR to an unprecedented level through the WTO TRIPS agreement, so extending the monopoly privileges enjoyed by their MNCs.[88]

China is again in the firing line here, frequently accused of counterfeiting and piracy to keep up a constant pressure for the implementation of IPR. US international business lobbies, undoubtedly exaggerating their losses through piracy, have demanded that the Chinese government be brought before the WTO to secure the stringent enforcement of copyright laws. Given that most Chinese consumers anyway could not afford the genuine version, this is hardly the most pressing issue in world trade,[89] yet it is one the US government is seriously pursuing.

Control over advanced technologies and scientific knowledge are key components of comprehensive national power (CNP), shaping the competition between developed countries and their ability to exploit the developing world. China's leaders recognise the question of IPR as one of the country's biggest challenges for the future. Technological collaboration with other developing countries is a vital part of the strategy to challenge the West's monopolisation of knowledge and find an alternative route for world economic development. Despite their weaker position in the global economy, some developing countries have become quite competitive in certain key areas of science and technology – China's space technology, India's IT and Brazil's rocket delivery technology – enhancing the scope for collaboration to give these countries leverage in dealing with Northern MNCs.[90]

TOWARDS A FAIR GLOBALISATION

China's agenda is for a fair globalisation, for the creation, through worldwide dialogue and cooperation, of a trading system that is 'public, fair, rational, transparent, open and nondiscriminatory' and of 'a stable and highly efficient financial environment conducive to global economic growth'.[91] To this end, China's leaders repeatedly urge the developed countries to 'give more' and not force the costs of adjustments on to others, to 'create a more favourable external environment for the economic growth of the developing countries' and 'assume increasing responsibility for preventing the negative effects of globalization and rendering the developing countries assistance in overcoming their difficulties'.[92]

For China, support for a fair globalisation defines the meaning of global responsibility, as is made clear in its statement on the Peaceful Development Road:

> The developed countries should shoulder greater responsibility for a universal, coordinated and balanced development of the world, while developing countries should make full use of their own advantages to achieve development.[93]

Tackling the monopolisation of knowledge also stands high on the agenda for a fair globalisation. Here China's view is that the smooth transfer of technology to developing countries through close cooperation with developed countries is essential to boost world development and achieve the goals of poverty reduction, sustainable development through the rational use of natural resources, and the fair and equal distribution of wealth between nations.[94] In collaborating with Western companies, China itself has favoured making agreements on royalty payments conditional on technology transfer.[95]

China's FTA agreement with ASEAN, in giving more room for poorer countries to develop, may come to serve as a model for wider multilateral agreements on rules-based trade and investment. In addition to this, China is beginning to demonstrate some further novel approaches in its own practices and proposals regarding aid, trade and investment as well as in relation to the international monetary system as it tackles the problems of monopoly, instability and inequality in the global economy.

New Approaches in Finance

As Sen has argued, China's own successful development based on a 'guided financial market' to ensure stability has been quite different from a situation where growth has been finance-led and where speculation dominates financial flows.[96] Now, as it becomes involved in development projects beyond its borders, China is demonstrating an approach to development finance which also contrasts with the West's prioritisation of 'debt sustainability'.

China's high-profile development assistance to Africa has met with widespread complaints in the West, primarily emanating from the United States, claiming that these loans are being extended irresponsibly and only add to the debt burden of the poorest developing countries. As Africa's main aid donors, OECD countries have gained unrivalled leverage over many governments to promote their own model of development, imposing, for example, stricter criteria for debt management as a condition of their write-off of debt. However, the World Bank reported recently that South–South financial flows had 'the potential of changing the landscape of overseas development assistance'.[97] What this means was made clear when Donald Kaberuka, president of the African Development Bank, which met in Beijing in 2007, received assurance from Chinese officials that China was 'alert to the dangers' but took a distinctive longer-term approach to the financing of development: debt sustainability was important but 'development sustainability is what we are after'.[98]

Reform of the international monetary system is clearly a necessary condition for a fair globalisation as its current subordination to the needs of the US domestic economy through the maintenance of dollar primacy comes at the expense of global economic stability.

China, on the other hand, has taken a responsible approach for example in diversifying its reserves by reducing new purchases of US Treasury bonds rather than dumping dollars, to avoid a global crash. It has also aimed to maintain currency stability both through the Asian financial crisis and through the current pressures from the United States to revalue, playing an increasingly important role as financial stabiliser in the East Asian region in what is seen by some as a 'second Bretton Woods system' of managed exchange rates in Asia.[99]

The anchoring role of the RMB undoubtedly helped here to underpin the currency swap arrangements agreed in the ASEAN+3 Chiang Mai Initiative of May 2000. Aiming to limit the scope for speculative flows of 'hot money', this agreement on exchanging reserves embodies a currency arrangement which does not privilege any one of its participants. Instead countries hold one another's currencies as reserves, allowing each other access to credit when needed. For Stiglitz, the initiative offers, at least in embryonic form, an alternative to the existing self-defeating international reserve system based on the dollar.[100] If it were to develop more fully as a form of reserve holding, it would potentially divert the financial flows from East Asia to the United States, so depriving the United States of cheap loans to ease its deficits and creating further pressures for reform of the international financial architecture. As a form of cooperative mutual insurance, the initiative potentially offers a different kind of financial model of mutual risk resistance and risk-sharing to tame the instability of globalising markets. Meanwhile, China's newly created sovereign wealth fund will, as a long term investor, also serve as a force for stability in global markets.

New Approaches to Trade

While China's exports are heavily import-dependent and their growth generates demand in exports from others, stimulating world trade, they are also a source of trade frictions with numbers of other countries. With the growing export sector serving as a crucial driver of employment for China, elements of disposing of unsold products below cost and aggressively seeking market share are evident in its trade drive.

To halt the dangers of a 'race to the bottom', China's aim is to transform its trade pattern by shifting towards higher-value industrial and agricultural processed goods at the upper end of R&D and customer services. However, in this way China will come to pose an increasing challenge to the United States, European Union and Japan. Developed and developing countries alike have expressed concern over the impact of China trade on local labour markets and the corrosive effects of cheaper Chinese imports on their own production capacity.

The stated goal of the Chinese government is for economic relations with other countries to produce balanced benefits: it has no particular aim to run a trade surplus. Its interest is in improving the international trade environment as a whole. Where trade conflicts do arise, China is committed to resolving these through 'dialogue on an equal footing',[101] to create a system of fair trading based on coordination for a new international economic order.

This new approach was demonstrated when frictions came to a head with the expiry of the Multi-Fibre Agreement (MFA) quota system on textiles in early 2005. There was widespread panic that China was going to wipe out the textile industry throughout the world as investors prepared to switch to China as an export platform for Western markets. The 'threat', however, in large part reflected the failure of countries to adapt and invest in their own industries since the removal of the MFA had ten years' advance warning.

The lifting of the MFA had a particularly adverse effect on smaller African countries which have lost protected markets in the United States and European Union. It was largely to mitigate their situation that the Chinese government granted zero tariffs and preferential treatment to the 26 least developed countries in Africa and Asia.[102] The Chinese government also set out to help industries in developing countries that export textiles by forming joint ventures and liberalising its own imports of clothing and textiles so as to share the benefits of the freer trade.[103]

In most cases, China has agreed to temporary restrictions on some of its own textile and clothing exports, and in this lie the seeds of a completely novel approach, since these limits on exports aim to allow the countries concerned a window of opportunity to turn around the problems of job loss and trade imbalance. Linked to its trade agreement with China, South Africa, for example, proposed to develop a full industrial strategy to modernise its own industry, plans in which its trade unions are very much involved.[104]

China's new approach to coordinated trade was revealed most clearly in its response to the 'shoe wars' and 'bra wars' launched by the European Union. From China's perspective, since some 70 per cent of the growth in its textile exports after the lifting of the quota system was from foreign-funded firms, the US and EU protectionist responses were seeking a double benefit for their own companies, first, in using China's low cost labour, then second, setting up barriers to imports so as to flood China's, and other countries' markets instead.[105] Trade protectionism, the Chinese government argued, would nevertheless lead to a lose–lose scenario, not only affecting hundreds of manufacturers in China and risking the jobs of millions of China's poorer workers but also damaging US cotton growers and exporters, as well as retailers and consumers in the United States and European Union, not to mention those companies exporting textile machinery and dyestuffs as well as outsourcing to China.

While making clear that it regarded anti-dumping measures as unfair, the Chinese government was prepared, in order to avoid trade frictions, to reduce exports by limiting investment in certain categories of textiles and garments, and also to regulate the disorderly expansion of its industry. These measures would also produce a win for China for while the majority of foreign-funded firms operated at the low-value end of production, with very small profits, and were of limited benefit to China, quota restrictions would drive producers to upgrade, helping to further government goals to ease competition at the low end by improving quality and standards and stepping up innovation and R&D.

On this basis, what the Chinese government proposed was in effect the coordination of a dual adjustment process. China itself, to reduce its own overwhelming reliance on low-value-added production, would coordinate the regulation of cut-throat competition at the lower end with a rise in the volume of high-end products, and this adjustment could itself be coordinated to produce a new mix of exports more complementary with the European Union, if in their turn the EU countries invested in improved competitiveness rather than protecting their declining textile sectors.[106]

Noting that both China and the European Union face problems of a big labour surplus and excessive production capacity, the idea was to open a new area for cooperation, with each seeking to use the other as an outlet for excessive capacity. In this way, trade partners would create buffer zones for each other in order to assist in industrial restructuring.

To facilitate this coordinated restructuring, China also proposed the creation of a mechanism to settle problems through negotiation and cooperation, in which both sides exchange opinions over any new issues arising in trade and investment and 'clarify each side's redline in the international division of labour and market openness'.[107] Such a mechanism would strengthen the settlement of disputes by establishing channels of dialogue and consultation between Chinese trade and business groups and trade unions, and their trading partner counterparts. This would help to eradicate differences and relieve pressures from domestic interest groups and ease worries over the

'China threat' among workers in these countries. Each side would then become aware of the others' difficulties and a deal could be negotiated.

China's approach to cooperative trade agreements based on win–win exchange points to an altogether different kind of global trading system. Neither protectionism nor a perfectly free trade, it seeks a negotiated order, facilitated by trade dialogue to coordinate a restructuring of the unequal world economic order towards a more equitable international division of labour. In place of the imperialist approach that has prevailed in the world economy for centuries, in which developed countries have used the developing world as a dumping ground for their excess production, what China proposes instead is that as its economy rises, trading partners supplement each other's markets and production in a fair globalisation based on fair trade and fair competition.

CONCLUSION

The United States and China are engaged in a 'smokeless war' over the direction of the global economy, the question of global imbalance and instability, and the nature of an international rules-based system based on dollar primacy or geared towards development.

China's response to moderate its revaluation stands in marked contrast to the compliance of both Germany and Japan in the 1980s when they allowed their own currencies to appreciate rapidly to suit the needs of the US economy but at the expense of their own economic growth. While withstanding the pressures from the exercise of dollar hegemony, China's initiatives also frustrate US efforts across a range of unequal policies to offload its economic problems on to other countries. At the same time, in response to the problem of its trade surplus with the United States and other developed countries, the Chinese government seeks to open new opportunities, by for example promoting 'green textiles' manufactured using energy-saving and environmentally friendly techniques to create a different kind of trade pattern, stepping up its own innovation and R&D, and increasing imports of advanced and new technologies to improve technical standards as well as increasing imports from developing countries, especially those least developed.[108]

While the system of dollar primacy underpins the monopoly position of the developed countries and their corporations and at the same time allows the United States to subordinate international monetary conditions to its own domestic requirements, creating global imbalances and instabilities, as China sees it, the situation overall is a reflection of the world's uneven development. This unevenness can only be resolved gradually over the longer term. In seeking a more balanced world development pattern, China is, by joining its own production systems to global production chains, placing itself strategically at the core of global restructuring in order to promote a coordination of industrial policies for global development complementary to its own domestic coordination of adjustments in its consumption, investment and exports.

Through mutually beneficial trade and investment, China is promoting South–South cooperation to strengthen the developing economies and enhance their voice in dialogue with the North. Fairly regulated globalisation will narrow the development gap between North and South, ensuring that investment serves production not speculation, trade liberalisation is balanced by technology transfer, and negotiated win–win agreements favour development such that the costs of the necessary global adjustments do not fall unfairly on the developing countries.

While the United States stands for the dominance of finance – financial liberalisation and the free flow of 'hot money' – China regards finance as the 'servant of the real economy'.[109] China's agenda for a fair and stable globalisation based on equal partnerships provides a challenge to the system of monopoly and finance capitalism, which as Lenin argued was the basis of the imperialist system.

The fair globalisation agenda carries forward the key elements of the 1974 UN call for a new international economic order against the prevailing system of unequal exchange: trade to aid development, a fair transfer of technology, and a greater role for developing countries in decision making in international financial organisations to ease debt burdens and obtain funds for development.

As China itself starts to take on the responsibilities of a major world power, it is beginning to set an example in areas where it has continually called on the other developed countries to take a lead: eliminating trade barriers, increasing development assistance and taking effective measures to improve the supervision and regulation of the flow of international financial capital.

The 'go global' strategy of China's 'national champions' and the creation of a US$200 billion sovereign wealth fund for investment are raising concerns amongst Western business elites about the lack of agreed framework for rules for foreign investments.[110] Returning from a visit to China in 2006, the German Chancellor Angela Merkel warned that the international community would face 'grave social disorder' if it failed to agree a global framework of rules to govern competition between old industrial and fast-developing economies.[111]

These may well be signs of a dawning recognition in the West that, with the United States less able to manipulate world economic conditions and its institutions, and China gaining bargaining power in trade and investment, the world needs to open a new debate, with a wider participation, on the rules of the global economy.

CONCLUSION

11 AN INTERNATIONAL NEW DEMOCRACY IN THE MAKING

China is everywhere. Wherever the United States seeks to consolidate and extend its power and influence globally, whether in geographical regions or in international institutions, China is there ready to adapt or deflect US moves with its own alternative initiatives for a more equitable world order across the wide spectrum of international affairs. This contention between the largest developed and the largest developing country represents the wider contest over world development and the rules of the international political economy, and has become the focus of an international trial of strength.

The United States is starting to find it more difficult to dominate the international agenda and to pass on its own economic difficulties to the international market, while as China's bargaining position strengthens, it is beginning to push harder for a new institutional architecture of global governance to support development with the United Nations at its centre.

A GAME OF GO

China's international path is quite different from that followed by the USSR. The Soviet aim to create an independent socialist bloc, separated from and counter to the dynamics of world capitalism, was only to end in failure when, forced to defend this bloc in an arms race, it was ultimately exhausted. Relying on ideological opposition, the Soviet leadership lacked strategic focus on the uneven conditions of imperialist development highlighted by Lenin. In contrast, China, grasping the key structural issue in the international situation, sees opposition to US hegemonism as the key to world peace, and recognising the competitive as well as cooperative aspect of relations between the major powers, has aimed to build as widely as possible on the recent worldwide opposition to US-led interventionism.

Chinese leaders are determined not to repeat the Soviet blunder of imposing an unbearable defence burden on their economy. With their view on the long term, they have sought to stay out of Washington's strategic headlights. Confrontational policies, as demonstrated by the experiences of Milosevic and Saddam Hussein, have proved futile in countering US hegemonism, like 'sticking your head out to be chopped off'.

China is by no means looking to supplant the United States directly within the world order. It will take decades for its economic, let alone technological, capacity to catch up, decades which are crucial in its transition to a more advanced socialism. What it seeks is a peaceful 'sharing of space' with the United States as between equal partners so that it can make its own distinct contribution in shaping the future world.[1] The challenge, as China sees it, is rather to 'figure out a way to make the US an ordinary member of the ... [world order] rather than a lawmaker'.[2]

What concerns China is the way the United States exercises its power, its strategic ambitions driven at once by its idealist liberal ideology and its pursuit of hegemonic domination. Seeking to transform its own relationship with the United States to one of equality, China's objectives are to minimise US unilateralism, deflect its hostile policy, and defuse the ideological element.

To this end, rather than separating itself off, China is using globalisation to make itself indispensable to the functioning of the world economy, promoting an interdependence which means it becomes increasingly difficult for the United States to impose a strategy of 'isolation and encirclement'. Instead the aim is to draw the United States into a much broader dialogue, beyond a narrowly defined human rights agenda, to engage with issues of fairer trade and more equitable development.

Pursuing a widespread diplomacy, China seeks to gain ground wherever and whenever US hegemony is at its weakest, looking to utilise the divisions within the US elite as well as cracks in the US-led alliances to secure some elbow room for manoeuvre, in order to be able to take the opportunity of counter-hegemonic moments to push forward the 'peace and development' agenda and accelerate the multipolar trend.

At its core, China's is a Leninist strategy whose cautious implementation is infused with the principles of protracted people's war: not overstepping the material limitations, but within those limits 'striving for victory'; being prepared to relinquish ground when necessary and not making the holding of any one position the main objective, focusing instead on weakening the opposing force; advancing in a roundabout way; using 'tit for tat' and 'engaging in no battle you are not sure of winning' in order to 'subdue the hostile elements without fighting'.

If the US camp and the Soviet bloc were ranged against each other like two sides in a game of chess during the Cold War, China's strategy of multilevel partnerships and initiatives aims to constrain US aggression more in the pattern of a game of Go with the world a board on which the hegemonist and anti-hegemonist strategies are played out, each seeking to turn the balance of contradictory relations in their favour. Amidst the flux, China is creating new networks for a more equitable and democratic international relations within the interstices of the US-dominated system.

CHINA AS A NASCENT IMPERIALIST POWER?

The key characteristics of China's emerging role as a responsible world power, based on its own structural innovation, are now becoming evident in its commitment to poverty reduction, to boosting world growth through investment in development in Africa and elsewhere, its adherence to international law, its contribution to UN peacekeeping, and its active support for the peaceful resolution of conflicts and for denuclearisation and disarmament. It is now also making serious efforts to address the problems of energy consumption, environmental protection and global warming.

However, as its companies start to expand investment overseas, this raises controversial questions about China's overall development trajectory: is its pursuit of South–South cooperation a cover for neocolonialism? Does it constitute a form of 'social imperialism' exploiting the working classes of other countries in the name of socialism?

Although China has so far proved amenable to adjusting to the needs of its trading partners, it clearly has the potential to exercise considerable power, particularly over smaller countries. Nevertheless, unlike the West, China is hardly in a position to set the rules of global trade and investment but can only meet its needs for development through win–win cooperation.

As has been seen, China is not alone amongst developing countries in 'going global': companies from India, South Africa, Brazil, Malaysia and elsewhere are similarly investing overseas. What drives this Third World globalisation is not so much efficiency-seeking as development goals. In China's case, most of its overseas investment is carried out by SOEs and much of it is resource-based, its companies involved generally as minor partners in joint ventures and as buyers of output under long-term contracts. The interest here is less in return on capital than in access to reliable supplies of raw materials whose prices have been driven sky high by the excess of dollars in international markets.[3] Chinese companies also need to familiarise themselves with the global environment as vital preparation for foreign competition in the domestic market. What they seek are strategic assets such as new technologies, brand names, design and organisational skills.[4] Looking for win–win deals, they are often prepared to accept low profit margins.

China's economic development is generally proving to be a 'rising tide which lifts all boats' within the global economy, and its expanding trade and investment has potential to change the North–South balance within the various developing regions. Nevertheless its economic relations with other developing countries are not unproblematic and, as Mbeki has suggested, will need to be worked on constantly.[5]

But what will happen in the future when China becomes stronger? Will it become less willing to accommodate others? Such concerns provide an argument for building a strong United Nations. As the New Zealand PM, Helen Clark, put it in 2003 when, expressing her opposition to the war on Iraq, she spoke of the dangers of the United States and UK setting a precedent for ignoring the United Nations:

> This is a century which is going to see China emerge as the largest economy, and usually with economic power comes military clout. In the world we are constructing, we want to know [that the system] will work whoever is the biggest and most powerful .... I don't want precedents set, regardless of who is seen as the biggest kid on the block .... We saw the UN [as] a fresh start for a world trying to work out its problems together rather than return to a 19th century world where the great powers carved it up .... Who wants to go back to the jungle?[6]

To extend this view further, the more China is now involved in international rule making, the greater its commitment to the system in the future.

TOWARDS A GLOBAL PROGRESSIVE DEMOCRATIC ALLIANCE

The new developmental agenda of Third World globalism is essentially captured in China's vision of a new democratic international order. This formulation recalls China's own period of New Democracy after 1949 and the policy of a united front with 'patriotic capitalists'.

The Chinese revolution was not only directed against its own parasitic elites but was a part of a world revolution against international capitalism which supported them. It nevertheless differed from Russia's October revolution in that the majority of China's own national capitalist class at that time were opposed to foreign domination and supported the mass movement for national self-determination. The goal in establishing the PRC in 1949 was to set up not a capitalist state but a republic of all anti-imperialist people.

However, under the New Democracy, without denying the contradictions, the CPC advocated the free development of a private capitalist economy within the framework of a mixed economy, free from the domination of foreign capital in which state and cooperative ownership were the predominant factors, so long as it did not 'hold in its grasp the livelihood of the people' but brought them benefits. While the objective demand on the one hand was to 'clear the path for the development of capitalism'; on the other hand, it was to 'clear the path even wider for socialism'.[7]

Today, the international priority is to create a new international order based on non-intervention and peaceful coexistence without arms races, in which all countries have an equal voice in shaping a more balanced globalisation geared to the human needs of peace, development and sustainability. The key themes and objectives here are set out in Table 11.1.

To realise this, as China recognises, requires the mobilisation not only of the broad movements for peace and social justice around the world but also the forces of indigenous capitalism in the global South, the locally rooted capitalist elites of the developing world whose regional and global strategies are helping to form the basis of a more effective multipolar world.

The New Democratic period in China unleashed political momentum for a transition to socialism in 1956. Although it is sometimes argued that this transition was too rapid, giving way to turbulence in the Great Leap Forward and the Cultural Revolution, nevertheless the CPC 'seized the time' and now today is in a far stronger position internationally to promote and stabilise the multipolar trend. By inserting itself into the global division of labour, albeit at the bottom rung, China is placing itself in a central position in any global economic and industrial restructuring, which, with its widening diversity of trade partners and as a growing state-controlled centre of finance for development, it will become increasingly able to shape. (See Table 11.2.)

China's approach to coordinated trade and investment is anathema to the longstanding US agenda of free trade and a private sector market-based global financial system. But more, in embracing a more equitable globalisation to share its growth with other developing countries, China is building the economic ground for a firmer global progressive alliance against the US dollar-based hegemonism, and the order of monopoly and finance capitalism it upholds.

While China's Asian regional initiatives may serve to mobilise new coalitions through South–South economic and technological cooperation, developing countries as a whole may find, in the opportunities created by China's rise, more room for flexibility to follow their own mix of state and market, and even to explore the socialist experiments they were forced to abandon by the International Monetary Fund (IMF) in the 1980s.

Table 11.1 Key Themes and Objectives for an NIPEO

UN as central coordinator in world affairs

- Maintain the centrality of the non-intervention principle.
- Strengthen the voice of developing countries.
- Broaden the agenda to cover all aspects of world affairs, including non-proliferation and economic matters, phasing out the role of the IMF, World Bank and G8.

Demilitarisation of world affairs

- Agreement on a Nuclear Weapons Convention and nuclear disarmament.
- End all military alliances; dismantle all overseas military bases.
- Treaty to prevent an arms race in outer space.

Regional organisation

- Regional solutions to regional problems within UN rules.

Equitable sharing of world markets among nations/regions

- Negotiated trade with graduated tariff adjustments in favour of poorer countries and economic sectors.
- Cooperation between producers and consumers of primary commodities, especially energy, to maintain security, stability and sustainability of supplies.
- Technology transfer on favourable terms to developing countries.
- UN regulation of global markets and MNCs.

Finance for development

- Limit the influence of stock exchanges and financial markets.
- Maximise productive, direct and long-term investment.
- Stabilisation of currency and commodity markets with controls on international flows of 'hot money' to reduce opportunities for speculation.

Stable international monetary system

- Negotiated coordination of exchange rate adjustment to reduce $ primacy steadily and promote a more balanced international currency regime.
- Regional currency mechanisms.
- A new international financial architecture based on mutual risk-resistance and risk-sharing.

Sustainable development

- Developed countries to take the lead in substantially reducing carbon emissions.
- Transfer of energy saving and environmental technologies to developing countries on favourable terms.
- Joint research between developed and developing countries on new environmental technologies.

Table 11.2 China's main trading partners: latest available figures

Country/region	Value ($ billion)	Year	2010 estimate ($ billion)
European Union	272	2007	
United States	270	2006	
Japan	207	2006	
South-East Asia	190	2007	
Latin America	80	2007	
Russia	48	2007	60–80
Africa	40	2005	100
India	39	2007	60
Gulf Co-operation Council	17	2003	

Source: *China Daily* (various dates).

LOOKING TO THE FUTURE

The Domestic Sphere

China's extraordinary rise from poverty serves as an inspiration to others. However, with its economy and society criss-crossed with faultlines, China is certainly no model: its policies are by no means ideal but limited by constraints on its choices for development in an unequal world. Nor is its success preordained. While the emergence of new urban elites adopting Western consumer lifestyles far removed from the rural poor makes compradorisation a constant danger, the route to reducing inequalities through a massive rural to urban population transfer is fraught with difficulties. The economy has good potential to sustain growth, which will help to minimise what are essentially transitional problems. Nevertheless the possibilities of development being derailed by domestic instability and political crisis are real.

Sympathetic Sinologists in the West often point to the Chinese leadership's capacity to 'muddle through'.[8] Yet this hardly does justice to the long-term vision and strategic thinking that has motivated and guided China's path of progress over the decades.

Socialism in China is very much a work in progress, a work of decades. The state has to a considerable extent shifted away from direct involvement in economic management through planning, but it remains intensively involved over a wide range of economic and social affairs. What defines Chinese socialism in the current stage is not just ownership per se, but the ability of the state to exercise control through regulation, while promoting innovation, managing state shares and maintaining macro-economic balance, to ensure a more equitable sharing of the benefits of development whilst strengthening the market system.

Delivering 'people first' growth demands changes in the practices of Party and government to become more responsive to people's immediate concerns and allow them a greater say. Today in China there is debate that was unthinkable ten years ago. Yet undeniably, there is still a long way to go in tackling corruption and authoritarian tendencies. However, socialist traditions valuing participation, social justice and egalitarianism remain strong in the Party, state and society at large. Following the 17th CPC Congress in October 2007, further plans are being floated to prepare the ground for a greater democratisation to take off after 2020 when economic security will be much more firmly assured and the working-class base of the country much enlarged. Already, proposals are being floated for a freer press and more representative parliament.[9]

Economic change and development have taken huge strides forward in a relatively short period but through a process of small steps, and it is likely that the transformation of the Chinese political landscape will proceed similarly, with periods of tightening up followed by greater relaxation. At some point, though not by any means in the foreseeable future, the problematic events of the past – the Great Leap Forward, the Cultural Revolution and the Tiananmen suppression of 4 June 1989 – will need to be opened up to wider scrutiny through an orderly public debate.

The International Sphere

The world is at an historical turning point, with a fundamental shift of wealth and power from West to East and North to South. The centuries of European and US imperialist hegemony are being reversed with the rise of the global majority. The United States has begun its historical decline, as witnessed by its economic instability and inability to win the wars in Iraq and Afghanistan; China is emerging as a determining factor in shaping the world in the twenty-first century.

The goal of a fairer, more equitable and democratic order, a multipolar world of equal and friendly relations, is, as Lanxin Xiang points out, what China has been desperately seeking since the Opium War of 1840.[10] It would represent the realisation of China's own struggle against imperialism and hegemonism. However, although in the last few years multipolarisation has gathered fresh impetus, the United States remains the world's pre-eminent military power by an enormous margin, with considerable leverage in the overall balance of power.[11] By Chinese calculations, US economic dominance will not be quickly eroded: the dollar will likely retain its position as the global reserve currency for the next 20 or 30 years.[12] Nor is it thought that the domination of the world's multilateral institutions by Western powers will be radically reformed or completely overthrown in this period. Instead 'violent debates surrounding the formulation and reform of international rules of conduct will proceed'.[13]

The Chinese strategic perspective sees multipolarisation, albeit developing unevenly, as moving through stages, looking forward by 2020 to a situation in which 'one superpower; four major powers' will be more evenly balanced, opening the way for the rise of regional groupings or new poles from the developing world.[14] In the present, most critical period, however, the multipolar trend is seen to lack the strength of an anti-hegemonic front whilst the United States continues to strive for permanent strategic supremacy.[15]

For the foreseeable future then, the game of international Go is likely to be at its most intense, caught between interdependence and major power rivalry, as the various strategies of hegemonism, balance of power and cooperative security are played out through the competing agendas of national militarist dominance, free trade globalisation and global peace, justice and environmental sustainability.

In this variable international geometry, the stance of the European Union and India are pivotal. There is less open talk now of an emerging China–Europe axis to balance the United States, with the European Union bowing more to US pressures, for example, in agreeing not to lift its embargo on arms to China. Nevertheless, Sino–EU relations have taken a quiet step forward with agreement to cooperate on preventing big exchange rate fluctuations.[16]

With regard to India, the signing of an agreement on a Sino–Indian strategic partnership in 2005 brings together the two biggest developing countries in a relationship of great potential global and strategic significance. Both countries have considerable common interests including finding a fair way internationally to tackle global warming. However, by signing up to the US nuclear deal, India's elite has demonstrated an apparent willingness to allow their country to be used to counterbalance China. India's non-aligned position is now on the line. On the other hand, the Indian prime minister has assured China that his country will not join a potential US alliance to contain China.[17]

In Africa, the US decision to establish a new military command outside UN structures is likely, as African commentators make clear, to militarise governments and 'inflame regional conflicts', making Africa a new focal point of international contention.[18]

But it is East Asia, where the multipolar situation is most advanced, that will provide the testing ground as to whether or not the United States accepts China's peaceful rise as a fact. Despite the United States gaining an agreement with Japan to cooperate on missile defence development, the complex international relations of the region are in other significant ways starting to tip in China's favour. The Taiwan issue has now been removed from the common strategic objectives of the US–Japan alliance,[19] while Australia has also given assurances that it will not join the US-led alliance of democracies to contain China.[20] With a non-aggression agreement between the United States and North Korea on the horizon and the resounding win for the KMT in the March 2008 election in Taiwan raising prospects of an eventual peace accord across the Taiwan Strait, the US-led post-Second World War Pacific order, built around these divisions to underpin its global hegemony, is threatening to come undone.

A new US administration brings hopes of a possible change in foreign policy to a less militarist path in line with international law. But the future is not guaranteed. While further US unilateral action in the forthcoming period cannot be ruled out, the question is also whether or not there is any significant adjustment in the current offensive aggressive 'sword and shield' nuclear posture.

A Cold War-type chill has begun to appear in Sino–US relations as the United States tries to seize back the moral high ground, encouraging anti-China ideological international campaigning to counter the growing influence of the soft power of the 'Beijing Consensus'.

China's ability to maintain stable relations with the United States to avert a collision remains critical. A lesson from history in patient diplomacy can be drawn here from the ambassadorial talks on the normalisation of Sino–US relations which took from 1955 to 1972, involving nearly 140 meetings before there were any concrete results.[21]

As it has done over the last 60 years, China will be looking to the zigzag process of multipolarisation, to rise with its tides, making the most of the opportunities to press ahead with the new international political and economic order (NIPEO) agenda, while riding out the ebbs. However, whereas up to now it has been the more passive element in the highly asymmetric relationship, as the international strategic background in relation to US primacy changes, China is likely now to become more and more active in exercising its global responsibilities, its choices not only shaping the future of Sino–US relations but also reshaping the world.

NOTES

CHAPTER 1: A WORLD TURNING UPSIDE DOWN

1 Giovanni Arrighi, *Adam Smith in Beijing: Lineages of the Twenty-First Century* (London: Verso, 2007), p.211.

2 Dan Plesch, 'Iraq first, Iran and China next', *Guardian*, 13 September 2002.

3 Bush's introduction to the White House's 2002 National Security Strategy advocates 'a single sustainable model of national success: freedom, democracy and free enterprise'. See *The National Security Strategy of the United States of America*, White House, Washington DC, 2002.

4 As quoted in 'The falsehood of monopolar theory: commentary', English.peopledaily.com.cn, 30 July 2003.

5 See 'Key quotes: Tony Blair's speech to US Congress', Simon Jeffrey, *Guardian*, 18 July 2003.

6 Lanxin Xiang 'China's Eurasian experiment', *Survival*, Vol. 46, No. 2, Summer 2005, p.118.

7 Samuel Huntington, 'The clash of civilizations?' *Foreign Affairs*, Summer 1993.

8 See for example, Paul Wolfowitz, 'Bridging centuries', *The National Interest*, 1 March 1997.

9 J. Mearsheimer, *The Tragedy of Great Power Politics* (London and New York: W.W. Norton, 2001), p.402.

10 Giovanni Arrighi, *Adam Smith in Beijing: Lineages of the Twenty-First Century*, p.211.

11 Siteresources.worldbank.org/DATASTATISTICS/Resources/GNIPC (accessed 15 October 2008). The figures quoted here are for GNI per capita. Figures based on PPP (purchasing power) are suspect since China does not participate in PPP exercises.

12 See 'Globalisation with a third-world face', *Economist*, 9 April 2005.

13 John Rees, 'Imperialism: globalization, the state and war', *International Socialism*, Issue 93, Winter 2001.

14 J. Petras, 'China in the context of globalization', *Journal of Contemporary Asia*, Vol. 30, No. 1, 2000. Compradore is a term used to describe capitalists who accept the subordination of their own country to economic domination by the imperialist powers.

15 Martin Hart-Landsberg and Paul Burkett, 'China and socialism: engaging the issues', *Critical Asian Studies*, Vol. 37, No. 4, December 2005.

16   A. Vanaik <www.tni.org/detail_page.phtml?page=archives_vanail_iran> (accessed 23 May 2007).

17   Mark Roden, 'US–China relations in the contemporary era: an international political economy perspective', *Politics,* Vol. 23, No. 3, 2003, p.198.

18   Joseph Stiglitz, *Globalization and Its Discontents* (London: Penguin, 2002).

19   Giovanni Arrighi, *Adam Smith in Beijing.*

20   Joshua Cooper Ramo, *The Beijing Consensus: Notes on the New Physics of Chinese Power* (London: Foreign Policy Centre, 2004).

21   In particular, Samir Amin's *Obsolescent Capitalism* (London: Zed Books, 2003).

22   'US dollar cause of currency instability – Fan Gang', *Reuters,* 29 August 2006.

23   David Ralston et al., 'Today's state owned enterprises of China: are they dying dinosaurs or dynamic dynamos?', *Strategic Management Journal,* Vol. 27, 2006.

24   Martin Jacques, 'A geopolitical sea change', *Guardian,* 22 February 2008.

25   UNDP Development Report 2007/2008 – Country Fact Sheets – China <http://hdrstats.undp.org/countries/country_fact_sheets/cty_fs_CHN.html>. The HDI considers the dimensions of a long and healthy life, having access to education, and a decent standard of living. The report refers to 2005.

26   Giovanni Arrighi, *Adam Smith in Beijing,* p.151.

27   Ibid., p.149.

28   Samir Amin, *Obsolescent Capitalism*, p.78.

29   Simon Bromley, 'American power and the future of the international order', in W. Brown, S. Bromley and S. Athreye (eds), *Ordering the International* (London: Pluto Press in association with the Open University, 2004), p.180.

30   Samir Amin, *Obsolescent Capitalism*, p.130.

31   Ibid., p.129.

32   Colin Parkins, 'North–south relations and globalization after the cold war', in C. Bretherton and G. Poynton (eds), *Global Politics: An Introduction* (Oxford: Blackwell, 1996), p.56.

33   Marianne Marchand, 'The political economy of north-south relations', in R. Stubbs and G. Underhill (eds), *Political Economy and the Changing Global Order* (Basingstoke: Macmillan, 1994), p.298.

34   See for example, the Brandt Report: *North-South: A Programme for Survival* (London: Pan, 1980).

35   Samir Amin, *Obsolescent Capitalism,* p.138.

36   This is illustrated well in the case of Burma in a recent book written by the grandson of the former UN Secretary General, U Thant: Thant Myint-U, *The River of Lost Footsteps* (London: Faber and Faber, 2007).

CHAPTER 2: US–CHINA RELATIONS IN THE GLOBAL DYNAMICS

1   *Quadrennial Defense Review Report*, Department of Defense, United States of America, 6 February 2006.

2   Yao Youzhi, head of the Dept. of Strategic Research in the Chinese Academy of Military Sciences, cited in Denny Roy, 'China's reaction to American predominance', *Survival*, Vol. 45, No. 3, Autumn 2003, p.58

3   Kate Hudson, *CND – Now More Than Ever* (London: Vision, 2005).

4   Ehsan Afrari, 'China's view of US 'lily pad' strategy', *Asian Times* <http://atimes.com/atimes/China/FH24Ad04.html> (accessed 2 April 2008).

5   R. Halloran, reporting on a speech by the commander of the American forces in the Asia-Pacific Region, 'Reading Beijing', *Far Eastern Economic Review,* 25 February 1999.

6   Patrick Martin, 'Spy plane standoff heightens US–China tensions', *World Socialist Web Site*, 3 April 2001 < http://www.wsws.org/articles/2001/apr2001/ spy-a03.shtml> (accessed 2 April 2008).

7   T. Kojima, 'China's "omni-directional diplomacy": cooperation with all, emphasis on major powers', *Asia-Pacific Review*, Vol. 8, No. 2, November 2001.

8   According to Chalmers Johnson, 'No longer the lone superpower: coming to terms with China', *TomDispatch.com*, 15 March 2005 <http://www.tomdispatch.com/post/2259/chalmers_johnson_coming_to_terms_with_china> (accessed 2 April 2008).

9   See Denny Roy, 'China's reaction to American predominance', *Survival*, Vol. 45, No. 3, Autumn 2003.

10   *Quadrennial Defense Review Report,* Department of Defense, United States of America, 30 September 2001.

11   *The National Security Strategy of the United States of America*, Section V111, White House, Washington DC, 2002 <http://www.whitehouse.gov/nsc/nssall. html> (accessed 2 April 2008).

12   Thomas Woodrow, 'The new great game', *Jamestown Foundation,* 11 February 2003 <http://www.jamestown.org/publications_details.php?volume_id=19&& issue_id=668> (accessed 2 April 2008).

13   Zbigniew Brzezinski, *The Grand Chessboard: American Primacy and its Geostrategic Imperatives* (New York: Basic Books, 1998).

14   Zbigniew Brzezinski, 'A geostrategy for Eurasia', *Foreign Affairs*, September/ October 1997.

15   John Rees, 'Imperialism: globalisation, the state and war', *International Socialism,* Issue 93, Winter 2001. See also Chris Harman, 'Analysing imperialism', *International Socialism*, Issue 99, Summer 2003.

16   Cited in R. Bailey, 'Energy independence', *reasononline*, 21 July 2004.

17   Yi Xiaoxiong, 'China's foreign policy in transition: understanding China's peaceful development', *Journal of East Asian Affairs*, Vol. 4, No. 1, Winter 2003.

18   Frank Gibney, 'Pacific ties: the United States of America and the emerging "Pacific community"?' in Anthony McGrew and Christopher Brook (eds), *Asia-Pacific in the New World Order* (London and New York: Routledge, 1998).

19   Nor for that matter did the United States ever raise any questions regarding Chinese claims of suzerainty over Tibet with the Chiang Kaishek regime between 1945 and 1949.

20   'The Far East: China', *Foreign Relations of the United States*, Vol. 8, 1949 (US Government Printing Office, Washington, 1978). Cited in W. Blum, *The CIA: A Forgotten History* (London and New Jersey: Zed, 1986).

21   Peter Townsend, *In China Now* (London: Union of Democratic Control, 1953).

22   This so-called invasion followed a provocative declaration by the US-backed government in the South that it in fact represented the whole of Korea.

23   These US-led forces operated under UN sanction according to an agreement

made at a UN Security Council meeting from which the Soviet Union was absent in protest at the refusal to grant the PRC its rightful place.

24 Peter Townsend, *In China Now*, p.25, footnote 8.
25 Liu Ji, 'Making the right choices in twenty-first century Sino–American relations', *Journal of Contemporary China*, Vol. 7, No. 17, March 1998.
26 For a discussion of allegations of a secret mutual defence agreement between China and North Korea see David Tsui, 'Did the CCP sign a secret document on mutual defense with the DPRK in 1949?' *Journal of Contemporary China*, Vol. 8, No. 20, March 1999, p.167.
27 For accounts of the threats of nuclear attacks by the United States on China see Ken Coates, 'China and the bomb', in Ken Coates (ed.), *China and the Bomb* (Nottingham: Spokesman, 1986) and Joseph Gerson, *Empire and the Bomb* (London and Ann Arbor: Pluto Press, 2007).
28 Chris Harman, 'Analysing imperialism', p.52.
29 See Robert Sutter, 'The dragon and the eagle: fated rivals?' *South China Morning Post*, 17 March 2003.
30 *Quadrennial Defense Review Report*, Department of Defense, United States of America, 6 February 2006.
31 Much of the following discussion draws on Dr Hannah Middleton, 'What is the US up to in the Pacific?' September 2007. Hannah Middleton is associated with the Australian Anti-Bases Campaign Coalition, info@anti-bases.org.
32 Keir A. Leiber and Daryl G. Press, 'The rise of US nuclear primacy', *Foreign Affairs*, March/April 2006.
33 Paul White 'Deteriorating relations', *Morning Star*, 12 December 2007.
34 'Bush plans new NATO partnership', *Morning Star*, 11 November 2006.
35 See for example Yong Deng, 'Hegemon on the offensive', *Political Science Quarterly*, Vol. 116, No. 3, Fall 2001.
36 Yan Wei, 'Relations in transition', *Beijing Review*, 22 February 2007.
37 See Philip Saunders (based on an interview with a senior Chinese analyst), 'Supping with a long spoon: dependence and interdependence in Sino–American relations', *China Journal*, No. 43, January 2000, p.80.
38 Wang Jisi, 'China's search for stability with America', *China Daily*, 8 February 2006.
39 Kenneth Lieberthal, 'Why is the US still so anxious about a robust China?', *Beijing Review*, 9 February 2006.

CHAPTER 3: HISTORICAL PERSPECTIVES ON MULTIPOLARISATION

1 Zhao Suisheng, 'Beijing's perception of the international system and foreign policy adjustment in the post-cold war world', *Journal of North East Asian Studies*, Vol. 11, Fall 1992.
2 This is according to Hu Jintao, 'Speech to commemorate the 60th anniversary of China's victory in the anti-Japanese war', Great Hall of the People, Beijing, 3 September 2005.
3 With the exception of Hong Kong.
4 Hu Jintao, 'Speech to commemorate the 60th anniversary of China's victory in the anti-Japanese war'.

5   Marianne Marchand, 'The political economy of north–south relations', in R. Stubbs and G. Underhill (eds), *Political Economy and the Changing Global Order* (Basingstoke: Macmillan, 1994), p.289.

6   B. C. Smith, *Understanding Third World Politics* (Basingstoke: Macmillan, 1996), p.121.

7. Ibid., p.124.

8   Eric Hobsbawm, *Age of Extremes: The Short Twentieth Century 1914–1991* (London: Michael Joseph, 1994), p.237.

9   Ibid., p.228.

10 Ibid., p.227.

11 See Walden Bello, *People and Power in the Pacific* (London: Pluto Press, 1992), p.14. Bello refers to the US National Security Document No. 68, published in 1950.

12 Eric Hobsbawm, *Age of Extremes*, p.238.

13 Marianne Marchand, 'The political economy of north–south relations', p.289

14 Colin Parkins, 'North–south relations and globalization after the cold war' in C. Bretherton and G. Poynton (eds), *Global Politics: An Introduction* (Oxford: Blackwell, 1996), pp.56–7.

15 Extracts from the final communique of the conference can be found in Claude Buss, *Southeast Asia and the World Today* (Van Nostrand, 1964), pp.101–4.

16 Marianne Marchand, 'The political economy of north–south relations', pp.291–2.

17 Eric Hobsbawm, *Age of Extremes*, p.245.

18 Michael Yahuda, *The International Politics of the Asia-Pacific, 1945–1995* (London and New York: Routledge, 1996), p.242.

19 Philip McMichael, *Development and Social Change* (California: Pine Forge Press, 2000, 2nd edn), p.124.

20 Marianne Marchand, 'The political economy of north–south relations', p.293.

21 Ibid., p.293. Marchand cites the work of Augelli and Murphy, *America's Quest for Supremacy and the Third World: A Gramscian Analysis* (London: Pinter, 1988), pp.149–50.

22 Eric Hobsbawm, *Age of Extremes*, p.245.

23 Kate Hudson, *CND – Now More Than Ever* (London: Vision, 2005), p.121.

24 Ibid., p.123.

25 Ibid., p.121.

26 Ibid., pp.144 and 153. Hudson cites the work of Laurence S. Wittner, *The Struggle Against the Bomb* Vol. 3 (Stanford, California: Stanford University Press, 2003).

27 Ibid., p.204.

28 Nkrumah cited by Jerry Jones, 'Global capitalism's imperial underbelly', *Morning Star*, 18 January 2006.

29. See for example, 'China steadily consolidates and strengthens its relations with other developing countries', Information Office of the State Council of the People's Republic of China, 1999.

30 See Deng Xiaoping, 'Speech at the Special Session of the U.N. General Assembly', 10 April 1974; online version: Deng Xiaoping Internet Archive (marxists.org) 2003 <http://www.marxists.org/reference/archive/deng-xiaoping/1974/04/10.htm> (accessed 5 April 2008).

31 *Chairman Mao's Theory of the Differentiation of the Three Worlds is a Major Contribution to Marxism-Leninism* (Peking: Foreign Languages Press, 1977).

32 France recognised China in 1964.

33 At the time of Nixon's visit to China in 1972 the United States had agreed to progressively reduce its forces and military installations on Taiwan. However, in 1979, the normalisation of relations was qualified by the Taiwan Relations Act which committed the United States to provide Taiwan with defensive weapons. The 1982 agreement was to reverse this but lacked a cut-off date for sales representing, according to some commentators at the time, a climbdown on China's part. Nevertheless, the agreement 'bought time' for China, and Deng was able to argue for prioritisation of economic growth for the foreseeable future, whilst recognising that the issue still remained to be resolved in US–China relations.

34 See Shen Shouyuan and Huang Zhongqing, 'The People's Republic of China: an independent foreign policy of peace', *Journal of Asian and African Studies*, Vol. 25, No. 1/2, January/April 1990, p.74.

35 See G. Segal, *The China Factor* (London: Croom Helm, 1982), p.37 for a discussion on the origins of the debate.

36 Ding Yuanhong, 'Vicissitudes in West European–US relations', in *China and the World*, No. 4 (Beijing; Beijing Review, 1983), p.95.

37 Chen Qimao, 'War and peace: a reappraisal', *Beijing Review*, Vol. 39, No. 23, 9 June 1986, p.24.

38. See Gerald Chan, *Chinese Perspectives on International Relations* (Basingstoke and London: Macmillan Press, 1999), p.121.

39 Huang Hua (foreign minister), 'Speech to the UN General Assembly Special Session on Disarmament', in *China and the World*, No. 2 (Beijing: Beijing Review, 1982), p.14.

40 Qian Qichen, 'Year marks improved world situation', *Beijing Review*, Vol. 32, No. 2, 26 December 1988 –1 January 1989.

41 Ibid.

42 Wu Baiyi, 'The Chinese security concept and its historical evolution', *Journal of Contemporary China*, Vol. 10, No. 27, May 2001, p.278.

43 Jin Canrong, 'The US global strategy in the post-cold war era and its implications for China–United States relations: a Chinese perspective', *Journal of Contemporary China*, Vol. 10, No. 27, May 2001, p.311.

44 Joseph Cheng, 'China's ASEAN policy in the 1990s: pushing for regional multipolarity', *Contemporary Southeast Asia*, Vol. 21, Issue 2, August 1999.

45 Brantly Womack, 'Asymmetry theory and China's concept of multipolarity', *Journal of Contemporary China*, Vol. 13, No. 39, May 2004, p.353.

CHAPTER 4: MANOEUVRING TOWARDS MULTIPOLARITY

1 G. Chan, *Chinese Perspectives on International Relations* (Basingstoke and London: Macmillan, 1999), pp.110–12.

2 J. Cheng, 'China's ASEAN policy in the 1990s', *Contemporary Southeast Asia*, Vol. 21, Issue 2, August 1999.

3 G. Chan, *Chinese Perspectives on International Relations*, pp.30–3. The extent to which CNP includes 'soft power' is one area of debate.

4   Ibid., p.103.

5   Chen Xiaogong, cited in Zhao Suisheng, 'Beijing's perception of the interna-
     tional system and foreign policy adjustment in the post-cold war world',
     Journal of North East Asian Studies, Vol. 11, Fall 1992.

6   Xin Hu, 'Characteristics of the world situation', *Beijing Review*, 11–17 January
     1993.

7   Xue Mouhong, 'The new world order: four powers and one superpower?',
     Beijing Review, Vol. 25, No. 9, 1 October 1995.

8   Zheng Bijian, 'Deng theory to lead China in 21st century', *China Daily*, 8
     December 1998.

9   'The falsehood of monopolar theory', *People's Daily*, 30 July 2003; Wang
     Jincun, '"Democracy" veils hegemony', *China Daily*, 28 May 1999.

10   Wang Jisi cited in Yong Deng, 'Hegemon of the offensive: Chinese perspectives
     on US global strategy', *Political Science Quarterly*, Vol. 116, No. 3, 2001,
     p.346.

11   Li Zhongwei, 'International security environment goes through changes'
     Beijing Review, 23 August 1999.

!2   'The characteristics of the world situation', *Beijing Review*, 28 December 1998.

13   Yong Deng, 'Hegemon of the offensive', p.347.

14   'American empire steps up fourth expansion', *People's Daily*, 12 March 2003.

15   See Yong Deng, 'Hegemon of the offensive', p.349; also 'China's national
     defense in 2000: the security situation' <http://www.fas.org/nuke/guide/china/
     doctrine/cnd0010china-001016wp.htm> (accessed 12 April 2008).

16   Wang Jincun, '"Democracy" veils hegemony'.

17   Cited in S. Blum, 'Chinese views of US hegemony', *Journal of Contemporary
     China*, Vol. 12, No. 35, May 2003, p.243.

18   Li Shaojun, 'The characteristics of relations among major powers and trends in
     international security at the turn of the century', unspecified source.

19   'Factors hindering US hegemonic moves', *Peoples Daily*, 8 April 2003.

20   S. Blum 'Chinese views of US hegemony', p.249.

21   Ibid., p.255.

22   M. Yahuda, 'Chinese dilemmas in thinking about regional security architecture',
     Pacific Review, Vol. 16, No. 2, 2003, p.193.

23   Denny Roy, 'China's reaction to American predominance' *Survival*, Vol. 45,
     No. 3, Autumn 2003, p.70.

24   'China's position paper on the new security concept', 31 July 2002, in *China
     Report*, Vol. 39, No. 1, 2003, pp.128–31.

25   These areas contain potential gas and oil reserves as well as busy sea lanes.
     China however had signed a code of conduct with other states concerned after
     a dispute in 1995. See Daojiong Zha and Mark J. Valencia, 'Mischief Reef:
     geopolitical and implications', *Journal of Contemporary Asia*, Vol. 31, No. 1,
     2001.

26   Deng and Moore, 'China views globalization: toward a new great power
     politics?' *Washington Quarterly*, Summer 2004, p.125.

27. Denny Roy, 'China's pitch for a multipolar world: the new security concept',
     Asia-Pacific Security Studies, Vol. 2, No. 1, May 2003, p.3.

28   Peter Van Ness, in the conclusion to M. Gurtov and P. Van Ness (eds),
     Confronting the Bush Doctrine (London and New York: Routledge Curzon,
     2005), p.264.

29 'China's national defense in 1998: the international security situation' <http://www.china.org.cn/e-white/5/5.1.htm> (accessed 12 April 2008).

30 Quoted in Roy, 'China's pitch for a multipolar world', p.3.

31 'China's position paper on the new security concept', 31 July 2002, in *China Report*, Vol. 39, No. 1, 2003.

32 Jiang Zemin's speech in December 1997 at an informal meeting of East Asian leaders in Kuala Lumpur on economic cooperation in East Asia. Quoted in *China Steadily Consolidates and Strengthens its Relations with other Developing Countries*, Information Office of the State Council of the PRC, 2000.

33 Pei Yuanying, 'The five principles of peaceful coexistence and the theory and practice of China's diplomacy in the new era', *China Institute of International Studies* < www.ciis.org.cn> (accessed 30 July 2004).

34 Ibid.

35 Chinese Foreign Minister, Li Zhaoxing, speech at the 12th ASEAN Regional Forum in Laos, 'China to forge security cooperation in Asia-Pacific region', *People's Daily*, 29 July 2005.

36 Chinese Foreign Minister, Li Zhaoxing, 'China's diplomacy contributes to world peace, development', *People's Daily*, 23 August 2005.

37 Qian Qichen, 'Nation will not seek hegemony', *China Daily*, 4 April 2004.

38 Pan Tao, 'Timeless theme of international relations', *Beijing Review*, 10 June 2004.

39 Neither China nor the United States has ratified the CTBT.

40 E. Medeiros and M. Taylor Fravel, 'China's new diplomacy', *Foreign Affairs*, November–December 2003, p.32.

41 Avery Goldstein, 'The diplomatic face of China's grand strategy', *China Quarterly*, 2001, p.852.

42 Ibid., p.855.

43 Wang Jisi, 'China's search for stability with the US', *China Daily*, 8 February 2006.

44 Avery Goldstein, 'The diplomatic face of China's grand strategy', p.852.

45 See David Lampton, *Same Bed, Different Dream: Managing US–China relations, 1989–2000* (Berkeley, Calif.: University of California Press, 2001).

46 *Financial Times* editorial for 22 March 2006.

47 Simon Tisdall, 'China and Russia flex their muscles as they join forces to play the war game', *Guardian*, 9 August 2005.

48 'Joint statement by the People's Republic of China and the Russian Federation on the multipolarisation of the world and the establishment of a new international order', *Beijing Review*, 12–18 May 1997.

49 President Jiang Zemin's speech at the Russian Duma, *Beijing Review*, 12–18 May 1997.

50 Phillip Saunders, 'China's America watchers: changing attitudes towards the United States', *China Quarterly*, No. 161, Spring 2000, p.62.

51 Avery Goldstein, 'The diplomatic face of China's grand strategy', pp.847, 850–1.

52 Yi Xiaoxiong, 'China's foreign policy in transition: understanding China's peaceful development', *Journal of East Asian Affairs*, Vol. 4, No. 1, Winter 2003, p.88.

53 Avery Goldstein, 'The diplomatic face of China's grand strategy', pp.846–7.

54 Denny Roy, 'China's pitch for a multipolar world', p.4.

55 S. Uyanayev, 'Relationships of Russia, China and India after 11 September event: facts and opinions', *China Report*, Vol. 39, No. 3, 2003.
56 Ibid.
57 Avery Goldstein, 'The diplomatic face of China's grand strategy', p.858.
58 'Bush, the new international order and China's choice', *People's Daily*, 22 November 2004.
59 'US global strategy foiled', *People's Daily*, 28 May 2004.
60 Ibid.
61 'The falsehood of monopolar theory', *People's Daily*, 30 July 2003.
62 'US global strategy foiled', *People's Daily*, 28 May 2004.
63 'The consequences of the Iraq War is worrying: A panel of experts', *People's Daily*, 25 March 2003.
64 'Factors hindering US hegemonic moves', *People's Daily*, 8 April 2003.
65. 'China's National Defence in 2004: The Security Situation' <http://www.fas.org/nuke/guide/china/doctine/natdef2004.html> (accessed 12 April 2008).
66 Ibid. See also 'Factors hindering US hegemonic moves'.
67 Cited in S. Blum, 'Chinese views of US hegemony', p.244.

CHAPTER 5: GLOBALISATION, IMPERIALISM AND MULTIPOLARISATION

1 Rong Ying, 'Economic globalization and the new international political and economic order', *China Report,* Vol. 38, No. 1, 2002, pp.115–16.
2 See 'China's National Defence in 2004: The Security Situation' <http://www.fas.org/nuke/guide/china/doctine/natdef2004.html> (accessed 12 April 2008).
3 Although the G7 became the G8 when Russia joined in 1997, the latter's role in economic decision making remains peripheral since it is not included in the financial ministerial meetings.
4 Joseph Stiglitz, *Making Globalization Work* (London: Allen Lane, 2006).
5 M. Hardt and A. Negri, *Empire* (Cambridge, Mass.: Harvard Univ. Press, 2000).
6 J. Petras, 'The imperial counter offensive: contradictions, challenges and opportunities', *Journal of Contemporary Asia*, Vol. 32, No. 3, 2002.
7 P. Anderson, 'Force and consent', *New Left Review*, No. 17, 2002, p.21.
8 See also for example Robert Griffiths, 'Generally speaking', *Morning Star*, 17 November 2001.
9 P. Anderson, 'Force and consent', pp.16–17.
10 John Rees, 'Imperialism: globalization, the state and war', *International Socialism*, Issue 93, 2001; Chris Harman, 'Analysing imperialism', *International Socialism*, Issue 99, 2003; Alex Callinicos, 'The grand strategy of the American empire', *International Socialism*, Issue 97, 2002.
11 John Rees, 'Imperialism: globalization, the state and war', pp.19–22.
12 Chris Harman, 'Analysing imperialism', p.65.
13 See Alex Callinicos, 'The grand strategy of the American empire', pp.30–1; Robert Griffiths, 'Generally speaking'.
14 Chris Harman, 'Analysing imperialism', pp.71–2.
15 Ibid., pp.71–2.

16 Peter Gowan, 'U.S. hegemony today', *Monthly Review*, July–August 2003, p.30.
17 Peter Gowan, *The Global Gamble* (London: Verso, 1999), p.23.
18 Peter Gowan, 'U.S. hegemony today', p.42.
19 Ibid.
20 Ibid.
21 Samir Amin, *Obsolescent Capitalism* (London: Zed, 2003), pp.77–8.
22 Ibid., pp.94 and 103.
23 Samir Amin, 'US imperialism, Europe and the Middle East', *Monthly Review*, November 2004.
24 Samir Amin, 'Confronting empire', *Monthly Review*, July–August 2003.
25 Samir Amin, *Obsolescent Capitalism*, p.95.
26 Samir Amin, cited in P. Bond, 'Facing the global apartheid', in A. Freeman and B. Kagarlitsky (eds), *The Politics of Empire* (London: Pluto Press, 2004), p.211.
27 W. Bello, 'Unraveling of the Atlantic alliance?', *Focus on the Global South*, 25 September 2002 <http://www.focusweb.org/unraveling-of-the-atlantic-alliance.html?Itemid=93> (accessed 11 April 2008).
28 B. Garrett, 'China faces, debates the contradictions of globalization', *Asian Survey*, Vol. 41, No. 3, May–June 2001, p.425; Zhu Wenli, 'International political economy from a Chinese angle', *Journal of Contemporary China*, Vol. 10, No. 26, 2001, pp.47–9.
29 Jiang Zemin, 'What we need is an all-win globalization', *Beijing Review*, 4 December 2000.
30 'Globalization is imperialism in its advanced and final stage', *Vanguard*, 28 January 2004.
31 Yuan Wenqi et al., 'International division of labor and China's economic relations with foreign countries', *Social Sciences in China*, No. 1, March 1980, p.42.
32 Rong Ying, 'Economic globalization', p.116.
33 Yuan Wenqi et al., 'International division of labor', p.45.
34 Ibid., p.29.
35 Long Yongtu, cited in Thomas Moore, 'China and globalization', in S. Kim (ed.), *East Asia and Globalization* (Rowman and Littlefield, 2000), p.116.
36 Rong Ying, 'Economic globalization', p.115; Chen Zuming, 'Economic globalization and China–Russia–India cooperation', *China Report*, Vol. 39, No. 3, 2003, p.372.
37 Pan Tao, 'Globalization and its effect on international relations', *Beijing Review*, 15 February 2001; Rong Ying, 'Economic globalization', p.118.
38 Zhu Qiwen, 'Participate in shaping the world', *China Daily*, 24 August 1998; Jiang Xianming, 'G77 plus China stress south–south cooperation', *China View*, 16 June 2005.
39 Rong Ying, 'Economic globalization', p.118.
40 Yuan Wenqi et al., 'International division of labor', p.27.
41 Zou Sanming, cited in S. Blum, 'Chinese views of US hegemony', *Journal of Contemporary China*, Vol. 12, No. 35, May 2003, p.257.
42 Rong Ying, 'Economic globalization', p.117; Zhu Qiwen, 'Participate in shaping the world'.
43 See Yong Deng, 'Hegemon on the offensive: Chinese perspectives on US global strategy', *Political Science Quarterly*, Vol. 116, No. 3, 2001, p.361.

44 Zhu Qiwen, 'Capitalising on global trade', *China Daily*, 22 April 1998.
45 Chen Zuming, 'Economic globalization and China–Russia–India cooperation', p.371.
46 Cheng Yu, 'China's foreign policy: opportunities and challenges', *Perspectives*, Vol. 2, No. 4 <http://www.oycf.org/Perspectives/10_022801/china.htm> (accessed 11 April 2008).
47 Rong Ying, 'Economic globalization', p.117.
48 Pan Tao, 'Globalization and its effect on international relations'.
49 Rong Ying, 'Economic globalization', p, 118; Qiu Wen, 'Two sides of globalization', *China Daily*, 13 April 2005.
50 Yu Zhou, 'Warning of an anti-globalization surge', *Beijing Review*, 23 August 2001.
51 Qiu Wen, 'Two sides of globalization'.
52 Rong Ying, 'Economic globalization', p.118-9; Yuan Wenqi et al, 'International division of labor', p.42.
53 'Make better use of globalization process', *China Daily*, 11 July 1998.
54 Chinese Foreign Minister, Li Zhaoxing, 'Banner of diplomacy stressed', *People's Daily*, 23 August 2005.
55 Jiang Zemin, 'What we need is an all-win globalization'.
56 Zhou Yihuang, 'Will China's rise trigger Sino–US confrontation?' *People's Daily* 26 December 2003 <http://english.people.com.cn/200312/26/print 20031226_131270html> (accessed 18 April, 2008); Cheng Yu, 'China's foreign policy: opportunities and challenges'.
57 Ibid.
58 Yan Xuetong, 'Globalization to shape millennium', *China Daily*, 9 July 1998.
59 Ibid.
60 Jin Yinan, 'Multipolarization irrevocable trend', *China Daily*, 15 July 2002.
61 'China's National Defense in 1998: The International Security Situation' <http://www.china.org.cn/e-white/5/5.1.htm> (accessed 12 April 2008).
62 Pan Tao, 'Globalization and its effect on international relations'.
63 Zhou Yihuang, 'Will China's rise trigger Sino–US confrontation?'
64 Yong Deng and T. G. Moore, 'China views globalization: toward a new great power politics?', *Washington Quarterly*, Summer 2004, p.118.
65 Ibid., p.127.
66 Jin Yinan, 'Multipolarization irrevocable trend'.
67 Jerry Harris, 'To be or not to be: the nation-centric world order under globalization', *Science and Society*, Vol. 69, No. 3, July 2005, pp.334–6.
68 Walden Bello and Marylou Malig, 'The crisis of the globalist project and the new economics of George Bush,' in Alan Freeman and Boris Kagarlitsky (eds), *The Politics of Empire* (London: Pluto Press, 2004), pp.88–9.
69 Ibid., pp.89–90.
70 P. Saunders, 'Supping with a long spoon: dependence and interdependence in Sino–American relations', *China Journal*, No. 43, January 2000, pp.77–8.
71 T. Cohn, *Global Political Economy* (New York: Longman, 2nd edn, 2003), p.430.
72 Ibid., p.44.
73 J. Kopstein, 'The transatlantic divide over democracy promotion', *Washington Quarterly*, Spring 2006, pp.96–7.
74 Peter Gowan, 'U.S. hegemony today'.

75   Lanxin Xiang, 'China's Eurasian experiment', *Survival*, Vol. 46, No. 2, Summer 2004, p.109.

76   J. Arias, 'China and Europe look ahead', *Beijing Review*, 6 October 2005.

77   Yu Xintuan, 'EU enlargement: an East Asian perspective', 8 July 2004 <www.rus.org.cn/newsp/shownews.asp?NewsID=266> (accessed 11 April 2008).

78   Cited in D. Shambaugh, 'The new strategic triangle: U.S. and European reactions to China's rise', *Washington Quarterly*, Summer 2005, p.22.

79   Lanxin Xiang, 'China's eurasian experiment', p.13.

80   Mai Zhaorong, 'Expanding and strengthening ties with the EU', *China Daily*, 12 April 2004.

81   Ibid.

82   Yu Xintuan, 'EU enlargement: an East Asian perspective'.

83   Ni Yanshuo, 'Diplomacy gathers steam', *Beijing Review*, 27 January 2005.

84   *China's EU Policy Paper*, PRC Ministry of Foreign Affairs, October 2003.

85   Wu Liming, 'Golden days for EU–US ties gone', 25 December 2004, Chinaview <www.chinaview.cn> <http://news.xinhuanet.com/english/2004-12/25/content_2379400.htm> (accessed 12 April 2008).

86   'EU moves toward independent military role', *People's Daily Online*, 19 December 2004 <english.peopledaily.com.cn/200412/19/eng20041219_167900.html> (accessed 11 April 2008).

87   Qian Qichen, 'US strategy to be blamed', *People's Daily Online*, 1 November 2004 <english.peopledaily.com.cn/200411/01/eng20041101_162331.html> (accessed 11 April 2008).

88   See interview with David Malone, Canada Assistant Deputy Minister of Foreign Affairs by Ni Yanshuo, 'Migration key issue for next 30–40 years', *Beijing Review*, 9 June 2005.

89   See Peter Symonds, 'Condoleezza Rice visits Australia and Indonesia to tighten US ties against China', *World Socialist Web Site*, 21 March 2006 <www.wsws.org/articles/2006/mar2006/rice-m21.shtml> (accessed 11 April 2008).

90   Chris Harman, 'Analysing imperialism', p.72.

91   Immanuel Wallerstein, 'The curve of American power', *New Left Review*, No. 40, July/August 2006, p.91.

92   Chen Zuming, 'Economic globalization and China–Russia–India cooperation', p.374.

93   Helen Nesadurai, 'Attempting developmental regionalism though AFTA', *Third World Quarterly*, Vol. 24, No. 2, 2003, p.236.

94   Zha Peixin 'China and Globalization' Speech at the Chinese Economic Association Annual Conference, 14 April 2003 <http://www.fmprc.gov.cn/ce/ceuk/eng/dsjh/t27161.htm> (accessed 17 October 2008).

95   Rong Ying, 'Economic globalization', p.119; Qiu Wen, 'Two sides of globalization'.

96   Chen Zhimin, 'NATO, APEC and ASEM: triadic interregionalism and global Order', *Asia–Europe Journal*, Vol. 3, No. 3, October 2005, pp.18–19.

97   Barry Lynn, 'The fragility that threatens the world's industrial systems', *Financial Times*, 11 October 2005. The same now goes for China which produces, for every computer in the world, at least one critical component.

98   'China urges G77 to play a role in new economic order', *Xinhua*, 12 June 2004.

99   Chen Zuming, 'Economic globalization and China–Russia–India cooperation',

p.374; Jiang Xianming, 'G77 plus China summit stresses south–south cooperation', *Xinhuanet*, 16 June 2005.

100 Jiang Zemin's Report to the 16th Congress of the CPC, 2002 <http://english.people.com.cn/200211/18/eng20021118_106983.shtml> (accessed 17 April 2008).

101 Chen Zhimin, 'NATO, APEC and ASEM: triadic interregionalism and global order'. ASEM was founded in 1996.

102 Ibid., pp.18–19.

103 Chris Harman, 'Analysing imperialism', p.69.

104 Alan Freeman and Boris Kagarlitsky 'Introduction: world empire – or a world of empires?' *The Politics of Empire* (London: Pluto Press, 2004), p.13–14.

105 Samir Amin, 2003, cited in P. Bond, 'Facing the global apartheid'.

106 Jerry Harris, 'To be or not to be'.

107 V. I. Lenin, 'Left-wing communism – an infantile disorder', cited in Chairman Mao's *Theory of the Differentiation of the Three Worlds is a Major Contribution to Marxism–Leninism* (Peking: Foreign Languages Press, 1977), p.74.

108 Ibid., p.59, citing Mao Zedong, 'On policy', 1940.

109 Ibid., p.15.

110 Ibid., p.56.

111 Ding Yuanhong, 'Vicissitudes in West European–US relations', in *China and the World* (4) (Beijing; Beijing Review, 1983), p.101.

112 'The falsehood of monopolar theory', *People's Daily*, 30 July 2003.

113 Alan Freeman and Boris Kagarlitsky, 'Introduction: world empire – or a world of empires?' p.32.

114 Bello and Malig, 'The crisis of the globalist project', p.89. Bello and Malig draw on Robert Brenner's work, *The Boom and the Bubble,* 2002.

CHAPTER 6: PROMOTING MULTIPOLARISATION: REGIONAL ORGANISATION IN ASIA

1   For further details see E. Medeiros and M. Taylor Frankel, 'China's new diplomacy', *Foreign Affairs*, November–December 2003. The main disputes remaining to be solved are with India, Japan (islands in the East China Sea) and Vietnam (islands in the South China Sea).

2   Pan Guang, 'A Chinese perspective on the Shanghai Cooperation Organization', in Alison J. K. Bailes et al., *The Shanghai Cooperation Organization*, SIPRI Policy paper No. 17, Stockholm International Peace Research Institute, May 2007.

3   Philip P. Pan, 'US accuses Uighur rebels of terror plot', *Guardian Weekly,* 5–11 September 2002. Some of these groups were thought to have links with the Taliban and Al-Qaeda.

4   Jabin Jacob, 'China's position on Iraq', *China Report*, Vol. 39, No. 3, July–September 2003.

5   Scott Parrish and William Potter, 'Central Asian states establish nuclear-weapon-free-zone despite U.S. opposition', *James Martin Centre for Nonproliferation Studies*, 5 September 2006 <http://cns.miis.edu/pubs/week/060905.htm> (accessed 13 April 2008); Merhat Sharipzhan, 'Central Asia: region pledges to remain free of nuclear weapons', Radio Free Europe/Radio

Liberty, September 2006 <http://www.rferl.org/featuresarticle/2006/09/fa5076ce-85df-46df-879d-ae78dba16429.html> (accessed 13 April 2008).

6   Pan Guang, 'A Chinese perspective on the Shanghai Cooperation Organization'.

7   Marcel de Haas, 'S.C.O. summit demonstrates its growing cohesion', *Power and Interest News Report,* 14 August 2007 <http://www.pinr.com/report.php?ac=view_report&report_id=673&language_id=1> (accessed 13 April 2008).

8   Text of speech by Mani Shankar Aiyar, Minister for Petroleum and Natural Gas, 13 January 2006 (source unknown).

9   Pan Guang, 'A Chinese perspective on the Shanghai Cooperation Organization'.

10 Isabel Gorst, 'CNPC oil link', *Financial Times*, 15 August 2007.

11 According to David Wall, regional expert at Chatham House. See Simon Tisdall, 'Putin aggression strains "Central Asian NATO"', *Guardian Weekly*, 17 August 2007. See also Simon Tisdall, 'China and Russia flex their muscles as they join forces to play the wargame', *Guardian Weekly*, 9 August 2005.

12 Alison J. K. Bailes and Pal Dunay, 'The Shanghai Cooperation Organization as a regional security institution', in Bailes et al., *The Shanghai Cooperation Organization*.

13 Steven Fidler and Jon Boone, 'Fields of little glory', *Financial Times*, 19 November 2007.

14 Isabel Gorst, 'Kyrgyzstan "cannot police borders"', *Financial Times*, 24 May 2006.

15 Amnesty International has raised concerns about the rate of executions carried out during the 'strike hard' campaigns. Since 2007, all death penalties imposed by provincial governments must now be reviewed by the Supreme People's Court to exert strict control over its use. See Li Li, 'Milestones mark new direction' *Beijing Review,* 22 March 2007.

16 Cheng Ruisheng, 'Some observations on the international situation since "September 11"', *China Report*, Vol. 39, No. 3, July–September 2003; B. Raman, 'Counter-terrorism: India–China–Russia cooperation', *China Report*, Vol. 40, No. 2, 2004.

17 Y. Zhu and D. Blatchford, 'China's fate as a multinational state: a preliminary assessment', *Journal of Contemporary China,* Vol. 14, No. 57, May 2006. Zhu and Blatchford cite recent research interviews in Xinjiang that found the desire for 'real autonomy' rather than independence as 'near universal'.

18 Alison J.K. Bailes, Preface to Bailes et al., *The Shanghai Cooperation Organization*.

19 Z. Brzezinski, 'A geostrategy for Eurasia', *Foreign Affairs*, September–October 1997.

20 Piotr Smolar and agencies, 'Kyrgyzstan opts for one-party solution', *Guardian Weekly*, 21 January 2007.

21 Bailes et al., *The Shanghai Cooperation Organization*.

22 Jonathan Watts, 'Cross-border maneouvres raise stakes in central Asia's power game', *Guardian Weekly,* 21–27 August 2003.

23 Mikhail Troitsky, 'A Russian perspective on the Shanghai Cooperation Organization', in Bailes et al., The Shanghai Cooperation Organization.

24 F. William Engdahl, 'The US's geopolitical nightmare', *Asian Times*, 9 May 2006 <http://www.atimes.com/atimes/China/HE09Ad01.html> (accessed 13 April 2008).

25 Pan Guang, 'A Chinese perspective on the Shanghai Cooperation Organization'.

26 S. Varadarajan, 'China, Russia and the Shanghai agenda', *The Hindu*, 4 July 2005

<www.hindu.com/2005/07/04/stories/2005070406291100.htm> (accessed 13 April 2008).
27 Europe is not included.
28 See Hou Hongyu, 'A brief report on the seminar on "Stability, Security and Cooperation in Northeast Asia"', *Peace* (Chinese People's Association for Peace and Disarmament), No. 78, March 2006.
29 See Joseph Gerson, *Empire and the Bomb* (London: Pluto Press, 2007).
30 Fred Goldstein, 'Nuclear crisis made in USA', *Workers World*, 12 October 2006.
31 Gavin McCormack, 'The umbrella and the mushroom: realism and extremism on North Korea', *Japan Focus,* 24 August 2005.
32 Anna Fifield, 'N Korea calls for end to all sanctions', *Financial Times*, 16 May 2007.
33 For a detailed discussion of the agreement see Hui Zhang, 'The North Korean nuclear crisis: negotiating a way out', *INESAP Bulletin*, No. 26, 2006.
34 Manoranjan Mohanty, 'Contrasting denuclearisation: Korea and Iran', *Economic and Political Weekly*, 8 October 2005.
35 Ibid.
36 Ibid.
37 There are two problematic issues still to be resolved. First, there is the question of North Korea's alleged uranium project, which Bush insisted in 2002 was being conducted in secret in violation of the 1994 agreement. It is widely considered now that this was greatly exaggerated with hostile intent. The second concerns the issue of the provision of the light water reactors which remain to be discussed. See Hui Zhang, 'The North Korean nuclear crisis: negotiating a way out'.
38 Shi Yongming, 'Relations at a crossroads', *Beijing Review*, 15 March 2007.
39 See the statement issued by the Global Partnership for the Prevention of Armed Conflict – North East Asia Regional Meeting in Ulaanbaatar Civil Society Six-Party talks, 25 May 2007; also Liu Yongjiang, 'Japan and Northeast Asia Security', *Peace* (Chinese People's Association for Peace and Disarmament), No. 78, March 2006.
40 In the words of Jabin Jacob, 'China's position on Iraq', *China Report*, Vol. 39, No. 3, July–September 2003.
41 Manoranjan Mohanty, 'Contrasting denuclearisation: Korea and Iran'.
42 Cited in Joseph Yu-shek Cheng, 'The ASEAN–China free trade area: genesis and implications', *Australian Journal of International Affairs*, Vol. 58, No. 2, June 2004.
43 Xiaoxiong Yi, 'China's foreign policy in transition: understanding China's peaceful development', *Journal of East Asian Affairs,* Vol. 4, No. 1, Winter 2003.
44 David Murphy, 'Softening at the edges', *Far Eastern Economic Review*, 4 November 2004.
45 John Burton, 'Call to speed South East Asian common market', *Financial Times*, 8 August 2006.
46 See Shen Hongfang, 'The building of the China–ASEAN free trade area: a case study of the Philippines' perspective', *China Report,* Vol. 42, No. 3, July–September 2006.
47 Martin Hart-Landsberg and Paul Burkett, 'China and socialism: engaging the issues', *Critical Asian Studies*, Vol. 37, No. 4, December 2005.

48 Ramkishen Rajan, 'Emergence of China as an economic power: what does it imply for South-East Asia?' *Economic and Political Weekly*, 28 June 2003.

49 Helen Nesadurai, 'Attempting developmental regionalism though AFTA', *Third World Quarterly*, Vol. 24, No. 2, 2003, p.236.

50 See Nicola Phillips' discussion of Mercosur, 'The rise and fall of open regionalism? Comparative reflections on regional governance in the Southern Cone of Latin America', *Third World Quarterly*, Vol. 24, No. 3, 2003.

51 J. Stiglitz, *Making Globalization Work* (London: Allen Lane, 2006), pp.260–1.

52 M. Vatikiotos, 'Military alliances: a diplomatic offensive', *Far Eastern Economic Review,* 5 August 2004.

53 R. McGregor, 'Beijing to sign ASEAN nuclear arms treaty', *Financial Times,* 31 October 2006.

54 John Burton, 'East Asia Summit being sidelined by ASEAN', *Financial Times,* 13 December 2005.

55 Ding Ying, 'A new stage of cooperation', *Beijing Review,* 9 August 2007.

56 'China, America and South East Asia', *International Institute for Strategic Studies*, Volume 11, No. 1, February 2005, pdf download from <www.iiss.org> (accessed 13 April 2008); David Rosenburg, 'Dire straits: competing security priorities in the South China Sea', *Znet,* 13 April 2005 <http://www.zmag.org/content/showarticle.cfm?ItemID=7632> (accessed 13 April 2008).

57 M. Vatikiotis and D. Murphy, 'Birth of a trading empire', *Far Eastern Economic Review*, 20 March 2003; Eoin Callan, 'China's shadow looms large over Doha failure', *Financial Times*, 23 June 2007.

58 Yao Chao Cheng, 'China's role in the Asian unification process', *Economic and Political Weekly*, 3 September 2005.

59 *The National Security Strategy of the United States of America,* White House, Washington DC, 2006, p.20 <http://www.whitehouse.gov/nsc/nssall.html> (accessed 2 April 2008).

60 International energy institutions have predicted that from 2002 to 2030 around 21 per cent of the world's new demand for energy resources will come from China, but this calculation does not take into account China's plans to increase energy efficiency.

61 Javier Blas and Ed Crooks, 'OPEC blames speculators for oil's rise', *Financial Times*, 16 October 2007.

62 Anne Krueger, 'China and global economic recovery', *Beijing Review*, 17 March 2005.

63 R. McGregor, 'China rounds on "unfair" criticism of its energy use', *Financial Times,* 8 March 2007.

64 OPEC's fear is that they will be left with massive overcapacity as they were during the 1980s after the 1970s oil-price shocks.

65 Wu Lei and Shen Qinyu, 'Will China go to war over oil?' *Far Eastern Economic Review*, April 2006.

66 Pan Guang, 'A Chinese perspective on the Shanghai Cooperation Organization'.

67 Joseph Yu-shek Cheng, 'The ASEAN–China free trade area: genesis and implications'.

68 Ibid.

69 To admit India and Pakistan to the SCO, for example, would cause problems since their status as de facto nuclear states contradicts the requirement of adherence to the NPT stipulated in the SCO's founding documents.

70 The SCO, for example, has signed up to a common programme to be achieved by 2020. See Oleg Sidorov, 'Member privileges', *Beijing Review*, 15 June 2006.
71 This suggestion was raised by Premier Zhu Rongji in 2002. See Arvinder Singh, 'Boao forum: Chinese imprint on pan-Asianism', *Economic and Political Weekly*, 27 July 2002.

CHAPTER 7: MAINTAINING SELF RELIANCE IN AN INDEPENDENT WORLD

1 Shaun Breslin, 'Globalisation, international coalitions and domestic reform', *Critical Asian Studies*, Vol. 36, No. 4, 2004, p.665.
2 Guo Sujian, 'Ownership reform in China: what direction and how far?', *Journal of Contemporary China*, Vol. 12, No. 36, August 2003.
3 Li Xing, 'Socialist foundations of market reform: assessing China's past', *Economic and Political Weekly*, 4 December 1999.
4 Ibid.
5 Deng Xiaoping, 'We shall concentrate on economic development', 18 September 1982 <http://english.people.com.cn/dengxp/vol3/text/c1030.html> (accessed 16 April 2008).
6 John Ross, 'Lessons of the Chinese economic reform', *Socialist Economic Bulletin*, April–May 1996.
7 Ibid.
8 Martin Khor, *Rethinking Globalization: Critical Issues and Policy Choices* (London and New York: Zed, 2001), p.94.
9 See for example Shaun Breslin, 'China: geopolitics and the political economy', in R. Stubbs and G. Underhill (eds), *Political Economy and the Changing Global Order* (Ontario: Oxford University Press, 2000), p.394.
10 *China's National Defence* (Beijing: Information Office of the State Council of the People's Republic of China, July 1998) <http://www.fas.org/nuke/guide/china/doctrine/cnd9807/index.html> (accessed 16 April 2008).
11 Zhu Wenli, 'International political economy from a Chinese angle', *Journal of Contemporary China*, Vol. 10, No. 26, February 2001, p.53.
12 Jiang Zemin, cited in Thomas Moore, 'China and globalization', in S. Kim (ed.), *East Asia and Globalisation* (Rowman & Littlefield, 2000), p.121.
13 Jiang Zemin's Report to the 15th Congress of the CPC, 1997 <www.fas.org/news/china/1997/970912-prc.htm> (accessed 17 April 2008).
14 Guo Sujian, 'Ownership reform in China', p.562.
15 See Long Yongtou, 'On economic globalization', cited in Thomas Moore, 'China and globalization', p.117.
16 Chen Wen, 'Fuelling the engine', *Beijing Review*, 16 March 2006, p.29.
17 'Make better use of globalization', *China Daily*, 11 July 1998.
18 Cited in Guy de Jonquieres, 'China's industrial policy should think small', *Financial Times,* 6 September 2006.
19 D. N. Ghosh, 'FDI and reform: significance and relevance of Chinese experience', *Economic and Political Weekly*, 15 December, 2005.
20 Martin Wolf, 'China has further to catch up with the world', *Financial Times*, 13 April 2006.

21 Cited in R. Buckman, 'Exaggerating the China threat', *Far Eastern Economic Review*, 15 May 2003.

22 Jiang Xiaojuan, 'China's foreign direct investment: its contribution to growth, structural upgrading and competitiveness', *Social Sciences in China*, Summer 2003.

23 Ibid.

24 J. Zhan, 'Export competitiveness and the role of FDI: the case of China', *Conference on Economy and Business in China: Now and future*, University of Lancaster, April 2003.

25 Jiang Xiaojuan, 'China's foreign direct investment'.

26 Gao Ting, 'China's FDI in perspective', *Harvard China Review*, Vol. 5; Li Yanjun, 'Coming to China', *Beijing Review*, 31 August 2006.

27 Shaun Breslin, 'Power and production: rethinking China's global economic role', *Review of International Studies*, No. 31, 2005.

28 Gautum Sen, 'Post-reform China and the international economy', *Economic and Political Weekly*, 11 March 2000.

29 Peter Nolan, *Transforming China: Globalization, Transition and Development* (London: Anthem Press, 2005), pp.210–14.

30 'Poor miss out as rich nations cream off their trade', *Guardian*, 30 April 2002.

31 Li Yanun, 'Coming to China', *Beijing Review*, 31 August 2006.

32 Geoff Dyer, 'Forbidden country? How foreign deals in China are hitting renewed resistance', *Financial Times*, 8 August 2006.

33 See Zha Daojiong, 'Comment: can China rise?' *Review of International Studies*, Vol. 31, 2005, pp.775–85.

34 Jing Xiaolei, 'Searching for supremacy', *Beijing Review*, 11 May 2006.

35 George Wehrfritz and Alexandra Seno, 'China pits competitors against each other', *Newsweek*, 23 June 2003.

36 B. Benoit, G. Dyer and R. Milne, 'Germany rejects call on funding for China rail link', *Financial Times*, 2 June 2006.

37 Mei Xinyu, 'BOA investment opens bank sector', *Beijing Review*, 7 July 2005.

38 Minxin Pei, 'China is stagnating in its "trapped transition"', *Financial Times*, 24 February 2006; Guy de Jonquieres, 'China's banking system needs a cultural revolution', *Financial Times*, 5 April 2006.

39 P. Ciccantell and S. Bunker, 'The economic ascent of China', *Journal of World-System Research*, Vol. 10, No. 3, Fall 2004, p.580.

40 B. Dolven, 'Making the whole world listen', *Far Eastern Economic Review*, 26 February 2004.

41 'China's champions', Survey of China, *Economist*, 8 January 2005.

42 Steve Ellis and Onet Gadiesh, 'Outsmarting China's start arounds', *Far Eastern Economic Review*, July/August 2006.

43 Lu Ling, 'Innovation rules', *Beijing Review*, 17 November 2005; Feng Jianhua, 'Ill-intended mergers?', *Beijing Review*, 13 April 2006.

44 'New Beijing legislation restricts monopolies', *Morning Star*, 31 August 2007.

45 Mark Konyu, 'China's controlled market is tough going', *Financial Times*, 11 September 2006.

46 Lu Ling, 'Innovation rules'.

47 C. Leadbetter and J. Wilsdon, 'Do not fear the rise of world-class science in Asia', *Financial Times*, 12 October 2005; G. Dyer, 'China overtakes Japan for R&D', *Financial Times*, 4 December 2006; Frederic Bobin, 'Mutually assured dependence', *Guardian Weekly*, 14–20 July 2006.

48 Guy de Jonquieres, 'China's high-tech success is not patently obvious', *Financial Times*, 25 October 2005.

49 Geoff Dyer, 'The dragon's lab – how China is rising through the innovation ranks', *Financial Times*, 5 April 2007.

50 Geoff Dyer, 'China overtakes Japan for R&D', *Financial Times*, 4 December 2006.

51 Eugene Bregolat, 'China's technological thrust poses formidable challenge', *Financial Times*, 21 June 2007; 'China's independent technology capability', *Beijing Review*, 23 March 2006.

52 Richard McGregor, 'OECD sees obstacles to China's high-tech drive', *Financial Times*, 28 August 2007.

53 A. Kuhn, 'China spins a new disc', *Far Eastern Economic Review*, 26 February 2004.

54 Guy de Jonquieres, 'To innovate, China needs more than standards', *Financial Times*, 13 July 2006.

55 P. Saunders, 'Supping with a long spoon: dependence and interdependence in Sino–American Relations', *China Journal*, No. 43, January 2000, p.70; Peter Nolan, *China's Rise, Russia's Fall* (Basingstoke: Macmillan, 1995), p.185.

56 Guo Sujian, 'Ownership reform in China', p.569.

57 Cited in Guo Sujian, 'Ownership reform in China', p.571.

58 For further discussion on China's approach to privatisation see Alok Ray, 'The Chinese economic miracle: lessons to be learnt', *Economic and Political Weekly*, 14 September 2002; T. T. Ram Mohan, 'Privatisation in China: softly, softly does it', *Economic and Political Weekly*, 6 November 2004.

59 'Survey of China', *Economist*, 25 March 2006.

60 Guy de Jonquieres, 'China's industrial policy should think small'.

61 Richard McGregor, 'Beijing launches state groups dividend plan', *Financial Times*, 31 May 2007.

62 'Survey of China', *Economist*.

63 Zhang Liwei, 'Are we prepared for a peaceful rise?' *Beijing Review*, 4 January 2007.

64 Barry Naughton and Adam Segal, 'China in search of a workable model', in W. W. Keller and R. J. Samuels (eds), *Crisis and Innovation in Asian Technology* (Cambridge: Cambridge University Press, 2003).

65 Li Li, 'Setting a precedent', *Beijing Review*, 4 January 2007; Richard McGregor, 'Farmers are the last to benefit from Chinese property law', *Financial Times*, 9 March 2007.

66 Jerry Harris, 'To be or not to be: the nation-centric world order under globalization', *Science and Society*, Vol. 69, No. 3, July 2005, p.338.

67 Mure Dickie, 'An area where imports outweigh exports', *Financial Times*, 12 December 2006.

68 Sundeep Tucker, 'Desperate rush for the entrance', *Financial Times*, 25 July 2007.

69 Premier Wen Jiabao, 'Turn your eyes to China', Remarks to Harvard University, 10 December 2003 < http://www.hno.harvard.edu/gazette/2003/12.11/10-wenspeech.html > (accessed 17 April 2008).

CHAPTER 8: DEVELOPMENT WITH CHINESE CHARACTERISTICS

1 Martin Hart-Landsberg and Paul Burkett, 'China and socialism', *Monthly Review*, Vol. 56, No. 3, July–August 2004, p.55 and 'China and socialism:

engaging the issues', *Critical Asian Studies*, Vol. 37, No. 4, 2005; J. Petras, 'The cultural revolution in historical perspective', *Journal of Contemporary Asia*, Vol. 27, No. 4, 1997.

2   Huang Wei, 'Working for harmony', *Beijing Review*, 17 March 2005.

3   'We permit some people and some regions to become prosperous first, for the purpose of achieving common prosperity faster'. Deng Xiaoping replies to the American TV correspondent Mike Wallace, *60 Minutes*, CBS TV, 2 September 1986.

4   Wen Jiabao, 'Development and peace hold key to national rejuvenation', *Beijing Review*, 8 March 2007.

5   Chris Bramall, 'Shedding darkness', *EastAsia@Sheffield*, No.11, December 2005, University of Sheffield. Bramall was responding to Jung Chang's charges of 70 million dead in the Mao period especially during the Great Leap Forward and Cultural Revolution. Even if one accepts the figures, he argues, by comparing the improvements in life expectancy in China with India during the Mao period 'one could plausibly argue that he saved between 200 million and 300 million from an early death …. Something which India cannot claim'. Whether Mao is to be held responsible for the deaths is also to be contested: these were the results of policy failures, not deliberate extermination campaigns. Not mentioned by Jung Chang is arguably Mao's worst failure: the neglect of population policy.

6   See J. Stiglitz, *Making Globalization Work* (London: Allen Lane, 2006), p.31; *Background Notes on Poverty Reduction in China*, November 2005, China Policy Institute, University of Nottingham. Using the $2-per-day measure, China's poverty rate dropped from 67 per cent to 47 per cent between 1987 and 2001: see J. Stiglitz, *Making Globalization Work*, p.297.

7   See *Towards Human Development with Equity* (the United Nations Development Programme China Report, 2005) <http://hdr.undp.org/en/reports/nationalreports/asiathepacific/china/name,3270,en.html> (accessed 27 April 2006). Adult male literacy was 95 per cent and female literacy 87 per cent in China in 2002, far better than India's at 73 per cent and 48 per cent respectively. See also M. Wolf, 'In this brave new world, Chindia's uneven rise continues', *Financial Times*, 21 March 2007.

8   R. McGregor, 'China's prosperity brings income gap', *Financial Times*, 9 August 2007. The gini coefficient is a summary measure of income inequality, the larger the coefficient the greater the inequality. China's gini coefficient has now increased to 0.45, greater than the United States (0.41), far more than India (0.33) but less than Brazil (0.54).

9   Lina Song, 'Policy initiatives on inequality in China', *China Discussion Paper*, Issue 3, 2005, China Policy Institute, University of Nottingham.

10   Around 150 million of these in fact form a 'floating population' of rural migrants in the urban areas.

11   Ian Cook and Trevor Dummer, 'Exploring China's rural health crisis: processes and policy implications', *Health Policy*, No. 84, 2007.

12   Feng Jianhua, 'Equal education', *Beijing Review*, 7 December 2006.

13   On comparative emissions see J. Stiglitz, *Making Globalization Work*.

14   Yongnian Zheng, 'The new policy initiatives in China's 11th 5-year plan', *China Briefing Series*, Issue 1, 2006, China Policy Institute, University of Nottingham, November 2005.

15 Interview with James W. Adams, World Bank Vice-President for the East Asia and Pacific Region, *Beijing Review*, 4 January 2007.

16 J. Watts, 'China admits first rise in poverty since 1978', *Guardian*, 20 July 2004.

17 Tang Qinghua, 'Give and take', *Beijing Review*, 30 November 2006.

18 J. Watts, 'Land seizures threaten social stability, warns China's leader', *Guardian*, 21 January 2006.

19 Huang Ping and Frank Pieke, 'Rural–urban migration: some policy issues', *Social Sciences in China*, Autumn 2005.

20 Zhang Xiaoshan, 'Turning government priorities for rural development into realities: how?' *Social Sciences in China*, Autumn 2005. The OECD reckons that between 70 million and 100 million rural workers will leave agriculture between 2000 and 2010; See also R. McGregor, 'OECD warning on rural China', *Financial Times*, 15 November 2005.

21 Wen Jiabao, 'Report on the work of the government', *5th session of the 10th NPC*, 5 March 2007.

22 Tan Wei, 'Where are the jobs?' *Beijing Review*, 10 August 2006.

23 Wu Jinglian, 'Does China need to change its industrialisation path?' in I. Gill et al., *East Asian Visions* (Washington/Singapore: World Bank/Institute of Policy Studies, 2007).

24 Alok Ray, 'The Chinese economic miracle: lessons to be learnt', *Economic and Political Weekly*, 14 September 2002.

25 Jiang Zemin, 'Report to the 16th Congress of the CPC', 2002 <http://english. people.com.cn/200211/18/eng20021118_106983.shtml> (accessed 17 April 2008).

26 Wu Jinglian, 'Does China need to change its industrialisation path?'

27 R. McGregor, 'China's five-year plan will underline Hu's agenda', *Financial Times*, 8 October 2005.

28 Xiao Zhuoji, 'Project of a harmonious society, *Beijing Review*, 17 March 2005.

29 Lan Xinzhen, 'Hoping for a spending spree', *Beijing Review*, 10 August 2006.

30 Huang Ping and Frank Pieke, 'Rural–urban migration: some policy issues'.

31 Li Li, 'Government tackles wealth gap', *Beijing Review*, 22 March 2007.

32 'China pledges pension plan for migrant rural workers', *Morning Star*, 12 June 2007.

33 'China defends its treatment of migrants', *Morning Star*, 2 March 2007.

34 M. Turner and F. Williams, 'Action on cities "has done little for slums"', *Financial Times*, 16 June 2006.

35 Wang Mengkui, 'Harmony in development', *Beijing Review*, 6 April 2006.

36 See Shaun Breslin, 'The virtual market', *China Review*, No. 17, Autumn–Winter 2000.

37 Wen Jiabao, 'Report on the work of the government', *5th session of the 10th NPC*, 5 March 2007.

38 Lan Xinzhen, 'China in 2010', *Beijing Review*, 13 April 2006; M. Dickie, 'China's country folk try co-operative cure', *Financial Times*, 4 October 2007.

39 Li Li, 'Government tackles wealth gap'.

40 A. Yeh, 'Tibet plans five-star treatment to draw high-end tourism', *Financial Times*, 24 February 2007.

41 Jonathan Watts, 'The spoiling of Shangri-la', *Guardian*, 30 August 2003; Geoff Dyer and Richard McGregor, 'Tibet untamed', *Financial Times*, 1 April 2008.

42 Thomas Abraham 'Little can be achieved through negotiations on Tibet', *Economic and Political Weekly*, 5 April 2008.

43 T. Mitchell, 'Shortage raises workers' stock', *Financial Times*, 3 May 2007.

44 'China's long road to riches', *Guardian Weekly*, 8 September 2006.

45 Lan Xinzhen, 'China in 2010'.

46 Quoted in Li Li, 'Greenhouse balancing act', *Beijing Review*, 14 June 2007.

47 R. Minder and K. Hille, 'Solar power looks to brighter future', *Financial Times*, 14 September 2007.

48 V. Mallet, 'China's chance to save our overheated planet', *Financial Times*, 6 July 2006.

49 Mure Dickie, 'China struggles on energy efficiency targets', *Financial Times*, 11 November 2007.

50 Yan Wei, 'Responsibility reaction to climate change', *Beijing Review*, 20 December 2007; Fiona Harvey, 'Yo, Kyoto', *Financial Times*, 2 October 2007.

51 'Constitution of the Communist Party of China, amended and adopted at the 16th CPC Congress', *Beijing Review Supplement*, 19 December 2002.

52 'White Paper on political democracy', *China Daily*, 19 October 2005 <http://www.chinadaily.com.cn/english/doc/2005-10/19/content_486206.htm> (accessed 25 April 2008).

53 Shaoguang Wang, 'Regulating death in coalmines: changing the mode of governance in China', *Journal of Contemporary China*, Vol. 15, No. 46, February 2006; Tim Wright, 'State capacity in contemporary China: closing the pits and reducing coal production', *Journal of Contemporary China*, Vol. 16, No. 51, May 2007.

54 Ibid.

55 'Constitution of the Communist Party of China, amended and adopted at the 16th CPC Congress'.

56 'Development and peace hold key to national rejuvenation', excerpts from an essay by Wen Jiabao', *Beijing Review*, 8 March 2007.

57 This section draws from Suisheng Zhao, 'Political liberalization without democratization', *Journal of Contemporary China*, Vol. 12, No. 35, May 2003.

58 China has signed both the international conventions on human rights: economic, social and cultural rights, and civil and political rights, but has not yet ratified the latter.

59 Liu Yunyun, 'No sexual harassment tolerated', *Beijing Review*, 21 July 2005. The laws on eliminating sexual discrimination in the workplace were strengthened in 2007. Women make up only 21.3 per cent of the total number of deputies to the NPC: see 'NPC deputies – facts and figures' *Beijing Review*, 27 March 2008. This compares with 22.6 per cent in 1975.

60 Qianfan Zhang, 'The People's Court in transition: the prospects of the Chinese judicial reform', *Journal of Contemporary China*, Vol. 12, No. 34, February 2003.

61 R. Ramesh, 'China's great leap forward', *Guardian Weekly*, 2–8 February 2007. China has more than four times the PC penetration of India. See A. Yee, 'India "will pay price" for high-tech sector neglect', *Financial Times*, 29 September 2006; Guobin Yang, 'The internet and civil society in China', *Journal of Contemporary China*, Vol. 12, No. 36, August 2003.

62 Xia Li Lollar, 'Assessing China's E-Government: information, service, transparency and citizen outreach of government websites', *Journal of Contemporary China*, Vol. 15, No. 46, February 2006.

63 As quoted in A. Stevenson-Yang, 'Can China co-opt the web?' *Far Eastern Economic Review*, October 2005.

64 A. Edgecliffe-Johnson, 'Google links hitches in China to problems with local net rivals', *Financial Times*, 27 January 2007.

65 'China's line of march', *Report of the Communist Party of Britain Delegation to China*, 2006.

66 Anita Chan, 'China and the International Labour Movement', *China Review*, No. 19, Summer 2001.

67 Zhang Yunqui, 'State power and labour–capital relations in foreign-invested enterprises in China: the case of Shandong Province', *Issues and Studies*, Vol. 36, No. 3, May–June 2000.

68 Zhang Yunqui, 'Law and labour in post-Mao China', *Journal of Contemporary China*, Vol. 14, No. 44, August 2005.

69 'The original draft gave employees more rights than UK workers according to C. Gill, 'Come the revolution', *Guardian*, 24 June 2006.

70 Feng Jianhua, 'Mixed reaction to workers' rights law', *Beijing Review*, 12 July 2007.

71 Paul White, 'Labour law with teeth', *Morning Star,* 26 February 2007.

72 Paul White, 'Model for China's exploited migrants', *Morning Star,* 16 July 2007.

73 'China vote for Wal-Mart trade union', *Morning Star*, 3 August 2006.

74 Feng Jianhua, 'Cheap labour', *Beijing Review,* 16 February 2006.

75 Tom Mitchell and Geoff Dyer, 'Labour law set to raise costs in China', *Financial Times*, 2 January 2008.

76 Liu Yunyun, 'How much am I worth?' *Beijing Review,* 14 December 2006.

77 Paul White, 'Workers' comeback', *Morning Star,* 23 April 2007.

78 Tom Mitchell, 'Chinese board structures "lead to confusion"', *Financial Times*, 3 April 2008.

79 D. Zweig and Chung Siu Fung, 'Elections, democratic values and economic development in rural China', *Journal of Contemporary China,* Vol. 16, No. 50, February 2007.

80 Official reports suggest that there have been more than a million illegal seizures between 1998 and 2005, although unofficial reports are higher. See G. Dyer, 'Taking the countryside: why agribusiness may reap profits and problems for China', *Financial Times,* 4 April 2007.

81 Zhang Xiaoshan, 'Turning government priorities for rural development into realities: how?'

82 Yu Jianrong, 'Social conflict in rural China today: observations and analysis on farmers' struggles to safeguard their rights', *Social Sciences in China*, Autumn 2005.

83 M. Dickie, 'Chinese farmers to get market rate for seized land', *Financial Times*, 9 March 2006; Tang Yuankai, 'Laws of the land', *Beijing Review*, 7 September 2007.

84 R. McGregor and M. Dickie, 'Jiangsu sets the pace of how to assess officials', *Financial Times*, 15 March 2007.

85 Feng Jianhua, 'End of an era', *Beijing Review,* 26 January 2006.

86 Zhang Rongchen, 'Getting the system right', *Beijing Review*, 7 September 2006.

87 According to Ministry of Health figures. Li Li, 'Health fix', *Beijing Review,* 14 November 2006.

88 Feng Jianhua, 'Hutong power', *Beijing Review*, 5 January 2006.
89 Feng Jianhua, 'AIDS prevention deepened', *Beijing Review*, 30 November 2006.
90 J. Anderlini and G. Dyer, 'Wary welcome for China's labour reform', *Financial Times*, 2 July 2007; M. Dickie, 'Pollution forces China water cut-off', *Financial Times*, 5 July 2007.
91 J. Anderlini, 'Campaign to clean the Yangtze under way', *Financial Times*, 10 July 2007; see also Jeffrey Sachs, 'Lecture 2, Survival in the Anthropocene', *Reith Lectures*, 2007 <http://www.bbc.co.uk/radio4/reith2007/lecture2. shtml#lecture2> (accessed 25 April 2008); Li Li, 'Eco warrior faces up', *Beijing Review*, 18 January 2007.
92 Reported in Feng Jianhua, 'Clean sweep', *Beijing Review*, 25 January 2007.
93 Ariana Eunjung Cha (*Washington Post*), 'Lobbyists move into China', *Guardian Weekly*, 12 October 2007.
94 '15,000 CPC members take top positions', *Morning Star,* 19 July 2007.
95 J. Haylett, 'China's long road', based on an interview with Liao Dong, Director General CPC International Department, *Morning Star,* 16 August 2006.
96 Yan Wei, 'Young bold', *Beijing Review*, 28 June 2007.
97 The Communist Party of Great Britain had private business members who were particularly active in the Second World War effort. Some of them went on to form the core of the 'Icebreakers' who persuaded the British government to open trade with both the USSR and China in the Cold War period of the 1950s.
98 'White Paper on Political Democracy', *China Daily.*
99 Ji Li, 'People's rights: an intrinsic part of harmony', *Beijing Review*, 30 November 2006.
100 Jiang Zemin, 'Report to the 16th Congress of the CPC'.
101 Ibid.
102 T. Mellen, 'Communists rally for slain comrades', *Morning Star*, 30 July 2007.
103 Jonathan Watts, 'Chinese party official in dock over rent-a-mob raid on villagers', *Guardian*, 17 December 2005.
104 Yongnian Zheng, 'The new policy initiatives in China's 11th 5-year plan'.
105 'Constitution of the Communist Party of China, amended and adopted at the 16th CPC Congress'.
106 'Enhancing governance capability of the party', resolution to the Fourth Plenum of the CC.CPC, September 2004, cited in M. Mohanty, 'China's focus on governance', *Economic and Political Weekly*, 9 October 2004.
107 K. Coyle, 'Hong Kong battleground for US assault on China', *Morning Star*, 4 October 2004.
108 A. So, 'Beyond the logic of capital and the polarisation model', *Critical Asian Studies*, Vol. 37, No. 3, 2005, p.491.
109 Ibid.
110 Huang Ping and Frank Pieke, 'Rural–urban migration: some policy issues'.
111 Ibid.
112 Li Peilin, 'Introduction: changes in social stratification in China since the reform', *Social Sciences in China*, Spring 2002.
113 For this point see Zhang Xiaoshan, 'Turning government priorities for rural development into realities: how?'

CHAPTER 9: TOWARDS A NEW INTERNATIONAL POLITICAL ORDER

1   Premier Wen Jiabao first put the conception of China's 'peaceful rise' forward in 'Turn your eyes to China', Remarks to Harvard University, 10 December 2003 <http://www.hno.harvard.edu/gazette/2003/12.11/10-wenspeech.html> (accessed 17 April 2008). This was later reformulated as 'peaceful development' when President Hu spoke at the Boao Forum in 2004 <http://www.china.org.cn/english/features/93897.htm> (accessed 27 April 2008).

2   Yi Xiaoxong, 'China's foreign policy in transition: understanding "China's peaceful development"', *Journal of East Asian Affairs*, Vol. 4, No. 1, Winter 2003, pp.75, 91; Deng and Moore, 'China views globalization: toward a new great power politics?', *Washington Quarterly*, Summer 2004, p.122.

3   Yu Xintian, *EU enlargement: An East Asian Perspective*, School of Advanced International and Area Studies, East China Normal University, 30 April 2004 <http://www.saias.ecnu.edu.cn/english/news/shownews.asp?NewsID=198> (accessed 27 April 2008).

4   Wang Jisi, 'China's search for stability with America', *Foreign Affairs*, September–October 2005.

5   Glenn Kessler, 'Rice puts Japan at centre of new U.S. vision of Asia', *Washington Post*, 19 March 2005.

6   Fu Mengzi, 'China's development and security concept', *Beijing Review*, 9 June 2007.

7   See for example John Gittings, 'Beijing stumped for an answer to Washington's new imperialism', *Guardian*, 2 October 2002.

8   For further discussion here see Jabin Jacob, 'China's position on Iraq', *China Report*, Vol. 39, No. 3, July–September 2003.

9   M. Turner, 'Beijing's UN envoy defends decision to back compromise resolution on Iraq', *Financial Times*, 19 October 2003.

10 Ibid.

11 'UN reforms should promote democracy, rule of law', *China View*, 13 June 2005 <http://german.china.org.cn/english/international/131745.htm> (accessed 27 April 2008).

12 'Position paper of the PRC on the UN reforms, June 7, 2005', *Beijing Review*, 11 August 2005.

13 Ibid.

14 Ni Yanshuo, 'G4 plan will split UN, Says China', *Beijing Review*, 16 June 2005.

15 China has used its veto sparingly: between 1971 and 2001, it cast only four vetoes on issues other than recommendations regarding the appointment of the Secretary General – compared with twelve by USSR/Russia, 14 by France, 25 by the UK and 73 by the United States. See S. Kim, 'China's path to great power status in the globalisation era', *Asian Perspective*, Vol. 27, No. 1, 2003, p.68.

16 Chen Xuling, 'Building a harmonious world', *Beijing Review*, 29 September 2005; 'UN reforms should promote democracy, rule of law'.

17 'Position paper of the PRC on the UN reforms'.

18 M. Turner, 'Beijing's UN envoy defends decision to back compromise resolution on Iraq'.

19 Shen Jiru cited in Ni Yanshuo, 'Pieces of eight', *Beijing Review*, 21 July 2005.
20 Wu Miaofa, 'TaiChi master at the helm', *Beijing Review*, 18 January 2007.
21 'Annan urges thorough UN reform', *Morning Star*, 22 March 2005.
22 'UN reforms should promote democracy, rule of law'.
23 Alsir Sidahmed, 'Sudan oil industry in American figures', *Sudan Tribune*, 12 May 2007 <www.sudantribune.com/spio.php?page+imprimable&id_ article=21848> (accessed 2 February 2008). According to Ed Crooks, the 'dirty secret' of China's controversial investment in Sudan is that is benefits US and European consumers by opening up a new source of supply of oil; see Ed Crooks, 'Centre of power is on the move', *Financial Times, 23 January 2008.
24 Richard McGregor, 'Beijing's Africa envoy to focus on Darfur', *Financial Times*, 11 May 2007.
25 Andrew Yeh, 'China rejects criticism of its trade ties with Sudan', *Financial Times*, 25 January 2007.
26 James Traub, 'The world according to China', *New York Times*, 3 September 2006.
27 Andrew England, 'Crisis in Darfur takes another turn for the worst', *Financial Times*, 18 December 2006.
28 Quoted by Andrew England, '"Apocalyptic" Darfur conflict finds new combatants – and victims', *Financial Times, 27 April 2007.
29 Jeffrey Sachs, 'Lecture 5, Global politics in a complex age', *Reith Lectures, 2007* <http://www.bbc.co.uk/radio4/reith2007/lecture5.shtml> (accessed 25 April 2008).
30 Paul White, 'The Spielberg situation', *Morning Star*, 21 February 2008.
31 Bryan Bender, 'US is top purveyor on weapons sales list', *Boston Globe*, 13 November 2006.
32 C. Bryson Hull, 'Darfur rebels meet, Sudan blasts France', *Reuters Africa, 5 August 2007* <africa.reuters.com/wire/news/usnBAN544360.html> (accessed 27 April 2008).
33 *Polity IV country reports* <http://www.systemicpeace.org/polity/polity4.htm> (accessed 27 April 2008).
34 Since the G8's Gleneagles commitment to double aid by 2010, the amount has in fact been falling. Meanwhile poor countries are still paying the rich world $100 million a day in debt repayments. See M. Bunting, 'Bono, Bob and G8's broken promises', *Guardian*, 8 June 2007.
35 'UN faces challenges and crisis in the new year', *China Daily*, 2 January 1999.
36 Russian and Chinese opposition in the UNSC has caused the United States to back down over action against Iran. See 'Bush calls for unity on Iran as allies argue', *Financial Times, 22 March 2006.
37 The United States succeeded in so doing on the notable occasion of the IAEA vote on referring the matter of Iran's compliance to the UNSC in September 2005. See D. Dombey and G. Smyth, 'Iran defiant in face of IAEA criticism over nuclear stance', *Financial Times*, 26 September 2005.
38 'Position paper of the PRC on the UN reforms'.
39 James Traub, 'The world according to China'.
40 J. Gerson, *Empire and the Bomb* (London: Pluto Press, 2007), p.249.
41 *The National Security Strategy of the United States of America*, White House, Washington DC, 2006, p.20 <http://www.whitehouse.gov/nsc/nssall.html> (accessed 2 April 2008).

42 Ibid., p.46.

43 David Isenberg, 'China's real nuclear capabilities', *Asia Times Online*, 14 December 2006 <http://www.atimes.com/atimes/china/hl14ad01.html> (accessed 27 April 2008).

44 Praful Bidwai and Achin Vanaik, *New Nukes* (Oxford: Signal Books, 2000), p.70. Bidwai and Vanaik reveal that China was equally prepared to supply India with each and every item they believed China had sold to Pakistan; that is, China's interest in supplying Pakistan with military technologies was purely commercial not strategic (p.74).

45 China was itself a victim of such weapons used by the Japanese in the Second World War.

46 Frank Ching, 'China's view of the world', *Far Eastern Economic Review,* 2 November 2000.

47 The United States has now withdrawn 5,000 of its warheads into storage and Russia has also made significant drawbacks, so it might be argued that China should now abide by its long-standing commitment. However, the remaining US nuclear force has been made more powerful and more effective, and while most US ballistic missiles are kept on high alert, none of China's long-range nuclear forces are believed to be on alert. See David Isenberg, 'China's real nuclear capabilities'.

48 Ye Ru'an, 'China's nuclear policy', *INESAP Bulletin* (International Network of Engineers and Scientists Against Proliferation), No. 24, December 2004.

49 Hou Hongyu, 'A brief review of international arms control and non-proliferation situation in 2005', *Peace* (periodical of the Chinese People's Association for Peace and Disarmament), No. 76, March 2006.

50 Pan Zhenqiang, 'China's non-proliferation policy and practices', *INESAP Bulletin,* No. 23, April 2004.

51 Zhang Liangui, 'Tighten the treaty', *Beijing Review*, 9 March 2006.

52 Ibid.

53 Hui Zhang, 'Action/reaction: U.S. space weaponization and China', *Arms Control Today*, December 2005.

54 Ibid.

55 The 2007 Conference of Disarmament (CD) meeting saw the United States taking up the FMCT with vigour in an apparent bid to wrongfoot China. Since all the recognised NWS except China have large stockpiles of fissile materials, and so would not have to make any sacrifices under the US proposals, the main aim would appear to be to bind China in to legal compliance on a moratorium. China informally has stopped production of fissile material but because of its reluctance to be legally bound on the question in the absence of PAROS, it has been made out as the main culprit in blocking progress against US endeavours to reinvigorate the CD and multilateralism in general. China has continued to maintain its stand on equal treatment of nuclear disarmament, FMCT and PAROS. See Jenni Rissanen, 'US to abandon package approach; China stands for a balanced approach', *Disarmament Diplomacy,* No. 83, Winter 2006 <www.acronym.org.uk/dd/dd83/83fissban.htm> (accessed 27 April 2008).

56 David Chandler, 'Confident China joins space elite', *New Scientist*, 25 October 2003.

57 David Shambaugh, 'The new strategic triangle: U.S. and European reactions to China's rise', *Washington Quarterly*, Summer 2005, p.9.

58 'Casus belli', *Economist*, 11 June 2005.

59 Stockholm International Peace Research Institute, *SIPRI Yearbook 2007* (Oxford: Oxford University Press 2007) <http://yearbook2007.sipri.org> (accessed 27 April 2008).

60 D. Sevastopulo, 'White House wraps star wars weapons in cloak of darkness', *Financial Times,* 20 May 2005.

61 Denny Roy, 'China's reaction to American predominance', *Survival*, Vol. 45, Autumn 2003, p.64.

62 S. Kim, 'China's path to great power status in the globalisation era', pp.47–9.

63 Goldstein cited in S. Kim, 'China's path to great power status in the globalisation era', p.47.

64 David Isenberg, 'China's real nuclear capabilities'.

65 Six years after Bush approved the Taiwan arms deal, the Taiwanese government has only allocated minor portions of the package, held up by opposition in parliament; see K. Hille, 'China's economic rise puts strain on US–Taiwan ties, *Financial Times*, 4 May 2007.

66 In his report to the 16th Congress of the CPC, Jiang Zemin stated that, on the premise of the one China principle, all issues could be discussed, including the international space in which Taiwan may conduct economic, cultural and social activities compatible with its status, and that, after reunification, Taiwan may keep its existing social system unchanged and enjoy a high degree of autonomy. Jiang Zemin's Report to the 16th Congress of the CPC, 2002 <http://english. people. com.cn/200211/18/eng20021118_106983.shtml> (accessed 17 April 2008).

67 A. Yeh, 'Chinese military spending to increase by 18%', *Financial Times*, 5 March 2007.

68 Yiwei Wang, 'China's defensive realism', *Asia Times*, 23 December 2004.

69 'US presses China to back stance on Iran's nuclear plans', *Financial Times*, 11 May 2006.

70 Yu Jun, 'Back in the spotlight', *Beijing Review*, 27 April 2006.

71 Yan Wei, 'Rising stakes', *Beijing Review*, 8 March 2007.

72 As stated in its Position Paper on UN reform, China stands for prudent use of sanctions. It also holds that IAEA inspections should respect the dignity and sovereignty of the country concerned.

73 Ruan Zongze, 'What we've learned from the latest nuclear crises', *China Daily*, 2 March 2007.

74 China's investment in infrastructure in developing countries to promote trade includes help in building port facilities in Pakistan and Myanmar. The Chinese navy will have access to these ports but whether they would constitute a permanent naval base as some argue facility is a moot point.

75 Hui Zhang, 'Action/reaction: U.S. space weaponization and China'.

76 Denny Roy, 'China's reaction to American predominance'.

CHAPTER 10: TOWARDS A NEW INTERNATIONAL ECONOMIC ORDER

1 Walden Bello and Marylou Malig, 'The crisis of the globalist project and the new economics of George Bush', in Alan Freeman and Boris Kagarlitsky (eds), *The Politics of Empire* (London: Pluto Press, 2004).

2   Ibid., pp.90–1.

3   E. Callan and K. Guha, 'China resists calls for reform', *Financial Times*, 26 May 2007; Liu Yumin, 'Some comments on China's economic development', *Peace*, No. 82, March 2007. The United States inflates figures to exaggerate China's trade surplus by counting in China's trade with Hong Kong, that is, transhipments from China to Hong Kong which reflect no value added to China.

4   Peter Garnham, 'Unloved dollar's hard times are not over yet', *Financial Times*, 27 July 2007.

5   Such is the claim for example of C. Fred Bergsten, of the Peterson Institute of International Economics. See Wang Lijun and Zhou Shijian, 'Strife over yuan', *Beijing Review*, 17 May 2007.

6   Approximately, $350 billion are held in US government bonds accounting for 8 per cent of the market. See K. Guha, 'Paulson "frustrated" at pace of renminbi reform', *Financial Times,* 1 February 2007.

7   Ben Bernanke, the chairman of the Federal Reserve, has branded China's undervalued currency as an 'effective subsidy'. See K. Guha et al., 'Fed calls renminbi "effective subsidy"', *Financial Times,* 16 January 2006.

8   Guy De Jonquieres, 'The rise of China has not killed off American factories', *Financial Times*, 4 April 2006.

9   R. Eckaus, 'Should China appreciate the yuan?' *Harvard China Review,* Vol. 5, No. 1, Spring 2004.

10   'Yuan step from the edge', *Economist,* 1 April 2006.

11   Richard McGregor, 'CNOOC willing to ask Beijing to reduce stake', *Financial Times*, 26 October 2007.

12   S. Kirchgaessner, 'US bans classified work on Chinese computers', *Financial Times*, 20 May 2006.

13   J. Sachs and W. T. Woo, 'China's economic growth after WTO membership', *Journal of Chinese Economic and Business Studies*, Vol.1, No. 1, 2003.

14   J. Lau and E. Alden, 'Cheap subsidized US cotton "threatens Chinese farmers"', *Financial Times*, 7 December 2005.

15   S. Schwab, 'Chinese voices that oppose reform grow louder', *Financial Times*, 11 December 2006.

16   Guy de Jonquieries, 'Why China's exporters are striking it rich', *Financial Times*, 8 March 2007.

17   Will Hutton, 'Low wage competition isn't to blame for western job losses and inequality', *Guardian*, 13 January 2007.

18   Will Hutton, 'Why 55m peasants scare the US', *Guardian*, 5 February 2006.

19   Richard McGregor, 'China says US and Europe are the main obstacle to global trade deficit', *Financial Times*, 13 March 2007.

20   Shaun Breslin, 'Power and production: rethinking China's global economic role', *Review of International Studies*, No. 31, 2005, p.743.

21   China's trade surplus with the EU for the first nine months of 2007 was $185.65 billion. See Richard McGregor, 'Pressure on China as trade surplus surges', *Financial Times*, 13 October 2007.

22   'China's peaceful development road', *Peoples Daily Online*, 22 December 2005 <http://english.people.com.cn/200512/22/eng20051222_230059.html> (accessed 28 April 2008).

23   Peter Gowan, 'U.S. hegemony today', *Monthly Review*, July–August 2003.

24   Wang Lijun and Zhou Shijian, 'Strife over yuan'.

25 Despite the sharp revaluation of the yen in 1985, US trade remained in deficit with Japan by $88.5 billion in 2006; see Wang Lijun and Zhou Shijian, 'Strife over yuan'. In China's case, since a large proportion of exports are reprocessed goods, a revaluation of the RMB would cheapen the imported inputs cancelling out the negative effects of higher export prices. Even if the profit margins of exporters were to be squeezed, production could be relocated to even lower cost locations elsewhere and Americans would simply end up buying textiles from say Bangladesh or Cambodia.

26 Wang Jisi, 'China's search for stability with the US', *China Daily*, 8 February 2006.

27 J. Stiglitz, *Making Globalization Work* (London: Allen Lane, 2006), p.258

28 Shaun Breslin, 'Power and production', p.741

29 Frederic Bobin, 'Mutually assured dependence', *Guardian Weekly*, 14–20 July 2006.

30 J. Stiglitz, *Making Globalization Work*, p.259.

31 K. Nordhaug, 'The United States and East Asia in an age of financialisation', *Critical Asian Studies*, Vol. 37, No. 1, 2005. When in January 2006, the Chinese government gave warning of its intention to diversify forex reserves away from US dollars and Treasury bonds, the European Union urged China to take its time, fearing a sudden reversal of capital flows would trigger a devaluation of the dollar relative to the euro.

32 'US deficit is so serious it threatens global crash', *Vanguard*, 9 February 2004.

33 R. McGregor and K. Guha, 'US cranks up the decibels while China plays it cool', *Financial Times,* 12 December 2006.

34 'US dollar cause of currency instability – Fan Gang', *Reuters*, 29 August 2006.

35 Zhao Xijun, 'Investing in foreign share options', *Beijing Review*, 23 November 2006.

36 T. Palley presents the arguments here in 'External contradictions of the Chinese development model: export-led growth and the dangers of global economic contraction', *Journal of Contemporary China*, Vol. 15, No. 1, February 2006.

37 See for example Lawrence Summers, 'History holds lessons for China and its partners', *Financial Times*, 26 February 2007.

38 The following discussion draws on K. Nordhaug, 'The United States and East Asia in an age of financialisation', pp.107–10.

39 Mei Xinyu, 'The downside of openness', *Beijing Review*, 22 March 2007.

40 Ba Shusong, 'How to deal with the US$ as a "spoiled child"?', *Peoples Daily*, 19 May 2006.

41 Ibid.

42 'Comparative advantage not cause of trade surplus', Interview with Justin Yifu Lin, *Beiing Review,* 16 August 2007; J. Anderlini, 'China hits out over "hot money"', *Financial Times*, 28 June 2007.

43 R. McGregor, 'Forex trading for renminbi nearer', *Financial Times*, 12 May 2006; Andrew Balls et al., 'Foreign exchanges: the American diplomacy behind China's revaluation', *Financial Times*, 25 July 2005.

44 R. McGregor, 'Beijing leaders see benefits of record reserves', *Financial Times*, 7 September 2006.

45 Zhao Xijun, 'Investing in foreign share options', *Beijing Review*, 23 November 2006.

46 S. Sen, 'Finance in China after WTO', *Economic and Political Weekly,* 5 February 2005.

47 Liu Yunyun, 'Hot money, hot potato', *Beijing Review*, 26 April 2007.

48 Mei Xinyu, 'The downside of openness'.

49 Ibid.

50 Zhang Wei, 'Just how big will China's forex reserves get?' *Beijing Review*, 23 November 2006.

51 K. Guha, 'US "impatient" at pace of progress in China talks', *Financial Times*, 23 May 2007. With the credit crunch reaching crisis proportions in September and October 2008, it is clear that the US has been completely mishandling the situation of its own trade deficits and the global economic imbalances. Rather than attempting to lecture China, Paulson would have been better off heeding the advice of its government which has continually warned of the serious implications of the weak dollar and US interest rate cuts. See for example, Richard McGregor 'Beijing lectures US on effect of weak dollar', *Financial Times,* 13 December 2007.

52 Mohamed El-Erian, 'Sit tight for a rollercoaster rise on global interest rates', *Financial Times*, 19 June 2007.

53 Richard McGregor, 'Weak dollar worries Beijing', *Financial Times*, 19 March 2008. According to one Chinese economist, commenting on the strengthening of the RMB, 'A small factor is the pressure from the US. A big factor is inflationary pressure in China'. See Richard McGregor, 'Inflation overtakes arm twisting as spur for currency's rise', *Financial Times,* 31 March, 2008.

54 Richard McGregor, 'Beijing lectures US on effect of weak dollar', *Financial Times,* 13 December 2007.

55 Tom Holland, 'An incredible balancing act', *Far Eastern Economic Review*, 18 March 2004.

56 Deng and Moore, 'China views globalization: toward a new great power politics?', *Washington Quarterly*, Summer 2004, p.131. The former managing director of the IMF, Rodrigo Rato, for one did not agree with a tough policy on China: see A. Balls and C. Giles, 'IMF in search of relevant strategies for benign times', *Financial Times*, 26 September 2005. He resigned unexpectedly in 2007 after the United States insisted on the IMF's stringent surveillance of currencies.

57 A. Seagar, 'Don't blame China for global trade imbalance, says UN', *Guardian Weekly*, 9–15 September 2005.

58 C. Giles, 'IMF to address global imbalance', *Financial Times,* 9 July 2006.

59 C. Giles et al., 'IMF voting wrangles likely to add to tensions with Asian states', *Financial Times*, 16 September 2006.

60 Vijay Joshi, 'Why we need to rethink the exchange rate system', *Financial Times*, 15 December 2006; J. G. Greive, 'A currency agreement could avert the dollar's collapse', *Financial Times*, 22 June 2006.

61 K. Guha, 'China tells IMF not to back US pressure', *Financial Times*, 21 June 2007.

62 'US dollar cause of currency instability – Fan Gang', *Reuters*.

63 Ibid.

64 Deng and Moore, 'China views globalization', p.124.

65 Martin Jacques, 'Globalisation has had its day', *Guardian Weekly*, 21–27 July 2006.

66 Ibid.

67 R. Higgott, 'US foreign policy and the "securitization" of economic globalization', *International Politics,* Vol. 41, No. 2, June 2004.

68   Lu Jianren, 'APEC crossroad', *Beijing Review*, 30 November 2006.
69   'Globalisation with a third-world face', *Economist*, 9 April 2005.
70   F. Williams, 'China overtakes Japan as third largest exporter', *Financial Times*, 15 April 2005.
71   W. Lam, 'China's encroachment on America's backyard', *China Brief*, Vol. 4, No. 23, 24 November 2004.
72   Jonathan Watts, 'Oil deal with China is a "Great Wall" that will stop the US, says Chavez', *Guardian*, 28 August 2006.
73   'China's peaceful development road', *Peoples Daily Online*.
74   See Piet Konings, 'China and Africa: building a strategic partnership', *Journal of Developing Societies*, Vol. 23, No. 3, 2007. He cites Moeletsi Mbeki, deputy chairman of the South Africa Institute of International Affairs.
75   Interview with Eleih-Elle Etian, Cameroon Ambassador to China, 'Increasing rapprochement', *Beijing Review*, 8 February 2007.
76   L. Barber and A. England, 'China's scramble for Africa finds a welcome in Kenya', *Financial Times,* 10 August 2006.
77   'China's African affair', *Financial Times* editorial, 26 June 2006.
78   Paul White, 'China diary', *Morning Star*, 21 August 2006.
79   Paul White, 'Chad goes to China', *Morning Star*, 8 August 2006.
80   Zan Jifang, 'Keeping a promise', *Beijing Review*, 22 February 2007.
81   Ibid.
82   Andrew Yeh, 'China ventures on rocky roads to trade with Africa', *Financial Times*, 20 June 2006.
83   Quentin Peel and James Lamont interview with President Thabo Mbeki, 'S Africa leader welcomes China investment', *Financial Times*, 25 May 2006.
84   Yao Graham, 'Africa and China: Looking beyond western anxieties', *Action* (World Development Movement), Spring 2007.
85   John Edwards, 'We must prepare for the march of China's giants', *Financial Times*, 17 January 2007.
86   C. Hoyos, 'A new era of nationalism', *Financial Times*, 19 June 2007.
87   Sundeep Tucker, 'Sinopec, ONGC buy Columbian stake', *Financial Times*, 15 August 2006.
88   Ha-Joon Chang, *Bad Samaritans* (London: Random House, 2007). As Chang makes clear, criticising the IPR regime as it exists today is not the same as arguing for the wholesale abolition of intellectual property itself (p.142).
89   A. Beattie, 'Ownership is not the real problem with China', *Financial Times*, 16 April 2007.
90   Rong Ying, 'Economic globalisation and the new international political and economic order', *China Report*, Vol. 38, No. 1, 2002, p.116.
91   'China's peaceful development road', *Peoples Daily Online*.
92   Qian Qichen, Minister of Foreign Affairs, 'Statement at the ASEAN summit', 1999 <www.aseansec.org/4249.htm> (accessed 28 April 2008).
93   Ibid.
94   'Experts fight global poverty', *China Daily*, 13 August 2003.
95   A. Bounds, 'China says it is powerless over surplus', *Financial Times*, 13 June 2007.
96   S. Sen, 'Finance in China after WTO'.
97   'Developing countries attract record levels of investment', *Morning Star*, 31 May 2007.

98   W. Wallis, 'China to eclipse donors with $20bn for Africa', *Financial Times*, 18 May 2007.
99   John Grieve Smith, 'A currency agreement could avert the dollar's collapse', *Financial Times*, 22 June 2006.
100   J. Stiglitz, *Making Globalization Work*, pp.260–1.
101   'China's peaceful development road', *Peoples Daily Online*.
102   Ibid.
103   Zhao Yumin, 'A setback or an opportunity?', *Beijing Review*, 2 June 2005.
104   <www.cosatu.org.za/press/2006/oct/press11.htm> (accessed 17 May 2007).
105   Zhao Yumin, 'A setback or an opportunity?'
106   Sun Xiaoqing, 'How to tackle an old problem', *Beijing Review,* 16 June 2005.
107   Ibid.
108   Lu Jianhua, 'Seeking a new trade pattern', *Beijing Review*, 23 March 2007.
109   Xu Xiaonian, 'Eyeing financial reform', *Beijing Review,* 4 May 2006.
110   John Edwards, 'We must prepare for the march of China's giants'.
111   B. Benoit and J. Thornhill, 'Merkel calls for rules on global trade', *Financial Times,* 26 January 2006.

CHAPTER 11: AN INTERNATIONAL NEW DEMOCRACY IN THE MAKING

1   'Bush, the new international order and China's choice', *Peoples Daily,* 22 November 2004.
2   Zhang Yansheng, cited in R. McGregor and E. Callan, 'Bejing's uncomfortable deal with America', *Financial Times,* 11 April 2007.
3   He Fan, 'Rediscovering Africa', *Beijing Review*, 24 January 2008.
4   Quentin Peel, 'The south's rise is hindered at home', *Financial Times*, 17 November 2005.
5   Quentin Peel and James Lamont, 'S. Africa leader welcomes China investment' (interview with Thabo Mbeki) *Financial Times,* 25 May 2006.
6   Charlotte Denny and Jonathan Freedland, 'New Zealand warns on "law of jungle"', *Guardian*, 3 May 2003.
7   Mao Zedong, 'On new democracy' (1940) *Selected Works of Mao Zedong Vol. 3* (London: Lawrence & Wishart, 1954) pp.111–12.
8   Barry Naughton and Adam Segal, 'China in search of a workable model', in W. W. Keller and R. J. Samuels (eds), *Crisis and Innovation in Asian Technology* (Cambridge: Cambridge University Press, 2003).
9   Richard McGregor, 'Party think-tank calls for checks on China's rulers', *Financial Times*, 20 February 2008.
10   Lanxin Xiang, 'China's Eurasian experiment', *Survival*, Vol. 46, No. 2, Summer 2005, p.117.
11   Giovanni Arrighi, *Adam Smith in Beijing* (London: Verso, 2007).
12   'Risks mount as forex reserves bulge', *People's Daily*, 2 June 2006.
13   Pan Tao, 'Globalization and its effect on international relations', *Beijing Review*, No. 7, 15 February 2001.
14   Yang Xiyue, 'Power relations in today's world', *Beijing Review*, 1–7 March 1999.

15 Wang Jisi, 'China's search for stability with America', *Foreign Affairs*, September/October 2005.

16 Tony Barber 'EU joins China in currency moves pact', *Financial Times*, 28 November 2007.

17 C. Raja Mohan, 'Washington embrace is warmer and closer', *Financial Times*, 25 January 2008.

18 Salim Lone, 'The last thing we need', *Guardian*, 12 March 2007.

19 Yan Wei, 'A complex signal', *Beijing Review,* 17 May 2007.

20 C. Raja Mohan, 'Washington embrace is warmer and closer', *Financial Times,* 25 January 2008; Peter Smith and Richard McGregor, 'Good days', *Financial Times*, 3 April, 2008.

21 Graham Rowbotham, 'A report of a talk by Guo Moro', *The East is Red*, SACU York, October 1971, No. 2.

INDEX